Real-Time Vision for Human-Computer Interaction

T0135144

Real-Time Vision
for Human-Computer
Interaction

Edited by

Branislav Kisačanin
Delphi Corporation

Vladimir Pavlović
Rutgers University

Thomas S. Huang
University of Illinois at Urbana-Champaign

 Springer

Branislav Kisačanin
Delphi Corporation

Vladimir Pavlović
Rutgers University

Thomas S. Huang
University of Illinois at Urbana-Champaign

Library of Congress Cataloging-in-Publication Data

A C.I.P. Catalogue record for this book is available
From the Library of Congress

ISBN 978-1-4419-3908-1   e-ISBN 978-0-387-27890-2

Printed in the United States of America

9 8 7 6 5 4 3 2 1

springeronline.com

To Saška, Milena, and Nikola

BK

To Karin, Irena, and Lara

VP

To Pei

TSH

Contents

Part III Looking Ahead

Foreword

2001's Vision of *Vision*

One of my formative childhood experiences was in 1968 stepping into the Uptown Theater on Connecticut Avenue in Washington, DC, one of the few movie theaters nationwide that projected in large-screen cinerama. I was there at the urging of a friend, who said I simply *must* see the remarkable film whose run had started the previous week. "You won't understand it," he said, "but that doesn't matter." All I knew was that the film was about science fiction and had great special effects. So I sat in the front row of the balcony, munched my popcorn, sat back, and experienced what was widely touted as "the ultimate trip:" *2001: A Space Odyssey*.

My friend was right: I didn't understand it... but in some senses that didn't matter. (Even today, after seeing the film 40 times, I continue to discover its many subtle secrets.) I just had the sense that I had experienced a creation of the highest aesthetic order: unique, fresh, awe inspiring. Here was a film so distinctive that the first half hour had no words whatsoever; the last half hour had no words either; and nearly all the words in between were banal and irrelevant to the plot – quips about security through Voiceprint identification, how to make a phonecall from a space station, government pension plans, and so on. While most films pose a problem in the first few minutes – Who killed the victim? Will the meteor be stopped before it annihilates earth? Can the terrorists's plot be prevented? Will the lonely heroine find true love? – in *2001* we get our first glimmer of the central plot and conflict nearly an hour into the film. There were no major Hollywood superstars heading the bill either. Three of the five astronauts were known only by the traces on their life support systems, and one of the lead characters was a bone-wielding ape!

And yet my eyes were riveted to the screen. Every shot was perfectly composed, worthy of a fine painting; the special effects (in this pre-computer era production) made life in space seem so *real*. The choice of music – from Johannes Strauss' spinning *Beautiful Blue Danube* for the waltz of the humongous space station and shuttle, to György Ligeti's dense and otherworldly *Lux Aeterna* during the StarGate lightshow near the end – was brilliant.

While most viewers focused on the *outer* odyssey to the stars, I was always more captivated by the film's other – *inner* – odyssey, into the nature of intelligence and the problem of the source of good and evil. This subtler odyssey was highlighted by the central and the most "human" character, the only character whom we really *care* about, the only one who showed "real" emotion, the only one whose death affects us: The HAL 9000 computer.

There is so much one could say about HAL that you could put an entire book together to do it. (In fact, I have [1] – a documentary film too [2].) HAL could hear, speak, plan, recognize faces, see, judge facial expressions, and render judgments on art. He could even read lips! In the central scene of the film, astronauts Dave Bowman and Frank Poole retreat to a pod and turn off all the electronics, confident that HAL can't hear them. They discuss HAL's apparent malfunctions, and whether or not to disconnect HAL if flaws remain. Then, referring to HAL, Dave quietly utters what is perhaps the most important line in the film: "Well I don't know what he'd think about it." The camera, showing HAL's view, pans back and forth between the astronauts' faces, centered on their mouths. The audience quickly realizes that HAL understands what the astronauts are saying – he's *lipreading!* It is a chilling scene and, like all the other crisis moments in the film, *silent.*

It has been said that *2001* provided the vision, the mold, for a technological future, and that the only thing left for scientists and technologists was to fill in the stage set with *real* technology. I have been pleasantly surprised to learn that many researchers in artificial intelligence were impressed by the film: *2001* inspired my generation of computer scientists and AI researchers the way *Buck Rogers* films inspired the engineers and scientists of the nascent NASA space program. I, for one, was inspired by the film to build computer lipreading systems [3]. I suspect many of the contributors to this volume, were similarly affected by the vision in the film.

So... how far have we come in building a HAL? Or more specifically, building a vision system for HAL? Let us face the obvious, that we are not close to building a computer with the full intelligence or visual ability of HAL. Despite the optimism and hype of the 1970s, we now know that artificial intelligence is one of the most profoundly hard problems in all of science and that general computer vision is AI complete.

As a result, researchers have broken the general vision problem into a number of subproblems, each challenging in its own way, as well as into specific applications, where the constraints make the problem more manageable. This volume is an excellent guide to progress in the subproblems of computer vision and their application to human-computer interaction. The chapters in Parts I and III are new, written for this volume, while the chapters in Part II are extended versions of all papers from the 2004 Workshop on Real-Time Vision for Human-Computer Interaction held in conjunction with IEEE Conference on Computer Vision and Pattern Recognition (CVPR) in Washington, DC.

Some of the most important developments in computing since the release of the film is the move from large mainframe computers, to personal computers, personal digital assistants, game boxes, the dramatic reduction in cost of computing, summarized in Moore's Law, as well as the rise of the web. All these developments added impetus for researchers and industry to provide natural interfaces, including ones that exploit real-time vision.

Real-time vision poses many challenges for theorist and experimentalist alike: feature extraction, learning, pattern recognition, scene analysis, multi-modal integration, and more. The requirement that fielded systems operate in real-time places strict constraints on the hardware and software. In many applications human-computer interaction requires the computer to "understand" at least something about the human, such as goals.

HAL could recognize the motions and gestures of the crew as they repaired the AE-35 unit; in this volume we see progress in segmentation, tracking, and recognition of arms and hand motions, including finger spelling. HAL recognized the faces of the crewmen; here we read of progress in head facial tracking, as well as direction of gaze. It is likely HAL had an internal map of the spaceship, which would allow him to coordinate the images from his many ominous red eye-cameras; for mobile robots, though, it is often more reliable to allow the robot to build an internal representation and map, as we read here. There is very little *paper* or hardcopy in *2001* – perhaps its creators believed the predictions about the inevitability of the "paperless office." In this volume we read about the state of the art in vision systems reading paper documents, scattered haphazardly over a desktop.

No selection of chapters could cover the immense and wonderfully diverse range of vision problems, but by restricting consideration to real-time vision for human-computer interaction, the editors have covered the most important components. This volume will serve as one small but noteworthy mile marker in the grand and worthy mission to build intelligent interfaces – a key component of HAL, as well as a wealth of personal computing devices we can as yet only imagine.

1. D G Stork (Editor). *HAL's Legacy: 2001's Computer as Dream and Reality.* MIT Press, 1997.
2. *2001: HAL's Legacy.* By D G Stork and D Kennard (InCA Productions). Funded by the Alfred P Sloan Foundation for PBS Television, 2001.
3. D G Stork and M Hennecke (Editors). *Speechreading by Humans and Machines: Models, Systems, and Applications.* Springer-Verlag, 1996.

David G. Stork
Ricoh Innovations and Stanford University

Preface

As computers become prevalent in many aspects of human lives, the need for natural and effective Human-Computer Interaction (HCI) becomes more important than ever. Computer vision and pattern recognition remain to play an important role in the HCI field. However, pervasiveness of computer vision methods in the field is often hindered by the lack of real-time, robust algorithms. This book intends to stimulate the thinking in this direction.

What is the Book about?

Real-Time Vision for Human-Computer Interaction or RTV4HCI for short, is an edited collection of contributed chapters of interest for both researchers and practitioners in the fields of computer vision, pattern recognition, and HCI. Written by leading researchers in the field, the chapters are organized into three parts. Two introductory chapters in Part I provide overviews of history and algorithms behind RTV4HCI. Ten chapters in Part II are a snapshot of the state-of-the-art real-time algorithms and applications. The remaining five chapters form Part III, a compilation of trend-and-idea articles by some of the most prominent figures in this field.

RTV4HCI Paradigm

Computer vision algorithms are notoriously brittle. In a keynote speech one of us (TSH) gave at the 1996 International Conference of Pattern Recognition (ICPR) in Vienna, Austria, he said that viable computer vision applications should have one or more of the following three characteristics:

1. The application is forgiving. In other words, some mistakes are tolerable.
2. It involves human in the loop. So human intelligence and machine intelligence can be combined to achieve the desired performance.

3. There is the possibility of using other modalities in addition to vision. Fusion of multiple modalities such as vision and speech can be very powerful.

Most applications in Human Computer Interface (HCI) possess all these three characteristics. By its very nature HCI systems have humans in the loop. And largely because of that, some mistakes and errors are tolerable. For example, if a person uses hand pointing to control a cursor in the display, the location estimation of the cursor does not have to be very accurate since there is immediate visual feedback. And in many HCI applications, a combination of different modalities gives the best solution. For example, in a 3D virtual display environment, one could combine visual hand gesture analysis and speech recognition to navigate: Hand gesture to indicate the direction and speech to indicate the speed (to give one possibility).

However, computer vision algorithms used in HCI applications still need to be reasonably robust in order to be viable. And another big challenge for HCI vision algorithms is: In most applications they have to be real-time (at or close to video rate). In summary: We need real-time robust HCI vision algorithms. Until a few years ago, such algorithms were virtually nonexistent. However, more recently a number of such algorithms have emerged; some as commercial products. But we need more!

Developing real-time robust HCI vision algorithms demands a great deal of "hack." The following statement has been attributed to our good friend Berthold Horn: "Elegant theories do not work; simple ideas do." Indeed, many very useful vision algorithms are pure hack. However, we think Berthold would agree that the ideal thing to happen is: An elegant theory leads to a very useful algorithm. It is nevertheless true that the path from elegant theory to useful algorithm is paved with much hack. It is our opinion that a useful (e.g., real-time robust HCI) algorithm is far superior to a useless theory (elegant or otherwise). We have been belaboring these points in order to emphasize to current and future students of computer vision that they should be prepared to do hack work and they had better like it.

Goals of this Book

Edited by the team that organized the workshop with the same name at CVPR 2004, and aiming to satisfy the needs of both academia and industry in this emerging field, this book provides food for thought for researchers and developers alike. By outlining the background of the field, describing the state-of-the-art developments, and exploring the challenges and building blocks for future research, it is an indispensable reference for anyone working on HCI or other applications of computer vision.

Part I – Introduction

The first part of this book, Introduction, contains two chapters. "RTV4HCI: A Historical Overview" by M. Turk reviews recent history of computer vision's role in HCI from the personal perspective of a leading researcher in the field. Recalling the challenges of the early 1980s when a "modern" VAX computer could not load a 512×512 image into memory at once, the author points to basic research questions and difficulties modern RTV4HCI faces. Despite significant progress in the past quarter century and growing interest in the field, RTV4HCI still lags behind other fields that emerged around the same time. Important issues such as the fundamental question of user awareness, practical robustness of vision algorithms, and the quest for a "killer app" remain to be addressed.

In their chapter "Real-Time Algorithms: From Signal Processing to Computer Vision," B. Kisačanin and V. Pavlović illustrate some algorithmic aspects of RTV4HCI while underlining important practical implementation and production issues an RTV4HCI designer faces. The chapter presents an overview of low-level signal/image processing and vision algorithms, given from the perspective of real-time implementation. It illustrates the concepts by examples of several standard image processing algorithms, such as DFT and PCA. The authors begin with standard mathematical formulations of the algorithms. They lead the reader to the algorithms' computationally efficient implementations, shedding the light on important hardware and production constraints that are easily overlooked by RTV4HCI researchers.

Part II – Advances in RTV4HCI

The second part of the book is a collection of chapters that describe ten applications of RTV4HCI. The task of "looking at people" is a common thread behind the ten chapters. An important aspect of this task are detection, tracking, and interpretation of the human hand and facial poses and movements.

"Recognition of Isolated Fingerspelling Gestures Using Depth Edges" by R. Feris et al. introduces an interesting new active camera system for fast and reliable detection of object contours. The system is based on a multi-flash camera and exploits depth discontinuities. The authors illustrate the use of this camera on a difficult problem of fingerspelling, showcasing the system's robustness needed for a real-time application.

S. Chandran and A. Sawa in "Appearance-Based Real-Time Understanding of Gestures Using Projected Euler Angles" consider sign language alphabet recognition where gestures are made with protruded fingers. They propose a simple, real-time classification algorithm based on 2D projection of Euler angles. Despite its simplicity the approach demonstrates that the choice of "right" features plays an important role in RTV4HCI.

M. Kölsch and M. Turk focus on another hand tracking problem in their "Flocks of Features for Tracking Articulated Objects" chapter. Flocks of Features is a method that combines motion cues with learned foreground color for tracking non-rigid and highly articulated objects such as the human hand. By considering a flock of such features, the method achieves robustness while maintaining high computational efficiency.

The problem of accurate recognition of hand poses is addressed by H. Zhou et al. in their chapter "Static Hand Posture Recognition Based on Okapi-Chamfer Matching." The authors propose the use of a text retrieval method, inverted indexing, to organize visual features in a lexicon for efficient retrieval. Their method allows very fast and accurate recognition of hand poses from large image databases using only the hand silhouettes. The approach of using simple models with many examples will, perhaps, lead to an alternative way of solving the gesture recognition problem.

A different approach to hand gesture recognition that uses a 3D model as well as motion cues is described in the chapter "Visual Modeling of Dynamic Gestures Using 3D Appearance and Motion Features" by G. Ye et al. Instead of constructing an accurate 3D hand model, the authors introduce simple 3D local volumetric features that are sufficient for detecting simple hand-object interactions in real time.

Face modeling and tracking is another task important for RTV4HCI. In "Head and Facial Animation Tracking Using Appearance-Adaptive Models and Particle Filters," F. Davoine and F. Dornaika propose two alternative methods to solve the head and face tracking problems. Using a 3D deformable face model, the authors are able to track moving faces undergoing various expression changes over long image sequences in close-to-real-time.

Eye gaze is sometimes easily overlooked, yet very important HCI cue. J. Magee et al. in "A Real-Time Vision Interface Based on Gaze Detection – EyeKeys" consider the task of detecting eye gaze direction using correlation-based methods. This simple approach results in a real-time system built on a consumer quality USB camera that can be used in a variety of HCI applications, including interfaces for the disabled.

The use of active vision may yield important benefits when developing vision techniques for HCI. In his chapter "Map Building from Human-Computer Interactions" A. Arsenio relies on cues provided by a human actor interacting with the scene to recognize objects and reconstruct the 3D environment. This paradigm has particular applications in problems that require interactive learning or teaching of various computer interfaces.

"Real-Time Inference of Complex Mental States from Facial Expressions and Hand Gestures" by R. el Kaliouby and P. Robinson considers the important task of finding optimal ways to merge different cues in order to infer the user's mental state. The challenges in this problem are many: accurate extraction of different cues at different spatial and temporal resolutions as well as the cues' integration. Using a Dynamic Bayesian Network modeling approach, the authors are able to obtain real-time performance with high recognition accuracy.

Immersive environments with projection displays offer an opportunity to use cues generated from the interaction of the user and the display system in order to solve the difficult visual recognition task. In "Epipolar Constrained User Pushbutton Selection in Projected Interfaces," A. Kale et al. use this paradigm to accurately detect user actions under difficult lighting conditions. Shadows cast by the hand on the display and their relation to the real hand allow a simplified, real-time way of detecting contact events, something that would be difficult if not impossible when tracking the hand image alone.

Part III – Looking Ahead

Current state of RTV4HCI leaves many open problems and unexplored opportunities. Part III of this book contains five chapters. They focus on applications of RTV4HCI and describe challenges in their adoption and deployment in both commercial and research settings. Finally, the chapters offer different outlooks on the future of RTV4HCI systems and research.

"Vision-Based HCI Applications" by E. Petajan provides an insider view of the present and the future of RTV4HCI in the consumer market. Cameras, static and video, are becoming ubiquitous in cell phones, game consoles and, soon, automobiles, opening the door for vision-based HCI. The author describes his own experience in the market deployment and adoption of advanced interfaces. In a companion chapter, "MPEG-4 Face and Body Animation Coding Applied to HCI," the author provides an example of how existing industry standards, such as MPEG-4, can be leveraged to deliver these new interfaces to the consumer markets of today and tomorrow.

In the chapter "The Office of the Past" J. Kim et al. propose their vision of the future of an office environment. Using RTV4HCI the authors build a physical office that seamlessly integrates into the space of digital documents. This fusion of the virtual and the physical spaces helps eliminate daunting tasks such as document organization and retrieval while maintaining the touch-and-feel efficiency of real paper. The future of HCI may indeed be in a constrained but seamless immersion of real and virtual worlds.

Many of the chapters presented in this book solely rely on the visual mode of communication between humans and machines. "Multimodal Human-Computer Interaction" by M. Turk offers a glimpse of the benefits that multimodal interaction modes such as speech, vision, expression, and touch, when brought together, may offer to HCI. The chapter describes the history, state-of-the-art, important and open issues, and opportunities for multimodal HCI in the future. In the author's words, "The grand challenge of creating powerful, efficient, natural, and compelling multimodal interfaces is an exciting pursuit, one that will keep us busy for some time."

The final chapter of this collection, "Smart Camera Systems Technology Roadmap" by B. Flinchbaugh, offers an industry perspective on the present and future role of real-time vision in three market segments: consumer electronics, video surveillance, and automotive applications. Low cost, low power, small size, high-speed processing and modular design are among the requirements imposed on RTV4HCI systems by the three markets. Embedded DSPs coupled with constrained algorithm development may together prove to play a crucial role in the development and deployment of smart camera and HCI systems of the future.

Acknowledgments

As editors of this book we had the opportunity to work with many talented people and to learn from them: the chapter contributors, RTV4HCI Workshop Program Committee members, and the Editors from the publisher, Springer: Wayne Wheeler, Anne Murray, and Ana Božičević. Their enthusiastic help and support for the book is very much appreciated.

Kokomo, IN   *Branislav Kisačanin*
Piscataway, NJ   *Vladimir Pavlović*
Urbana, IL   *Thomas S. Huang*
February 2005

Part I

Introduction

RTV4HCI: A Historical Overview

Matthew Turk

University of California, Santa Barbara
mturk@cs.ucsb.edu

Computer vision has made significant progress in recent decades, with steady improvements in the performance and robustness of computational methods for real-time detection, recognition, tracking, and modeling. Because of these advances, computer vision is now a viable input modality for human-computer interaction, providing visual cues to the presence, identity, expressions, and movements of users. This chapter provides a personal view of the development of this intersection of fields.

1 Introduction

Real-time vision for human-computer interaction (RTV4HCI) has come a long way in a relatively short period of time. When I first worked in a computer vision lab, as an undergraduate in 1982, I naively tried to write a program to load a complete image into memory, process it, and display it on the lab's special color image display monitor (assuming no one else was using the display at the time). Of course, we didn't actually have a camera and digitizer, so I had to read in one of the handful of available stored image files we had on the lab's modern VAX computer. I soon found out that it was a foolish thing to try and load a whole image – all 512×512 pixel values – into memory all at once, since the machine didn't have that much memory. When the image was finally processed and ready to display, I watched it slowly (very slowly!) appear on the color display monitor, a line at a time, until finally the whole image was visible. It was a painstakingly slow and frustrating process, and this was in a state of the art image processing and computer vision lab.

Only a few years later, I rode inside a large instrumented vehicle – an eight-wheel, diesel-powered, hydrostatically driven all-terrain undercarriage with a fiberglass shell, about the size of a large van, with sensors mounted on the outside and several computers inside – the first time it successfully drove along a private road outside of Denver, Colorado completely autonomously, with no human control. The vehicle, "Alvin," which was part of the DARPA-sponsored

Autonomous Land Vehicle (ALV) project at Martin Marietta Aerospace, had a computer onboard that grabbed live images from a color video camera mounted on top of the vehicle, aimed at the road ahead (or alternatively from a laser range scanner that produced depth images of the scene in front of the vehicle). The ALV vision system processed input images to find the road boundaries, which were passed onto a navigation module that figured out where to direct the vehicle so that it drove along the road. Surprisingly, much of the time it actually accomplished this. A complete cycle of the vision system, including image capture, processing, and display, took about two seconds.

A few years after this, as a PhD student at MIT, I worked on a vision system that detected and tracked a person in an otherwise static scene, located the head, and attempted to recognize the person's face, in "interactive-time" – i.e., not at frame-rate, but at a rate fast enough to work in the intended interactive application [24]. This was my first experience in pointing the camera at a person and trying to compute something useful about the person, rather than about the general scene, or some particular inanimate object in the scene. I became enthusiastic about the possibilities for real-time (or interactive-time) computer vision systems that perceived people and their actions and used this information not only in security and surveillance (the primary context of my thesis work) but in interactive systems in general. In other words, real-time vision for HCI. I was not the only one, of course: a number of researchers were beginning to think this could be a fruitful endeavor, and that this area could become another driving application area for the field of computer vision, along with the other applications that motivated the field over the years, such as robotics, modeling of human vision, medical imaging, aerial image interpretation, and industrial machine vision.

Although there had been several research projects over the years directed at recognizing human faces or some other human activity (most notably the work of Bledsoe [3], Kelly [11], Kanade [12], Goldstein and Harmon [9]; see also [18, 15, 29]), it was not until the late 1980s that such tasks began to seem feasible. Hardware progress driven by Moore's Law improvements, coupled with advances in computer vision software and hardware (e.g., [5, 1]) and the availability of affordable cameras, digitizers, full-color bitmapped displays, and other special-purpose image processing hardware, made interactive-time computer vision methods interesting, and processing images of people (yourself, your colleagues, your friends) seemed more attractive to many than processing more images of houses, widgets, and aerial views of tanks.

After a few notable successes, there was an explosion of research activity in real-time computer vision and in "looking at people" projects – face detection and tracking, face recognition, gesture recognition, activity analysis, facial expression analysis, body tracking and modeling – in the 1990s. A quick subjective perusal of the proceedings of some of the major computer vision conferences shows that about 2% of the papers (3 out of 146 papers) in CVPR 1991 covered some aspect of "looking at people." Six years later, in CVPR

1997, this had jumped to about 17% (30 out of 172) of the papers. A decade after the first check, the ICCV 2001 conference was steady at about 17% (36 out of 209 papers) – but by this point there were a number of established venues for such work in addition to the general conferences, including the Automatic Face and Gesture Recognition Conference, the Conference on Audio and Video Based Biometric Person Authentication, the Auditory-Visual Speech Processing Workshops, and the Perceptual User Interface workshops (later merged with the International Conference on Multimodal Interfaces). It appears to be clear that the interest level in this area of computer vision soared in the 1990s, and it continues to be a topic of great interest within the research community.

Funding and technology evaluation activities are further evidence of the importance and significance of these activities. The Face Recognition Technology (FERET) program [17], sponsored by the U.S. Department of Defense, held its first competition/evaluation in August 1994, with a second evaluation in March 1995, and a final evaluation in September 1996. This program represents a significant milestone in the computer vision field in general, as perhaps the first widely publicized combination of sponsored research, significant data collection, and well-defined competition in the field. The Face Recognition Vendor Tests of 2000 and 2002 [10] continued where the FERET program left off, including evaluations of both face recognition performance and product usability. A new Face Recognition Vendor Test is planned for late 2005, conducted by the National Institute of Standards and Technology (NIST) and sponsored by several U.S. government agencies.

In addition, NIST has also begun to direct and manage a Face Recognition Grand Challenge (FRGC), also sponsored by several U.S. government agencies, which has the goal of bringing about an order of magnitude improvement in performance of face recognition systems through a series of increasingly difficult challenge problems. Data collection will be much more extensive than previous efforts, and various image sources will be tested, included high resolution images, 3D images, and multiple images of a person. More information on the FERET and FRVT activities, including reports and detailed results, as well as information on the FRGC, can be found on the web at http://www.frvt.org.

DARPA sponsored a program to develop Visual Surveillance and Monitoring (VSAM) technologies, to enable a single operator to monitor human activities over a large area using a distributed network of active video sensors. Research under this program included efforts in real-time object detection and tracking (from stationary and moving cameras), human and object recognition, human gait analysis, and multi-agent activity analysis.

DARPA's HumanID at a Distance program funded several groups to conduct research in accurate and reliable identification of humans at a distance. This included multiple information sources and techniques, including face, iris, and gait recognition.

These are but a few examples (albeit some of the most high profile ones) of recent research funding in areas related to "looking at people." There are many others, including industry research and funding, as well as European, Japanese, and other government efforts to further progress in these areas. One such example is the recent European Union project entitled Computers in the Human Interaction Loop (CHIL). The aim of this project is to create environments in which computers serve humans by unobtrusively observing them and identifying the states of their activities and intentions, providing helpful assistance with a minimum of human attention or distraction.

Security concerns, especially following the world-changing events of September 2001, have driven many of the efforts to spur progress in this area – particularly those with person identification as their ultimate goal – but the same or similar technologies may be applied in other contexts. Hence, though RTV4HCI is not primarily focused on security and surveillance applications, the two areas can immensely benefit each other.

2 What is RTV4HCI?

The goal of research in real-time vision for human-computer interaction is to develop algorithms and systems that sense and perceive humans and human activity, in order to enable more natural, powerful, and effective computer interfaces. Intuitively, the visual aspects that matter when communicating with another person in a face-to-face conversation (determining identity, age, direction of gaze, facial expression, gestures, etc.) may also be useful in communicating with computers, whether stand-alone or hidden and embedded in some environment. The broader context of RTV4HCI is what many refer to as *perceptual interfaces* [27], *multimodal interfaces* [16], or *post-WIMP interfaces* [28] central to which is the integration of multiple perceptual modalities such as vision, speech, gesture, and touch (haptics). The major motivating factor of these thrusts is the desire to move beyond graphical user interfaces (GUIs) and the ubiquitous mouse, keyboard, and monitor combination – not only for better and more compelling desktop interfaces, but also to better fit the huge variety and range of future computing environments.

Since the early days of computing, only a few major user interface paradigms have dominated the scene. In the earliest days of computing, there was no conceptual model of interaction; data was entered into a computer via switches or punched cards and the output was produced, some time later, via punched cards or lights. The first conceptual model or paradigm of user interface began with the arrival of command-line interfaces in perhaps the early 1960s, with teletype terminals and later text-based monitors. This "typewriter" model (type the input command, hit carriage return, and wait for the typed output) was spurred on by the development of timesharing systems and continued with the popular Unix and DOS operating systems.

In the 1970s and 80s the graphical user interface and its associated desktop metaphor arrived, and the GUI has dominated the marketplace and HCI research for over two decades. This has been a very positive development for computing: WIMP-based GUIs have provided a standard set of direct manipulation techniques that primarily rely on recognition, rather than recall, making the interface appealing to novice users, easy to remember for occasional users, and fast and efficient for frequent users [21]. The GUI/direct manipulation style of interaction has been a great match with the office productivity and information access applications that have so far been the "killer apps" of the computing industry.

However, computers are no longer just desktop machines used for word processing, spreadsheet manipulation, or even information browsing; rather, computing is becoming something that permeates daily life, rather than something that people do only at distinct times and places. New computing environments are appearing, and will continue to proliferate, with a wide range of form factors, uses, and interaction scenarios, for which the desktop metaphor and WIMP (windows, icons, menus, pointer) model are not well suited. Examples include virtual reality, augmented reality, ubiquitous computing, and wearable computing environments, with a multitude of applications in communications, medicine, search and rescue, accessibility, and smart homes and environments, to name a few.

New computing scenarios, such as in automobiles and other mobile environments, rule out many of the traditional approaches to human-computer interaction and demand new and different interaction techniques. Interfaces that leverage natural human capabilities to communicate via speech, gesture, expression, touch, etc., will complement (not entirely replace) existing interaction styles and enable new functionality not otherwise possible or convenient. Despite technical advances in areas such as speech recognition and synthesis, artificial intelligence, and computer vision, computers are still mostly deaf, dumb, and blind. Many have noted the irony of public restrooms that are "smarter" than computers because they can sense when people come and go and act accordingly, while a computer may wait indefinitely for input from a user who is no longer there or decide to do irrelevant (but CPU intensive) work when a user is frantically working on a fast approaching deadline [25].

This concept of *user awareness* is almost completely lacking in most modern interfaces, which are primarily focused on the notion of *control*, where the user explicitly does something (moves a mouse, clicks a button) to initiate action on behalf of the computer. The ability to see users and respond appropriately to visual identity, location, expression, gesture, etc. – whether via implicit user awareness or explicit user control – is a compelling possibility, and it is the core thrust of RTV4HCI.

Human-computer interaction (HCI) – the study of people, computer technology, and the ways they influence each other – involves the design, evaluation, and implementation of interactive computing systems for human use. HCI is a very broad interdisciplinary field with involvement from computer science, psychology, cognitive science, human factors, and several other disciplines, and it involves the design, implementation, and evaluation of interactive computer systems in the context of the work or tasks in which a user is engaged [7]. The user interface – the software and devices that implement a particular model (or set of models) of HCI – is what people routinely experience in their computer usage, but in many ways it is only the tip of the iceberg. "User experience" is a term that has become popular in recent years to emphasize that the complete experience of the user – not an isolated interface technique or technology – is the final criterion by which to measure the utility of any HCI technology. To be truly effective as an HCI technology, computer vision technologies must not only work according to the criteria of vision researchers (accuracy, robustness, etc.), but they must be useful and appropriate for the tasks at hand. They must ultimately deliver a better user experience.

To improve the user experience, either by modifying existing user interfaces or by providing new and different interface technologies, researchers must focus on a range of issues. Shneiderman [21] described five human factors objectives that should guide designers and evaluators of user interfaces: time to learn, speed of performance, user error rates, retention over time, and subjective satisfaction. Researchers in RTV4HCI must keep these in mind – it's not just about the technology, but about how the technology can deliver a better user experience.

3 Looking at People

The primary task of computer vision in RTV4HCI is to detect, recognize, and model meaningful communication cues – that is, to "look at the user" and report relevant information such as the user's location, expressions, gestures, hand and finger pose, etc. Although these may be inferred using other sensor modalities (such as optical or magnetic trackers), there are clear benefits in most environments to the unobtrusive and unencumbering nature of computer vision. Requiring a user to don a body suit, to put markers on the face or body, or to wear various tracking devices, is unacceptable or impractical for most anticipated applications of RTV4HCI.

Visually perceivable human activity includes a wide range of possibilities. Key aspects of "looking at people" include the detection, recognition, and modeling of the following elements [26]:

- Presence and location – Is someone there? How many people? Where are they (in 2D or 3D)? [Face and body detection, head and body tracking]
- Identity – Who are they? [Face recognition, gait recognition]
- Expression – Is a person smiling, frowning, laughing, speaking . . . ? [Facial feature tracking, expression modeling and analysis]
- Focus of attention – Where is a person looking? [Head/face tracking, eye gaze tracking]

- Body posture and movement – What is the overall pose and motion of the person? [Body modeling and tracking]
- Gesture – What are the semantically meaningful movements of the head, hands, body? [Gesture recognition, hand tracking]
- Activity – What is the person doing? [Analysis of body movement]

The computer vision problems of modeling, detecting, tracking, recognizing, and analyzing various aspects of human activity are quite difficult. It's hard enough to reliably recognize a rigid mechanical widget resting on a table, as image noise, changes in lighting and camera pose, and other issues contribute to the general difficulty of solving a problem that is fundamentally ill-posed. When humans are the objects of interest, these problems are magnified due to the complexity of human bodies (kinematics, non-rigid musculature and skin), and the things people do – wear clothing, change hairstyles, grow facial hair, wear glasses, get sunburned, age, apply makeup, change facial expression – that in general make life difficult for computer vision algorithms. Due to the wide variation in possible imaging conditions and human appearance, robustness is the primary issue that limits practical progress in the area.

There have been notable successes in various "looking at people" technologies over the years. One of the first complete systems that used computer vision in a real-time interactive setting was the system developed by Myron Krueger, a computer scientist and artist who first developed the VIDEO-PLACE responsive environment around 1970. VIDEOPLACE [13] was a full body interactive experience. It displayed the user's silhouette on a large screen (viewed by the user as a sort of mirror) and incorporated a number of interesting transformations, including letting the user hold, move, and interact with 2D objects (such as a miniature version of the user's silhouette) in real-time. The system let the user do finger painting and many other interactive activities. Although the computer vision was relatively simple, the complete system was quite compelling, and it was quite revolutionary for its time. A more recent system in a similar spirit was the "Magic Morphin Mirror / Mass Hallucinations" by Darrell et al. [6], an interactive art installation that allowed users to see modified versions of themselves in a mirror-like display. The system used computer vision to detect and track faces via a combination of stereo, color, and grayscale pattern detection.

The first computer programs to recognize human faces appeared in the late 1960s and early 1970s, but only in the past decade have computers become fast enough to support real-time face recognition. A number of computational models have been developed for this task, based on feature locations, face shape, face texture, and combinations thereof; these include Principal Component Analysis (PCA), Linear Discriminant Analysis (LDA), Gabor Wavelet Networks (GWNs), and Active Appearance Models (AAMs). Several companies, such as Identix Inc., Viisage Technology Inc., and Cognitec Systems, now develop and market face recognition technologies for access, security, and surveillance applications. Systems have been deployed in public locations such as airports and city squares, as well as in private, restricted access environments. For a comprehensive survey of face recognition research, see [34].

The MIT Media Lab was a hotbed of activity in computer vision research applied to human-computer interaction in the 1990s, with notable work in face recognition, body tracking, gesture recognition, facial expression modeling, and action recognition. The ALIVE system [14] used vision-based tracking (including the Pfinder system [31]) to extract a user's head, hand, and foot positions and gestures to enable the user to interact with computer-generated autonomous characters in a large-screen video mirror environment. Another compelling example of vision technology used effectively in an interactive environment was the Media Lab's KidsRoom project [4]. The KidsRoom was an interactive, narrative play space. Using computer vision to detect the locations of users and to recognize their actions helped to deliver a rich interactive experience for the participants. There have been many other compelling prototype systems developed at universities and research labs, some of which are in the initial stages of being brought to market. A system to recognize a limited vocabulary of American Sign Language (ASL) was developed, one of the first instances of real-time vision-based gesture recognition using Hidden Markov Models (HMMs).

Other notable research progress in important areas includes work in hand modeling and tracking [19, 32], gesture recognition [30, 22], facial expression analysis [33, 2], and applications to computer games [8].

In addition to technical progress in computer vision – better modeling of bodies, faces, skin, dynamics, movement, gestures, and activity, faster and more robust algorithms, better and larger databases being collected and shared, the increased focus on learning and probabilistic approaches – there must be an increased focus on the HCI aspects of RTV4HCI. Some of the critical issues include a deeper understanding of the semantics (e.g., when is a gesture a gesture, how is contextual information properly used?), clear policies on required accuracy and robustness of vision modules, and sufficient creativity in design and thorough user testing to ensure that the suggested solution actually benefits real users in real scenarios. Having technical solutions does not guarantee, by any means, that we know how to apply them more appropriately – intuition may be severely misleading. Hence, the research agenda for RTV4HCI must include both development of individual technology components (such as body tracking or gesture recognition) and the integration of these components into real systems with lots and lots of user testing.

Of course, there has been great research in various areas of real-time vision-based interfaces at many universities and labs around the world. The University of Illinois at Urbana-Champaign, Carnegie Mellon University, Georgia Tech, Microsoft Research, IBM Research, Mitsubishi Electric Research Laboratories, the University of Maryland, Boston University, ATR, ETL, the University of Southampton, the University of Manchester, INRIA, and the University of Bielefeld are but a few of the places where this research has flourished. Fortunately, the barrier to entry in this area is relatively low; a PC, a digital camera, and an interest in computer vision and human-computer interaction are all that is necessary to start working on the next major breakthrough in the field. There is much work to be done.

4 Final Thoughts

Computer vision has made significant progress through the years (and especially since my first experience with it in the early 1980s). There have been notable advances in all aspects of the field, with steady improvements in the performance and robustness of methods for low-level vision, stereo, motion, object representation and recognition, etc. The field has adopted more appropriate and effective computational methods, and now includes quite a wide range of application areas. Moore's Law improvements in hardware, advancements in camera technology, and the availability of useful software tools (such as Intel's OpenCV library[1]) have led to small, flexible, and affordable vision systems that are available to most researchers. Still, a rough back-of-the-envelope calculation reveals that we may have to wait some time before we really have the needed capabilities to perform very computationally intensive vision problems well in real-time. Assuming relatively high speed images (100 frames per second) in order to capture the temporal information needed for humans moving at normal speeds, relatively high resolution images (1000×1000 pixels) in order to capture the needed spatial resolution, and an estimated 40k operations per pixel in order to do the complex processing required by advanced algorithms, we are left needing a machine that delivers 4×10^{12} operations per second [20]. If Moore's Law holds up, it's conceivable that we could get there within a (human) generation. More challenging will be figuring out what algorithms to run on all those cycles! We are still more limited by our lack of knowledge than our lack of cycles. But the progress in both areas is encouraging.

RTV4HCI is still a nascent field, with growing interest and awareness from researchers in computer vision and in human-computer interaction. Due to how the field has progressed, companies are springing up to commercialize computer vision technology in new areas, including consumer applications. Progress has been steadily moving forward in understanding fundamental issues and algorithms in the field, as evidenced by the primary conferences and journals. Useful large datasets have been collected and widely distributed, leading to more rapid and focused progress in some areas. An apparent "killer app" for the field has not yet arisen, and in fact may never arrive; it may be the accumulation of many new and useful abilities, rather than one particular application, that finally validates the importance of the field. In all of these areas, significant speed and robustness issues remain; real-time approaches tend to be brittle, while more principled and thorough approaches

---

[1] http://www.intel.com/research/mrl/research/opencv

tend to be excruciatingly slow. Compared to speech recognition technology, which has seen years of commercial viability and has been improving steadily for decades, RTV4HCI is still in the Stone Age.

At the same time, there is an increased amount of cross-pollination between people in the computer vision and HCI communities. Quite a few conferences and workshops have appeared in recent years devoted to intersections of the two fields. If the past provides an accurate trajectory with which to anticipate the future, we have much to look forward to in this interesting and challenging endeavor.

References

1. M Annaratone et al. The Warp computer: architecture, implementation and performance. *IEEE Trans Computers*, pp 1523–1538, 1987.
2. M Black and Y Yacoob. Tracking and recognizing rigid and non-rigid facial motions using local parametric models of image motion. *Proc ICCV*, 1995.
3. W W Bledsoe. Man-machine facial recognition. Technical Report PRI 22, Panoramic Research Inc., 1966.
4. A Bobick et al. The KidsRoom: A perceptually-based interactive and immersive story environment. *PRESENCE: Teleoperators and Virtual Environments*, pp 367–391, 1999.
5. P J Burt. Smart sensing with a pyramid vision machine. *Proceedings of the IEEE*, pp 1006–1015, 1988.
6. T Darrell et al. A Magic Morphin Mirror. *SIGGRAPH Visual Proc*, 1997.
7. A Dix et al, *Human-Computer Interaction, Second Edition*. Prentice Hall, 1998.
8. W Freeman et al. Computer vision for computer games. *Proc Int Conf on Automatic Face and Gesture Recognition*, 1996.
9. A J Goldstein et al. Identification of human faces. *Proceedings of the IEEE*, pp 748–760, 1971.
10. P J Grother et al. Face Recognition Vendor Test 2002 Performance Metrics. *Proc Int Conference on Audio Visual Based Person Authentication*, 2003.
11. M D Kelly. Visual identification of people by computer. Stanford Artificial Intelligence Project Memo AI-130, 1970.
12. T Kanade. Picture processing system by computer complex and recognition of human faces. Doctoral Dissertation, Kyoto University, 1973.
13. M W Krueger. *Artificial Reality II*. Addison-Wesley, 1991.
14. P Maes et al. The ALIVE system: wireless, full-body interaction with autonomous agents. *ACM Multimedia Systems*, 1996.
15. J O'Rourke and N Badler. Model-based image analysis of human motion using constraint propagation. *IEEE Trans PAMI*, pp 522–536, 1980.
16. S Oviatt et al. Multimodal interfaces that flex, adapt, and persist. *Comm ACM*, pp 30–33, 2004.
17. P J Phillips et al. The FERET evaluation methodology for face recognition algorithms. *IEEE Trans PAMI*, pp 1090–1104, 2000.
18. R F Rashid. Towards a system for the interpretation of Moving Light Displays. *IEEE Trans PAMI*, pp 574–581, 1980.

19. J Rehg and T Kanade. Visual tracking of high DOF articulated structures: An application to human hand tracking. *Proc ECCV*, 1994.
20. S Shafer. Personal communication, 1998.
21. B Shneiderman. *Designing the User Interface: Strategies for Effective Human-Computer Interaction, Third Edition.* Addison-Wesley, 1998.
22. M Stark and M Kohler. Video based gesture recognition for human computer interaction. In: W D Fellner (Editor). *Modeling – Virtual Worlds – Distributed Graphics.* Infix Verlag, 1995.
23. M Turk. Computer vision in the interface. *Comm ACM*, pp 60–67, 2004.
24. M Turk. Interactive-time vision: face recognition as a visual behavior. PhD Thesis, MIT Media Lab, 1991.
25. M Turk. Perceptive media: Machine perception and human computer interaction. *Chinese Computing J*, 2001.
26. M Turk and M Kölsch. Perceptual interfaces. In: G Medioni and S B Kang (Editors). *Emerging Topics in Computer Vision.* Prentice Hall, 2004.
27. M Turk and G Robertson. Perceptual user interfaces. *Comm ACM*, pp 33–34, 2000.
28. A van Dam. Post-wimp user interfaces. *Comm ACM*, pp 63–67, 1997.
29. J A Webb and J K Aggarwal. Structure from motion of rigid and jointed objects. *Artificial Intelligence*, pp 107–130, 1982.
30. C Vogler and D Metaxas. Adapting Hidden Markov Models for ASL recognition by using three-dimensional computer vision methods. *Proc IEEE Int Conf on Systems, Man, and Cybernetics*, 1997.
31. C R Wren et al. Pfinder: Real-time tracking of the human body. *IEEE Trans PAMI*, pp 780–785, 1997.
32. Y Wu and T S Huang. Hand modeling, analysis, and recognition. *IEEE Signal Proc Mag*, pp 51–60, 2001.
33. A Zelinsky and J Heinzmann. Real-time visual recognition of facial gestures for human-computer interaction. *Proc Int Conf on Automatic Face and Gesture Recognition*, 1996.
34. W Zhao et al. Face recognition: A literature survey. *ACM Computing Surveys*, pp 399–458, 2003.

Real-Time Algorithms:
From Signal Processing to Computer Vision

Branislav Kisačanin[1] and Vladimir Pavlović[2]

[1] Delphi Corporation
   b.kisacanin@ieee.org
[2] Rutgers University
   vladimir@cs.rutgers.edu

In this chapter we aim to describe a variety of factors influencing the design of real-time vision systems, from processor options to real-time algorithms. By touching upon algorithms from different fields, from data and signal processing to low-level computer vision and machine learning, we demonstrate the diversity of building blocks available for real-time vision design.

1 Introduction

In general, when faced with a problem that involves constraints on both the system response time and the overall system cost, one must carefully consider all problem assumptions, simplify the solution as much as possible, and use the specific conditions of the problem. Very often, there is much to gain just by using an alternative algorithm that provides similar functionality at a lower computational cost or in a shorter time.

In this chapter we talk about such alternatives, *real-time algorithms*, in computer vision. We begin by discussing different meanings of *real-time* and other related terminology and notation. Next, we describe some of the hardware options available for real-time vision applications. Finally, we present some of the most important real-time algorithms from different fields that vision for HCI (Human-Computer Interaction) relies on: data analysis, digital signal and image processing, low-level computer vision, and machine learning.

2 Explaining Real-Time

What do we mean by *real-time* when we talk about real-time systems and real-time algorithms? Different things, really, but similar and related. These separate uses of *real-time* have evolved over the years, and while their differences might cause a bit of confusion, we do not attempt to rectify the situation.

Researchers have been investigating much more complex topics without first defining them properly. To quote Sir Francis Crick and Christof Koch [8]:

> If it seems like a cop-out, try defining the word "gene" – you will not find it easy.

We will not completely avoid the subject either: we will *explain*, rather than *define*, what is usually meant by *real-time*. At the same time we will introduce other common terminology and notation.

There are at least two basic meanings to *real-time*. One is used in the description of software and hardware systems (as in *real-time operating system*). We will discuss this and related terminology shortly, in Sect. 2.1.

The other meaning of *real-time* is employed in the characterization of algorithms, when it is an alternative to calling an algorithm *fast* (e.g., Fast Fourier Transform – FFT). This meaning is used to suggest that the *fast* algorithm is more likely to allow the entire system to achieve *real-time* operation than some other algorithm. We talk about this in Sect. 2.2.

2.1 Systems

For systems in general, the time it takes a system to produce its output, starting from the moment all relevant inputs are presented to the system, is called the *response time*. We say that a system is *real-time* if its response time satisfies constraints imposed by the application. For example, an automotive air-bag must be deployed within a few milliseconds after contact during a crash. This is dictated by the physics of the event. Air-bag deployment systems are an example of *hard real-time* systems, in which the constraints on the response time must always be satisfied.

Some applications may allow deadlines to be occasionally missed, resulting in performance degradation, rather than failure. For example, your digital camera may take a bit longer than advertised to take a picture of a low-light scene. In this case we say its performance degrades with decreasing illumination. Such systems are called *soft real-time* systems. Real-time HCI systems can often be soft real-time. For example, a 45 ms visual delay is not noticeable, but anything above that will progressively degrade visual interfaces [38].

2.2 Algorithms

To illustrate the use of *real-time* to qualify algorithms, consider the Discrete Fourier Transform. It can be implemented directly from its definition

$$X_k = \sum_{m=0}^{n-1} x_m e^{-j2\pi km/n} \quad (k = 0, 1, \ldots, n-1) \tag{1}$$

This implementation, let us just call it the DFT algorithm for simplicity, requires $3n^2$ real multiplications. This is true if we assume that exponential factors are calculated offline and the complex multiplication is implemented so that the number of real multiplications is minimized:

$$(a + jb)(p + jq) = ap - bq + j(aq + bp)$$
$$= ap - bq + j((a + b)(p + q) - ap - bq)$$

Usually we are most concerned with the number of multiplications, but the number of additions is also important in some implementations. In any case, we say that DFT is an $O(n^2)$ algorithm. This so-called O-notation [7] means there is an upper bound on the worst case number of operations involved in execution of the DFT algorithm, and that this upper bound is a multiple of n^2, in this case $3n^2$.

In general, an algorithm is $O(f(n))$ if its execution involves $\leq \alpha f(n)$ operations, where α is some positive constant. This notation is also used in discussions about NP-completeness of algorithms [7].

This same function, the Discrete Fourier Transform, can also be implemented using one of many algorithms collectively known as FFT, such as Cooley-Tukey FFT, Winograd FFT, etc. [10, 30, 45]. Due to the significant speed advantage offered by these algorithms, which are typically $O(n \log n)$, we say that the FFT is a *real-time* algorithm. By this we mean that the FFT is more likely than DFT to allow the entire system to achieve real-time.

Note that the O-notation is not always the best way to compare algorithms, because it only describes their asymptotic behavior. For example, with sufficiently large n we know that an $O(n^3)$ algorithm will be slower that an $O(n^2)$ algorithm, but this notation tells us very little about what happens for smaller values of n. This is because the O-notation absorbs any multiplicative constants and additive factors of lesser order.

Often we do not work with a "sufficiently large n" and hence must be careful not to jump to conclusions. A common example is the matrix multiplication. The standard way to multiply two $n \times n$ matrices requires $O(n^3)$ scalar multiplications. On the other hand, there are matrix algorithms of lesser asymptotic complexity. Historically, the first was Strassen's $O(n^{2.81})$ algorithm [41]. However, due to the multiplicative constants absorbed by the O-notation, the Strassen's algorithm should be used only for $n \approx 700$ and greater. Have you ever had to multiply matrices that big? Probably not, but if you have they were probably sparse or had some structure. In that case one is best off using a matrix multiplication algorithm designed specifically for such matrices [11, 19].

2.3 Design Considerations

Designing a real-time system is often a complex task. It involves multiple trade-offs, such as choosing the right processor: one that will offer enough "horsepower" to do the job in a timely manner, but will not cost a lot or consume too much power. We discuss processor selection in Sect. 3.

Needless to say, we can make any system real-time by using faster resources (processors, memory, sensors, I/O) or waiting for them to become available, but that is not the way to design for success. This is where we need real-time algorithms, to allow us to use less expensive hardware while still achieving real-time performance. We discuss real-time algorithms in Sect. 4.

Other things to consider when designing a real-time system: carefully determine real-time deadlines for the system, make sure the system will meet these deadlines even in the worst case scenario, and choose development tools to enable you to efficiently design your real-time system (for example, compiling the software should not take hours). One frequently overlooked design parameter is the *system lag*. For example, an interactive vision system may be processing frames at a frame rate, but if the visual output lags too much behind the input, it may be useless or nauseous. This often happens because of the delay introduced by the frame-grabbing pipeline and similarly, the video output pipeline.

3 Hardware Options

Before discussing real-time algorithms (Sect. 4), we must discuss hardware options. Algorithms do not operate in a vacuum, they are implemented either directly in hardware or in software that operates on hardware.

Given a design problem, one must think about what kinds of processing will be required. Different types of processing have varying levels of success mapping onto different hardware architectures. For example, a chip specifically designed to efficiently handle linear filtering will not be the best choice for applications requiring many floating-point matrix inversions or large control structures.

3.1 Useful Hardware Features

In general, since computer vision involves processing of images, and image processing is an extreme case of digital signal processing, your design will benefit from using fast memory, wide data busses with DMA, and processor parallelism:

- **Fast memory.** Fast, internal (on-chip) memory is required to avoid idle cycles due to read and write latencies characteristic of external memory. Configuring the internal memory as cache helps reduce the memory size requirements and is often acceptable in image processing, because imaging functions tend to have a high locality of reference for both the data and the code.

- **Wide data bus with DMA.** Considering the amount of data that needs to be given to the processor in imaging and vision applications, it is understandable that wide data busses (at least 64-bit wide) are a must. Another must is having a DMA (Direct Memory Access) unit, which performs data transfers in the background, for example from the frame buffer to the internal memory, freeing the processor to do more complex operations.

- **Parallelism.** Regarding the processor parallelism, we distinguish [39]: temporal parallelism, issue parallelism (superscalar processors), and intra-instruction parallelism (SIMD, VLIW):

  - **Temporal.** The temporal parallelism is now a standard feature of microprocessors. It refers to pipelining the phases of instruction processing, commonly referred to as Fetch, Decode, Execute, and Write.

  - **Superscalar processors.** The issue parallelism is achieved using superscalar architectures, a commonplace for general purpose microprocessors such as Pentium and PowerPC families. Superscalar processors have special-purpose circuitry that analyzes the decoded instructions for dependences. Independent instructions present an opportunity to parallelize their execution. While this mechanism is a great way to increase processor performance, the associated circuitry adds significantly to the chip complexity, thus increasing the cost.

  - **SIMD, VLIW.** Intrainstruction parallelism is another way to parallelize processing. SIMD (Single Instruction Multiple Data) refers to multiple identical processing units operating under control of a single instruction, each working on different input data. A common way to use this approach is, for example, to design 32-bit multipliers so that they can also do 4 simultaneous 8-bit multiplications. VLIW (Very Long Instruction Word) refers to a specific processor architecture employing multiple non-identical functional units running in parallel. For example, an 8-way VLIW processor has eight parallel functional units (e.g., two multipliers and six arithmetic units). To support their parallel execution it fetches eight 32-bit instructions each cycle. The full instruction is then up to 256 bits long, thus the name, VLIW. Note that unlike superscalar processors, which parallelize instructions at run-time, the VLIW processors are supported by sophisticated compilers that analyze the code and parallelize at compile-time.

3.2 Making a Choice

While there is no universal formula to determine the best processor for your application, much less a processor that would best satisfy all combinations of requirements, there are things that you can do to ensure you are making a good choice. Here are some questions to ask yourself when considering hardware options for your computer vision problem:

- **Trivial case.** Are you developing for a specific hardware target? Your choice is then obvious. For example, if you are working on lip reading software for the personal computer market, then you will most likely work with a chip from the Pentium or PowerPC families.

- **High volume: > 1,000,000.** Will your product end up selling in high volumes? For example, if you expect to compete with game platforms such as PlayStation, or if your product will be mounted in every new car, then you should consider developing your own ASIC (Application Specific Integrated Circuit). This way you can design a chip with exactly the silicon you need, no more, no less. In principle, you do not want to pay for silicon you will not use. Only at high volumes can the development cost for an ASIC be recovered. You may find it useful to start your development on some popular general purpose processor (e.g., Pentium). Soon you would migrate to an FPGA (Field Programmable Gate Array), and finally, when the design is stable, you would produce your own ASIC. Tools exist to help you with each of these transitions. Your ASIC will likely be a fairly complex design, including a processor core and various peripherals. As such, it qualifies to be called a System-on-a-Chip (SoC).

- **Medium volume: 10,000–100,000.** Are you considering medium volume production? Is your algorithm development expected to continue even after the sales start? In this case you will need the mix of flexibility and cost effectiveness offered by a recently introduced class of processors, called *media processors*. They typically have a high-end DSP core employing SIMD and VLIW methodologies, married on-chip with some typical multimedia peripherals such as video ports, networking support, and other fast data ports. The most popular examples are TriMedia (Philips), DM64x (TI), Blackfin (ADI), and BSP (Equator).

- **Low volume: < 1,000.** Are you working on a military or aerospace application or just trying to quickly prove the concept to your management or customer? These are just a few examples of low volume applications and situations in which the system cost is not the biggest concern or development time is very short. If so, you need to consider using a general purpose processor, such as Pentium or PowerPC. They cost more than media processors, but offer more "horsepower" and mature development tools. With available SIMD extensions (MMX/SSE/SSE2 and AltiVec) they are well suited for imaging and vision applications. Pentium's MMX/SSE/SSE2 and PowerPC's AltiVec can do two and eight floating-point operations per cycle, respectively. You may find it useful to add an FPGA for some specific tasks, such as frame-grabbing and image preprocessing. Actually, with ever-increasing fabric density of FPGAs and the availability of entire processing cores on them, an FPGA may be all you need. For example, the brains of NASA's Mars rovers *Spirit* and *Opportunity* have been implemented on radiation-tolerant FPGAs [51]. Furthermore, FPGAs may be a viable choice for even slightly higher volumes. As their cost is getting lower every year, they are competing with DSPs and media chips for such markets.

- **Difficult case.** If your situation lies somewhere in between the cases described above, you will need to learn more about different choices and decide based on the specific requirements of your application. You may need to benchmark different chips using a few representative pieces of your code. It will also be useful to understand the primary application for which the chips have been designed and determine how much common ground there is (in terms of types of processing and required peripherals) with your problem.

Recently, much attention has been given to two additional classes of processors: highly parallel SIMD arrays of VLIW processors [26, 33, 42, 43] and vision engines (coprocessors) [29, 49]. With respect to cost, performance, and flexibility, they are likely to be between the media processors and ASICs.

Another thing you may want to consider is the choice between fixed-point and floating-point processors. Typically, imaging and vision applications do most of their processing on pixels, which are most often 8-bit numbers. Even at higher precision, fixed-point processors will do the job. If the fixed-point processor is required to perform floating-point operations, vendor-supplied software libraries usually exist that emulate floating-point hardware. Since hardware floating-point is much more efficient than software emulation, if you require a lot of floating-point operations, you will have to use a floating-point processor. Also, the cost of floating-point hardware is usually only 15–20% higher than the corresponding fixed-point hardware. The ease of development in a floating-point environment may be a sufficient reason to pay the extra cost.

Before finalizing your choice, you should make sure the chip you are about to select has acceptable power consumption, appropriate qualifications (military, automotive, medical, etc.), mature development tools, defined roadmap, and is going to be supported and manufactured in the foreseeable future. Last, but certainly not least, make sure the official quoted price of the chip at volume is close to what you were initially told by vendor's marketing.

3.3 Algorithms, Execution Time, and Required Memory

Next, we discuss the mapping of algorithms onto hardware. In more practical terms, we address the issue of choosing among different algorithms and processors. If we have a choice of several algorithms for the same task, is there a theoretical tool or some other way to estimate their execution times on a particular processor? Of course, we are trying to avoid making actual time measurements, because that implies having to implement and optimize all candidate algorithms. Alternatively, if we are trying to compare execution times of several processors for the same algorithm, can we do it just based on processor architecture and algorithm structure? Otherwise we would have to implement the algorithm on all candidate processors. An even more difficult problem is when we have two degrees of freedom, i.e., if we can choose between both algorithms and processors. Practice often deals us even greater problems by adding cost and other parameters into the decision making process.

In general, unfortunately, there is no such tool. However, for some processing architectures and some classes of algorithms we can perform theoretical analysis. We will discuss that shortly, in Sect. 3.4. A trivial case is, for example, comparing digital filtering on several media processors. By looking at how many MAC (Multiply and Accumulate) operations the chip can do every cycle and taking into account the processor clock frequency, we can easily compare their performance. However, this analysis is valid only for data that can fit into the on-chip memory. The analysis becomes much more complex and non-deterministic if the on-chip memory has to be configured as cache [28]. The problem becomes even more difficult if our analysis is to include superscalar processors, such as Pentium and PowerPC. Even if these major obstacles could disappear, there would remain many other, smaller issues, such as differences between languages, compilers, and programming skills.

The memory required by different algorithms for the same task may also be important. For example, as will be discussed in Sect. 4, Quicksort is typically up to two times faster than Heapsort, but the latter does sorting in-place, i.e., it does not require any memory in addition to the memory containing the data. This property may become critical in cases when the available fast (on-chip) memory is only slightly larger than the data to be sorted: Quicksort with external memory will likely be much slower than the Heapsort with on-chip memory.

3.4 Tensor Product for Matching Algorithms and Hardware

For a very important class of algorithms there is a theoretical tool that can be of use in comparing different algorithms as they map on different processor architectures [13, 14, 45]. This tool applies to digital filtering and transforms with a highly recursive structure. Important examples are [13]:

- Linear convolution, e.g., FIR filtering, correlation, and projections in PCA (Principal Component Analysis)
- Discrete and Fast Fourier Transform
- Walsh-Hadamard Transform
- Discrete Hartley Transform
- Discrete Cosine Transform
- Strassen Matrix Multiplication

To investigate these algorithms, the required computation is first represented using matrix notation. For example, DFT (Discrete Fourier Transform) can be written as

$$X = F_n x$$

where X and x are $n \times 1$ vectors representing the transform and the data, respectively, while F_n is the so-called DFT matrix

$$F_n = \begin{bmatrix} 1 & 1 & 1 & \cdots & 1 \\ 1 & \omega & \omega^2 & \cdots & \omega^{n-1} \\ 1 & \omega^2 & \omega^4 & \cdots & \omega^{2(n-1)} \\ \vdots & \vdots & \vdots & \ddots & \vdots \\ 1 & \omega^{n-1} & \omega^{2(n-1)} & \cdots & \omega^{(n-1)^2} \end{bmatrix}$$

where $\omega = e^{-j2\pi/n}$. This representation is equivalent to (1).

The recursive structure of algorithms implies the decomposability of the associated matrices. For example, for the DFT matrix F_n numerous decompositions can be found, each corresponding to a different FFT algorithm. For example, the Cooley-Tukey FFT (radix-2 decimation-in-time) algorithm can be derived for $n = 2^r$ from the following recursive property:

$$F_n = \begin{bmatrix} I_{n/2} & I_{n/2} \\ I_{n/2} & -I_{n/2} \end{bmatrix} \begin{bmatrix} I_{n/2} & 0 \\ 0 & D_{n/2} \end{bmatrix} \begin{bmatrix} F_{n/2} & 0 \\ 0 & F_{n/2} \end{bmatrix} P_{n,2} \qquad (2)$$

where

$$D_{n/2} = \mathrm{diag}(1, \omega, \ldots, \omega^{n/2-1})$$

$I_{n/2}$ is the size-$n/2$ unity matrix, and $P_{n,2}$ is the stride-by-two permutation matrix representing the familiar data shuffling in the FFT.

At this point the formalism of the tensor product (also known as Kronecker or direct product) of matrices becomes useful. If A and B are $p \times q$ and $r \times s$ matrices, respectively, their tensor product is denoted by $A \otimes B$. If A and B are given by

$$A = \begin{bmatrix} a_{11} & a_{12} & \cdots & a_{1q} \\ a_{21} & a_{22} & \cdots & a_{2q} \\ \vdots & \vdots & \ddots & \vdots \\ a_{p1} & a_{p2} & \cdots & a_{pq} \end{bmatrix} \quad \text{and} \quad B = \begin{bmatrix} b_{11} & b_{12} & \cdots & b_{1s} \\ b_{21} & b_{22} & \cdots & b_{2s} \\ \vdots & \vdots & \ddots & \vdots \\ b_{r1} & b_{r2} & \cdots & b_{rs} \end{bmatrix}$$

their tensor product is a $pr \times qs$ matrix defined as

$$A \otimes B = \begin{bmatrix} a_{11}B & a_{12}B & \cdots & a_{1q}B \\ a_{21}B & a_{22}B & \cdots & a_{2q}B \\ \vdots & \vdots & \ddots & \vdots \\ a_{p1}B & a_{p2}B & \cdots & a_{pq}B \end{bmatrix}$$

Using this formalism, the recursive property (2) can be written as

$$F_n = (F_2 \otimes I_{n/2})\mathrm{diag}(I_{n/2}, D_{n/2})(I_2 \otimes F_{n/2})P_{n,2}$$

Applying the same recursion to $F_{n/2}, F_{n/4}, \ldots$ down to F_2 we find a fast algorithm for DFT and see that it can be explained using this decomposition of F_n into a product of sparse matrices.

In particular, this recursion shows us that $T(n)$, the number of operations required for the size-n problem using the fast algorithm, can be described recursively by

$$T(n) = \begin{cases} 0 & n = 1 \\ 2T(n/2) + \alpha n & n > 1 \end{cases}$$

where α is some constant. The solution of this recursion [7] is an $O(n \log n)$ function. Therefore, FFT is an $O(n \log n)$ algorithm.

Alternative decompositions yield different FFT algorithms [45]. A similar formalism exists for other algorithms [13]. Most importantly, this same formalism can be used to determine which one of many mathematically equivalent algorithms is most suitable for a particular processor architecture [14].

For example, consider a part of an algorithm involving multiplication by a $pr \times pr$ block diagonal matrix C whose p blocks are all equal to an $r \times r$ matrix B

$$C = \begin{bmatrix} B & & & \\ & B & & \\ & & \ddots & \\ & & & B \end{bmatrix}$$

This can be written using the tensor product notation as $C = I_p \otimes B$ and can be efficiently implemented on a SIMD architecture involving p functional units, each performing multiplication by B.

Unfortunately, this method does not take into account non-deterministic effects of cache memory and superscalar issue parallelism.

4 Real-Time Algorithms

In this section, we present some of the most important real-time algorithms from the fields related to vision for HCI: data analysis, optimization, signal and image processing, computer vision, and machine learning. The selection and depth of coverage are a trade-off between several conflicting requirements: limited space, need for versatility and depth, and desire to cover the fundamental techniques while providing a glimpse at some related developments. Since most of the described algorithms are available as function calls in standard software libraries, we do not provide any code. Our goal is to illustrate enough for understanding and practical application of these algorithms. For interested readers we provide a number of references.

4.1 Sorting

A common task in data analysis is sorting of data in numerical order. Theoretical analysis and practice [7, 34] show that for problems with small-size data ($n < 20$) the best choice is *straight insertion* [25], for medium-size data ($20 \leq n \leq 50$) the best approach is *Shell's method* [25], while for larger data sets ($n > 50$) the fastest sorting algorithm is Sir C. A. R. Hoare's *Quicksort* algorithm [18]. Instead of Quicksort, one may prefer to use J. W. J. Williams' *Heapsort* algorithm [50], which is slightly slower (typically around half the speed of Quicksort) but does an in-place sorting and has better worst-case asymptotics. In Table 1 we show some more information on asymptotic complexity.

Table 1. Guide to choosing a sorting algorithm

algorithm	worst case	average	best for
Straight insertion	$O(n^2)$	$O(n^2)$	$n < 20$
Shell's method	$O(n^{1.5})$	$O(n^{1.25})$	$20 \leq n \leq 50$
Quicksort	$O(n^2)$	$O(n \log n)$	$n > 50$ and high speed
Heapsort	$O(n \log n)$	$O(n \log n)$	$n > 50$ and low memory

For a detailed explanation of these and other sorting algorithms we refer the reader to [7, 25, 34].

4.2 Golden Section Search

Frequently we need to optimize a function, for example to find the maximum of some index of performance. Minimization of $f(x)$ can be done by maximization of $-f(x)$. Here we present a simple but very effective algorithm to find a maximum of a function: Golden Section Search [4, 34]. Our basic assumption is that getting the value of the function is expensive because it involves extensive measurements or calculations. Thus, we want to estimate the maximum of $f(x)$ using the minimum number of actual values of $f(x)$ as possible. The only prerequisites are that $f(x)$ is "well-behaved" (meaning that it does not have discontinuities or other similar mathematical pathologies), and that by using some application-specific method, we can guarantee that there is one, and only one, maximum in the interval given to the algorithm.

At all times, the information about what we learned about the maximum of function $f(x)$ will be encoded by three points: $(a, f(a)), (b, f(b)), (c, f(c))$, with $a < b < c$. After each iteration we will get a new, narrower triplet, $(a', f(a')), (b', f(b')), (c', f(c'))$, which can be used as input to the next iteration, or can be used to estimate the peak of $f(x)$ by fitting a parabola to the three points and finding the maximum of the parabola. This assumes that $f(x)$ is a "well-behaved" function and looks like a parabola close to the peak.

If we know that the maximum is in the interval (a, c), we start by measuring or calculating $f(x)$ at the interval boundaries, $x = a$ and $x = c$, and at a point $x = b$ somewhere inside the interval. We will specify what "somewhere" means shortly. Now we begin our iterative procedure (see Fig. 1): A new measurement, at $x = m$, is made inside the wider of the two intervals (a, b) or (b, c).

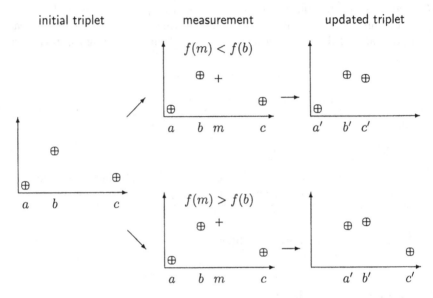

Fig. 1. Each iteration of the Golden Section Search algorithm results in shrinking of the interval containing the desired maximum. Iterations start from the input triplet, take a new measurement, and output the updated triplet, which can be used in the next iteration or in the final step – fitting a parabola and finding its peak

Assume $m \in (b, c)$. If $f(m) < f(b)$, we set the resulting triplet so that $a' = a$, $b' = b$, and $c' = m$, otherwise, for $f(m) > f(b)$, we set the resulting triplet so that $a' = b$, $b' = m$, and $c' = c$. Similar rules hold for $m \in (a, b)$.

How should b and m be selected? Let b divide the interval (a, c) in proportions α and $1 - \alpha$, i.e.,

$$\frac{b - a}{c - a} = \alpha \quad \text{and} \quad \frac{c - b}{c - a} = 1 - \alpha$$

and let m be such that

$$\frac{m - b}{c - a} = \beta$$

For all iterations to be the same, we want the rules for choosing b and m to be identical, i.e.,

$$\frac{\beta}{1 - \alpha} = \alpha$$

Additionally, we want to maximize the worst-case rate of convergence (the rate of interval shrinking). This is done by setting the two larger intervals equal, $c - m = b - a$, when

$$\beta = 1 - 2\alpha$$

The only solution in interval $(0, 1)$ for α, and correspondingly for $1 - \alpha$, is

$$\alpha = \frac{3 - \sqrt{5}}{2} \quad \text{and} \quad 1 - \alpha = \frac{\sqrt{5} - 1}{2}$$

Note that $1 - \alpha$ equals $\phi = 0.618\ldots$, a mathematical constant called the *golden section*, which is related to Fibonacci numbers and appears in many unexpected places (geometry, algebra, biology, architecture, ...) [12, 22]. After n iterations, the interval width is $c^{(n)} - a^{(n)} \leq \phi^n(c - a)$.

Note that a similar method, called Fibonacci search, achieves a slightly better convergence rate by not employing the same rule for the new measurement in each iteration [4]. In the Fibonacci search the rule used in the k-th iteration is based on the ratio of consecutive Fibonacci numbers (1, 1, 2, 3, 5, 8, 13, 21, 34, ...; in general $F_{n+2} = F_{n+1} + F_n$ with $F_1 = F_2 = 1$). If we allow a total of n iterations, then

$$\alpha_k = 1 - \frac{F_{n-k+1}}{F_{n-k+2}}$$

Since the ratio of consecutive Fibonacci numbers quickly converges to ϕ, most α_k are very close to $\alpha = 1 - \phi$.

4.3 Kalman Filtering

Kalman filter is an estimator used to estimate states of dynamic systems from noisy measurements. While the attribute "filter" may be a bit confusing, according to Mohinder Grewal and Angus Andrews [15] the method itself is

> ... certainly one of the greater discoveries in the history of statistical estimation theory and possibly the greatest discovery in the twentieth century.

Invented by R. E. Kalman in 1958, and first published in [20], it has been quickly applied to the control and navigation of spacecraft, aircraft, and many other complex systems. Kalman filter offers a quadratically optimal way to estimate system states from indirect, noisy, and even incomplete measurements.

In the context of estimation theory, it represents an extension of recursive least-squares estimation to problems in which the states to be estimated are governed by a linear dynamic model. What makes this method particularly attractive is the recursive solution, suitable for real-time implementation on a digital computer.

The fact that the solution is recursive means that at each time instant the estimate is formed by updating the previous estimate using the latest measurement. If there was no recursive solution, we would have to calculate the current estimate using all measurements.

Consider a discrete-time linear dynamic system that is fully described by an $n \times 1$ state vector x. If these states are not directly measurable, we can estimate them from a noisy $m \times 1$ measurement vector y, provided the system is observable [15, 23] and the noise has certain properties. Let the system be described by the following variables and parameters

$$
\begin{aligned}
x[k] \quad &\ldots \quad n \times 1 \quad \text{state vector} \\
u[k] \quad &\ldots \quad m \times 1 \quad \text{deterministic input vector} \\
y[k] \quad &\ldots \quad r \times 1 \quad \text{measurement vector} \\
w[k] \quad &\ldots \quad n \times 1 \quad \text{system noise vector} \\
e[k] \quad &\ldots \quad r \times 1 \quad \text{measurement noise vector} \\
A \quad &\ldots \quad n \times n \quad \text{state transition matrix} \\
B \quad &\ldots \quad n \times m \quad \text{input coupling matrix} \\
C \quad &\ldots \quad r \times n \quad \text{measurement sensitivity matrix}
\end{aligned}
$$

The dynamic model consists of update and measurement equations

$$
\begin{aligned}
x[k+1] &= Ax[k] + Bu[k] + w[k] \\
y[k] &= Cx[k] + e[k]
\end{aligned}
$$

where the system noise $w[k]$ and the measurement noise $e[k]$ are zero-mean, white, and Gaussian. Furthermore, $w[k]$ is uncorrelated with $e[k]$. If the noise covariances are

$$
\begin{aligned}
E\{w[k]w'[l]\} &= Q\delta[k-l] \\
E\{e[k]e'[l]\} &= R\delta[k-l]
\end{aligned}
$$

then the steady-state Kalman estimator is given by

$$
\hat{x}[k] = z[k] + L(y[k] - Cz[k])
$$

where

$$
z[k] = A\hat{x}[k-1] + Bu[k-1] \quad (z[0] = x[0] = x_0)
$$

and the gain L is given by $L = PC'(R + CPC')^{-1}$, where P is a solution of the algebraic Riccati equation

$$
P = Q + APA' - APC'(R + CPC')^{-1}CPA
$$

The algebraic Riccati equation is solved offline. MATLAB and other development and simulation tools offer functions to solve this equation and determine the steady-state Kalman filter gain L. As can be seen from these equations, the estimate $\hat{x}[k]$ is recursive. In other words, it is based on the previous estimate, $\hat{x}[k-1]$, and the latest measurement, $y[k]$.

A slightly more complicated formulation may be useful, in which the Kalman filter gain L is not treated as a constant matrix, but is determined for each recursion, as L_k. In that case we do not solve the algebraic Riccati equation ahead of time. Instead, we recursively calculate P_k at each stage. In that case P_k can be interpreted as the covariance matrix of the estimate $\hat{x}[k]$. More details can be found in [15, 23].

In computer vision one often encounters the following dynamic model used in object tracking. For the $x-$axis (c_x is the $x-$coordinate, v_x is the associated velocity, and T is the sampling period), we write

$$\begin{bmatrix} c_x[k+1] \\ v_x[k+1] \end{bmatrix} = \begin{bmatrix} 1 & T \\ 0 & 1 \end{bmatrix} \begin{bmatrix} c_x[k] \\ v_x[k] \end{bmatrix} + \begin{bmatrix} w_{cx}[k] \\ w_{vx}[k] \end{bmatrix}$$

$$y[k] = \begin{bmatrix} 1 & 0 \end{bmatrix} \begin{bmatrix} c_x[k] \\ v_x[k] \end{bmatrix} + e[k]$$

Similar equations can be written for the $y-$ and $z-$axes. These equations model object motion as random. The noise covariances determine how much weight is given to the new measurement $y[k]$ and how much to the previous estimate, $\hat{x}[k-1]$, as they are combined to form the new estimate, $\hat{x}[k]$.

Since the above model is only order-2, the matrix calculations involved in its implementation are almost trivial. Many more details on efficient implementation of higher-order Kalman filters, which involve matrix factorization and matrix inversion, can be found in [11, 15, 19]. This is useful, for example, in application of Kalman filtering to model complex articulated structures, such as human body [35].

Other, more complicated formulations of Kalman filter exist [15]: some allow colored noise, others can account for unknown system model parameters, and some can deal with nonlinearities (extended Kalman filter). In recent years, a more general framework called *particle filtering* has been used to extend applicability of Kalman's approach to non-Gaussian stochastic processes [1, 32].

The main idea is to recursively propagate the conditional probability distribution function for the value of the state vector, given all measurements. In the case of a linear dynamic system and Gaussian noise, this becomes the Kalman filter. In general, for nonlinear models and non-Gaussian noise, the equations only have approximate solutions.

4.4 FFT

Fast Fourier Transform (FFT) is a common name for a number of $O(n \log n)$ algorithms used to evaluate the Discrete Fourier Transform (DFT) of n data points. The DFT itself was initially most important to physicists in modeling and analysis of periodic phenomena (string vibrations, planetary orbits, tides, daily temperature variations, etc.). Since the 1940s crystallographers used DFT, actually its inverse, to infer the crystal structure and properties from X-ray diffraction patterns. For example, in 1953, the calculations that Rosalind Franklin made from diffraction images of DNA taken by her and Maurice Wilkins, confirmed the brilliant double-helix hypothesis proposed earlier that year by James Watson and Francis Crick. Not knowing which algorithm she used for her calculations, we can only speculate that she would have made the big discovery herself had she used the FFT.

The discovery of FFT algorithms has a fascinating history [6]. Like many other mathematical discoveries it can be traced back to Carl Friedrich Gauss [17], who developed it to analyze the orbit parameters of the asteroid Pallas in 1805. He used $N = N_1 N_2$ astronomical observations and performed the DFT analysis (he didn't call it DFT – Fourier himself entered the scene only in 1807) by dividing calculations into smaller blocks, thus having to do only $N(N_1 + N_2)$ calculations instead of N^2. He commented on the computational savings and also on the possibility to improve his method by dividing factors of N further into smaller factors. This work was published much later, posthumously, in 1866. In the meantime, better methods for orbit determination had been developed. Thus, Gauss' method fell into oblivion. As it happens, the algorithm was rediscovered, used, and forgotten on several later occasions.

It was rediscovered one last time, in 1964, by James Cooley and John Tukey [5] and almost immediately gained wide acceptance. The time was ripe because many fields of science and engineering had an immediate application for such an algorithm. At the same time, the use of digital computers was on the rise, providing an ideal platform for implementation. The Cooley-Tukey FFT was soon followed by other FFT algorithms [10, 30, 45].

The FFT is commonly available as a function in signal/image processing libraries. Additionally, the body of literature dedicated to implementation details is proportional to its importance, to list just a few [2, 10, 30, 36, 45]. Therefore, we move on to the topics more relevant to real-time vision, to describe several ways the FFT can be used to speed up seemingly unrelated operations, such as convolution, correlation, and morphological operations. We also mention some other fast algorithms for convolution that are non-FFT based.

Fast convolution and correlation. We limit the following discussion to sequences, but note that these methods are easily generalized to two dimensions and higher. Convolution of two sequences $u = (u_0, \ldots, u_m)$ and $h = (h_0, \ldots, h_n)$ yields a new sequence $y = u * h = (y_0, \ldots, y_{m+n})$ given by

$$y_k = \sum_{i=0}^{k} u_i h_{k-i} \quad (k = 0, \ldots, m+n) \tag{3}$$

We assume that a sequence equals zero outside the specified range. For example, $h_{-1} = h_{n+1} = 0$. Convolution has diverse uses, for example, as representation for digital filtering or for multiplication of polynomials.

Correlation of sequences u and h produces another sequence c given by

$$c_k = \sum_{i=0}^{k} u_i h_{n+i-k} \quad (k = 0, \ldots, m+n) \tag{4}$$

Although correlation is used differently than convolution, the formal similarity between (3) and (4) allows fast convolution algorithms to be adapted for fast correlation.

To simplify the notation, let $m = n$. Then calculation of sequence y directly from (3) requires $O(n^2)$ multiplications. There are, however, $O(n \log n)$ algorithms to do this using several different approaches [2, 30, 36]. Very much like the FFT, a large convolution can be written in terms of shorter convolutions, yielding computational savings.

There is also a fast convolution algorithm based on the FFT. It uses the following property of the DFT and convolution. If sequences A, B, and C are $(m+n+1)$-length DFTs of a, b, and c, respectively, and $c = a * b$, then

$$C_k = A_k B_k \quad (k = 0, \ldots, m+n)$$

The FFT-based fast convolution algorithm is not faster than many of the non-FFT algorithms. It may also suffer from round-off errors on fixed-point processors, whereas many of the non-FFT algorithms typically do not. However, FFT-based fast convolution has a major advantage: due to wide applicability of the FFT itself, the FFT routines are widely available, while non-FFT fast convolution algorithms are generally not.

Windowing and data transfers. As noted earlier, an $O(n \log n)$ algorithms is not always more efficient than an $O(n^2)$ algorithm, due to multiplicative constants that are absorbed by the O-notation. Such is the case for convolutions in which one sequence (or image) is much shorter (smaller) than the other sequence (image). Then the implementation directly from (3) is computationally more efficient.

Processors with SIMD functionality (as discussed in Sect. 3.1) are well suited to do convolution as in (3), but one may find that data throughput is the limiting factor. The technique to be presented next improves the execution time by significantly reducing the number of data transfers.

In order to be able to use SIMD operations, one usually needs to ensure that the input data is aligned with 32-bit boundaries in the memory. This is trivial when, for example, we need to calculate the absolute difference (AD) of two images: we just make sure that both images start at 32-bit boundaries, and the rest is automatic, because each SIMD operation will use 4 bytes from each image, hence the next SIMD call will again be on the 32-bit boundary.

However, if we need to find the best match for a small image (mask) within a bigger image, then we need to slide the mask over the bigger image and calculate some measure of fit, e.g., sum of absolute differences (SAD) or normalized cross-correlation (NCC), for each displacement. As we move the mask over the image, the data in the mask remains in the same place in memory. Therefore, if the mask data is initially aligned, there will be no misalignment issues. However, the image data under the mask is misaligned in 3 out of 4 possible cases, (b), (c), and (d) in Fig. 2.

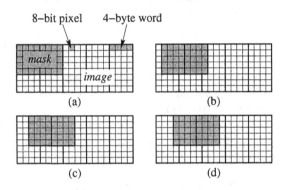

Fig. 2. Illustration of memory alignment issues: as the mask slides over the image, the image data is ready for SIMD operations only in one of four cases (a), when aligned with 32-bit word boundaries

The simplest solution is to copy the image data under the mask to a different part of memory that is 32-bit aligned and then invoke the SIMD operation. This, as we discuss below, is a rather inefficient solution. If the image is $M \times N$ while the mask is $m \times n$, then for 3 out of 4 mask displacements we need to copy $m \times n$ bytes of image data for realignment. Since there are $(M - m + 1) \times (N - n + 1)$ different mask displacements, this amounts to $\frac{3}{4}(M - m + 1)(N - n + 1)mn$ byte transfers.

For example, implementing the minimum SAD module in this way on TI's popular media processor DM642 with $M = 128$, $N = 64$, $m = 72$, and $n = 48$, requires transfer of 2.5 million bytes. The module takes 16.5 ms to execute, which is far from acceptable in an application that needs to do many more things and has a 25 or 30 Hz video refresh rate. We need something much faster.

The main idea is to create three additional copies of the entire image, each copy shifted by one byte compared to the previous copy. Let the original image be denoted by A, its 1-byte-shifted copy by B, B's 1-byte-shifted copy by

C, and C's 1-byte-shifted copy by D. Then we use A for mask displacements that have no misalignment (cases typified by (a) in Fig. 2), B for mask displacements causing 1-byte misalignments (such as (b) in Fig. 2), C for mask displacements causing 2-byte misalignments (such as (c) in Fig. 2), and D for mask displacements causing 3-byte misalignments (such as (d) in Fig. 2).

The only data transfer in this method occurs during creation of three shifted copies of the original image, requiring only $3MN$ byte transfers. Using this technique, the minimum SAD module requires only around 25,000 byte transfers and the execution time is around 0.75 ms.

Fast morphology. Binary dilation and erosion are basic operations in mathematical morphology, a branch of image processing [16, 37]. Dilation of image A by a structuring element S causes all binary objects in A to expand (dilate), with S providing the prescription for this growth through the following definition

$$D(x,y) \;=\; A \oplus S \;=\; \max_{S(u,v)=1} A(x-u, y-v)$$

Similarly, erosion of image A by structuring element S shrinks (erodes) binary objects in A as defined by

$$E(x,y) \;=\; A \ominus S \;=\; \min_{S(u,v)=1} A(x-u, y-v)$$

All other morphological operators are constructed from dilation and erosion, for example

$$O \;=\; A \circ S \;=\; (A \ominus S) \oplus S \qquad \text{opening}$$

$$C \;=\; A \bullet S \;=\; (A \oplus S) \ominus S \qquad \text{closing}$$

$$T \;=\; \hat{A}_S \;=\; A - (A \circ S) \qquad \text{top-hat}$$

$$B \;=\; \check{A}_S \;=\; (A \bullet S) - A \qquad \text{bottom-hat}$$

where "$-$" denotes the set-theoretic difference.

Morphological operators are nonlinear, and as defined above, operate on binary images. There are corresponding operators defined for grayscale images as well.

It may be unexpected to see that morphological operations, which are nonlinear, can be represented using convolution, a linear operation, and binarization (thresholding) [21]

$$A \oplus S = \mathrm{bin}_{1/2}(A * S)$$

This representation is the basis for a fast algorithm for dilation, using fast convolution, either FFT or non-FFT type. There is a similar representation for erosion, relating it to correlation.

4.5 PCA Object Detection and Recognition

Principal Component Analysis (PCA), also known as eigenpictures or eigenfaces, is a popular computer vision technique for object detection and classification, especially in the context of faces [40, 46]. It has its roots in statistical and signal processing methods known as Karhunen-Loeve Transform (KLT) or Hotelling Transform. The first example of KLT in computer vision was for compression of images from a face database. To quote Lawrence Sirovich and Michael Kirby [40]:

> ... we demonstrate that any particular face can be economically represented in terms of a *best* coordinate system that we term *eigenpictures.* These are the eigenfunctions of the averaged covariance of the ensemble of faces. To give some idea of the data compression gained from this procedure, we first observe that a fairly acceptable picture of a face can be constructed from the specification of gray levels at 2^{14} pixel locations. Instead of this, we show, through actual construction, that roughly 40 numbers giving the admixture of eigenpictures characterize a face to within 3% error.

Historically, the next big step was to apply these ideas to face detection and recognition. Here we quote Matthew Turk and Alex Pentland [47]:

> ... It occurred to us that if a multitude of face images can be reconstructed by weighted sums of a small collection of characteristic images, then an efficient way to learn and recognize faces might be to build the characteristic features from known face images and to recognize particular faces by comparing the feature weights needed to (approximately) reconstruct them with the weights associated with the known individuals.

The success of this approach inspired a vast amount of further research and development. A simple search for "eigenface" on *IEEExplore*, the IEEE online digital library, produces more than a hundred results.

Reduced dimensionality. The reason we consider PCA to be a real-time technique is the reduction in problem dimensionality. In general, if we work with $M \times N$ images, the problem has dimensionality $m = MN$. Since images of objects contain a lot of redundancies, we can use the energy-compaction property of KLT to significantly reduce the dimensionality of the problem, down to $r \ll m$. This is done by keeping only r eigenvectors ϕ_k of the data covariance matrix corresponding to r largest eigenvalues λ_k. In order to estimate how many eigenvectors are sufficient to give enough variance coverage (i.e., what reduced order r to use), the following formula for the ratio of the covered variance σ_r^2 and the total variance of the class σ^2 is useful

$$\frac{\sigma_r^2}{\sigma^2} = \frac{\sum_1^r \lambda_k}{\sum_1^n \lambda_k}$$

Matrix trick. In order to construct eigenpictures for a class, one needs to start from a set of n training $M \times N$ images of objects from the class. Typically, $n \ll m = MN$. After reshaping, they form n column vectors $x(1), \ldots, x(n)$. First we need to estimate the mean μ and covariance matrix C of the class from the training data. We use the sample mean as an estimate of μ, so let

$$\mu = \frac{1}{n} \sum_{k=1}^{n} x(k)$$

If we form a centered data matrix

$$D = [\, x(1) - \mu \quad \ldots \quad x(n) - \mu \,]$$

then C can be estimated as the sample covariance, so let

$$C = \frac{1}{n-1} DD^T$$

This is an $m \times m$ matrix, typically huge. Fortunately, all that is needed are the eigenvectors and eigenvalues of C, nothing else. The non-zero eigenvalues λ_k coincide with the eigenvalues of a much smaller matrix [23, 46],

$$L = \frac{1}{n-1} D^T D$$

which is $n \times n$. Recall that $n \ll m$. For numerical stability, this calculation is usually accomplished using the singular value decomposition (SVD) of D, because the singular values of D are by definition the square roots of eigenvalues of its Gram matrix, $D^T D$. The eigenvectors of C can be determined from the eigenvectors of L, here denoted by ψ_k, as follows

$$\phi_k = D\psi_k \qquad (k = 1, \ldots, n)$$

This is important to know for offline calculation of eigenpictures and may be useful to know for some online learning scheme, where the computational savings could be critical.

Pythagorean trick. The most common PCA classification scheme is based on the reconstruction error. The image data is reformatted into an $m \times 1$ vector x, this vector is centered using the average of the object class μ and projected into the eigenspace using the $r \times m$ matrix Φ, formed from the first $r \ll m$ of the appropriately ordered eigenvectors – by the magnitude of their respective eigenvalues, $\Phi = [\phi_1 \ldots \phi_r]$. The result are r weights

$$w = [w_1 \ldots w_r]^T = \Phi^T (x - \mu) \tag{5}$$

Next, the eigenspace reconstruction $\hat{x}$ of the data x is calculated

$$\hat{x} = \mu + w_1 \phi_1 + \ldots + w_r \phi_r = \mu + \Phi w \tag{6}$$

Finally, the reconstruction error is calculated as

$$e^2 = \|x - \hat{x}\|^2 = \sum_{i=1}^{m}(x_i - \hat{x}_i)^2 \qquad (7)$$

Note that it is computationally more efficient to use the formula derived using the Pythagorean theorem. Instead of constructing $\hat{x}$ as a weighted sum of eigenvectors ϕ_k as in (6) and then using it to calculate the reconstruction error as in (7), the orthonormality of eigenvectors is used to determine this error directly as

$$e^2 = \|x - \mu\|^2 - \sum_{k=1}^{r} w_k^2 \qquad (8)$$

A simple comparison of formulas (7) and (8) shows that (8) requires approximately half of the computations implied in (7). To prove (8) we start from the definition of the reconstruction error

$$e^2 = \|y - \hat{y}\|^2 = \|y - (\mu + \Phi w)\|^2 = \|(y - \mu) - \Phi w\|^2$$

Since Φw is the orthogonal projection of $(y - \mu)$ onto the eigenspace, we can use the Pythagorean Theorem to write

$$e^2 = \|y - \mu\|^2 - \|\Phi w\|^2$$

Finally, since the columns of Φ are orthonormal we obtain (8). Similar reasoning can be found in [46].

Fixed-point PCA. If PCA is implemented using a set of orthonormal eigenvectors, this implies use of the floating-point precision. This is not good news if you are using a fixed-point processor, such as TI's DM642. However, projections in PCA can be viewed in terms of linear filtering, because (5) is a matrix formulation of a linear filter. Linear filtering is often done using fixed-point hardware [31]. Thus, by sacrificing some precision, we can significantly improve the execution time, typically around 70 times [24].

To represent the eigenvectors in fixed-point we first scale them so that their components are between -128 and $+127$, then round them to the nearest integer:

$$\tilde{\phi}_k = \text{round}\left[\frac{127\phi_k}{\max_i |\phi_k^{(i)}|}\right] \qquad (k = 1, \ldots, r)$$

After that all projection calculations are done using 8-bit operations. Of course, the results are scaled back using the reciprocal of that same scale factor. On a TI DM642 processor, this technique has reduced the execution time of PCA classification by a factor of seventeen. The execution time is further reduced (by a factor of four) when utilizing the SIMD operations available on the chip. These operations utilize 32-bit multipliers and adders to do four simultaneous 8-bit operations.

To estimate the numerical error introduced by fixed-point representation we can model the quantization error as uniform noise with variance [31]

$$\sigma_e^2 = \frac{2^{-2B} X_m}{12}$$

where $B + 1$ is the number of bits in the representation, hence $B = 7$, and $X_m = 128$ (the maximum amplitude). As a result of going from a 32-bit floating-point representation to an 8-bit fixed-point representation, the SNR change due to quantization error is $\Delta(\text{SNR}) = 20 \log 2^{B_0 - B_1} \approx -144\,\text{dB}$, where $B_0 = 8$ bit and $B_1 = 32$ bit. By itself this may seem like a large degradation, but we are still left with around 48 dB of SNR (corresponding to quantization noise in 8-bit representation). Is that sufficient? The best way to answer that question is to compare the performance of the system with and without quantization. In general, unless your design relies on marginal differences between classes, you do not have to worry about losing accuracy and robustness [24].

Scanning. So far we discussed PCA-based object recognition, in which a candidate image is analyzed and classified as belonging or not belonging to one of the classes. The projections in (5) are simple dot-products and there is not much that can be done to speed them up, other than using the Fixed-point PCA.

Object detection is a related but different problem of finding candidate images to be used in recognition. PCA can be used for detection as well [46], when the entire scene is scanned by sliding the PCA classifier in search of objects such as faces. In this case, projections in (5) turn into correlations. As we discussed earlier in this section, fast correlation algorithms exist, similar to fast convolution algorithms, based on FFT or other approaches.

5 Conclusions

In this chapter we discussed two different meanings of *real-time*, one very precise, related to system specification, the other a bit vague, used to characterize algorithms as suitable for real-time systems. After introducing relevant terminology and notation we described a variety of factors that must be considered for real-time vision design in general. They range from processor selection to real-time algorithms.

We chose to describe algorithms coming from diverse fields, as diverse as computer vision itself. We begun by discussing algorithms for sorting and optimization. This was followed by a summary of Kalman filtering. Then we described the FFT and its application to fast convolution and correlation and fast morphology. Finally, we analyzed some computational aspects of PCA-based classification.

Numerous references have been provided for the interested reader, because there is so much to learn from what others have done. Most importantly, this chapter is designed to provide the reader with a sample of the building blocks available for real-time vision. Hopefully, this will provide the inspiration to cultivate new ideas and research.

Acknowledgments

The authors wish to thank Eric Yoder, Mathias Kölsch, and Matthew Turk for their helpful comments and suggestions.

References

1. M S Arulampalam et al. A tutorial on particle filters for online nonlinear/non-Gaussian Bayesian tracking. *IEEE Trans Signal Proc*, pp 174–188, 2002.
2. R E Blahut. *Fast Algorithms for Digital Signal Processing.* Addison-Wesley, 1985.
3. C M Brown and D Terzopoulos (Editors). *Real-Time Computer Vision.* Cambridge University Press, 1994.
4. E K P Chong and S H Zak. *An Introduction to Optimization.* Wiley, 2001.
5. J W Cooley and J W Tukey. An algorithm for the machine calculation of the complex Fourier series. *Math Comput,* pp 297–301, 1965.
6. J W Cooley. How the FFT gained acceptance. *IEEE Signal Proc Mag,* pp 10–13, 1992.
7. T H Cormen et al. *Introduction to Algorithms.* MIT Press, 1990.
8. F Crick and C Koch. The problem of consciousness. *Special Issue of Scientific American: Mind and Brain.* W H Freeman, 1992.
9. E R Dougherty and P A Laplante. *Introduction to Real-Time Imaging.* IEEE Press, 1995.
10. H K Garg. *Digital Signal Processing: Number Theory, Convolution, Fast Fourier Transforms, and Applications.* CRC Press, 1998.
11. G H Golub and C F Van Loan. *Matrix Computations, Second Edition* The Johns Hopkins University Press, 1989.
12. R L Graham et al. *Concrete Mathematics: A Foundation for Computer Science.* Addison-Wesley, 1989.
13. J Granata et al. Recursive fast algorithm and the role of the tensor product. *IEEE Trans Signal Proc,* pp 2921–2930, 1992.
14. J Granata et al. The tensor product: A mathematical programming language for FFTs and other fast DSP operations. *IEEE Signal Proc Mag,* pp 40–48, 1992.
15. M S Grewal and A P Andrews. *Kalman Filtering.* Wiley, 2001.
16. R Haralick et al. Image analysis using mathematical morphology. *IEEE Trans PAMI,* pp 523–550, 1987.

17. M T Heideman et al. Gauss and the history of Fast Fourier Transform. *IEEE ASSP Mag*, pp 14–21, 1984.
18. C A R Hoare. Quicksort. *Computer Journal*, pp 10–15, 1962.
19. T Kailath and A H Sayed. *Fast Reliable Algorithms for Matrices With Structure*. SIAM, 1999.
20. R E Kalman. A new approach to linear filtering and prediction problems. *ASME J of Basic Engineering*, pp 34–45, 1960.
21. B Kisačanin and D Schonfeld. A fast thresholded convolution representation of morphological operators. *IEEE Trans Image Proc*, pp 455–457, 1994.
22. B Kisačanin. *Mathematical Problems and Proofs*. Plenum, 1998.
23. B Kisačanin and G C Agarwal. *Linear Control Systems*. Kluwer, 2001.
24. B Kisačanin and G J Witt. Getting ahead of competition with real-time computer vision. *Proc Delphi Technical Conf*, 2004.
25. D E Knuth. *The Art of Computer Programming Vol 3: Sorting and Searching*. Addison-Wesley, 1973.
26. S Kyo et al. A 51.2-GOPS scalable video recognition processor for intelligent cruise control based on a linear array of 128 four-way VLIW processing elements. *IEEE J Solid-State Circuits*, pp 1992–2000, 2003.
27. P A Laplante and A D Stoyenko. *Real-Time Imaging*. IEEE Press, 1996.
28. C C McGeoch. Experimental analysis of algorithms. *Notices of Am Math Soc*, pp 304–311, 2001.
29. www.mobileye.com
30. H Nussbaumer. *Fast Fourier Transform and Convolution Algorithms*. Springer, 1982.
31. A Oppenheim and R Schafer. *Discrete-Time Signal Processing*. Prentice Hall, 1989.
32. P Pérez et al. Data fusion for visual tracking with particles. *Proceedings of the IEEE*, pp 495–513, 2004.
33. D Pham et al. The design and implementation of a first-generation CELL processor. *Proc ISSCC*, 2005.
34. W H Press et al. *Numerical Recipes in C*. Cambridge University Press, 1992.
35. J Rehg and T Kanade. Visual tracking of high DOF articulated structures: An application to human hand tracking. *Proc ECCV*, 1994.
36. M Schroeder. *Number Theory in Science and Communication, Third Edition* Springer, 1997.
37. J Serra. *Image Analysis and Mathematical Morphology*. Academic Press, 1982.
38. T B Sheridan and W R Ferrell. Remote manipulative control with transmission delay. *IEEE Trans Human Factors in Electronics*, pp 25–29, 1963.
39. D Sima. Decisive aspects in the evolution of microprocessors. *Proceedings of the IEEE*, pp 1896–1926, 2004.
40. L Sirovich and M Kirby. Low-dimensional procedure for the characterization of human faces. *J Opt Soc Am A*, pp 586–591, 1987.
41. V Strassen. Gaussian elimination is not optimal. *Numer Math*, pp 354–356, 1969.
42. J Tanabe et al. Visconti: Multi-VLIW image recognition processor based on configurable processor. *Proc IEEE Custom Integrated Circuits Conf*, 2003.
43. A Techmer et al. A 100 GOPS vision platform for intelligent vehicles. *Proc IEEE Intelligent Vehicles Symp*, 2003.
44. M O Tokhi et al. *Parallel Computing for Real-Time Signal Processing and Control*. Springer, 2003.

45. R Tolimieri et al. *Algorithms for Discrete Fourier Transform and Convolution.* Springer, 1989.
46. M Turk and A Pentland. Eigenfaces for recognition. *J Cognitive Neuroscience,* 1991.
47. M Turk and A Pentland, Face recognition using eigenfaces. *Proc CVPR,* 1991.
48. J Vanhoof et al. *High-Level Synthesis for Real-Time Digital Signal Processing.* Kluwer, 1993.
49. G van der Wal et al. The Acadia vision processor. *Proc IEEE Int Workshop on Computer Architectures for Machine Perception,* 2000.
50. J W J Williams. Algorithm 232 (heapsort). *Comm ACM,* pp 347–348, 1964.
51. www.xilinx.com

## Part II

Advances in RTV4HCI

Recognition of Isolated Fingerspelling Gestures Using Depth Edges

Rogerio Feris[1], Matthew Turk[1], Ramesh Raskar[2], Kar-Han Tan[3], and Gosuke Ohashi[4]

[1] University of California, Santa Barbara
    `rferis@cs.ucsb.edu`
    `mturk@cs.ucsb.edu`
[2] Mitsubishi Electric Research Labs
    `raskar@merl.com`
[3] University of Illinois at Urbana-Champaign
    `tankh@vision.ai.uiuc.edu`
[4] Shizuoka University
    `tegooha@ipc.shizuoka.ac.jp`

Although steady progress has been made on developing vision-based gesture recognition systems, state-of-the-art approaches are still limited to discriminate hand configurations with high amounts of finger occlusions, a common scenario in most fingerspelling alphabets. In this article, we propose a novel method for recognition of isolated fingerspelling gestures based on depth edge features. Our approach is based on a simple and inexpensive modification of the capture setup: a multi-flash camera is used with flashes strategically positioned to cast shadows along depth discontinuities in the scene, allowing efficient and accurate extraction of depth edges. We then use a shift and scale invariant shape descriptor for fingerspelling recognition, demonstrating great improvement over methods that rely on features acquired by traditional edge detection and segmentation algorithms.

1 Introduction

Sign language is the primary communication mode used by most deaf people. It consists of two major components: 1) word level sign vocabulary, where gestures are used to communicate the most common words and 2) fingerspelling, where the fingers on a single hand are used to spell out more obscure words and proper nouns, letter by letter. Facial expressions can also be employed to distinguish statements, questions and directives.

Over the past decade, great effort has been made to develop systems capable of translating sign language into speech or text, aiming to facilitate

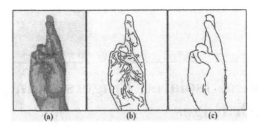

Fig. 1. (a) Letter 'R' in ASL alphabet. (b) Canny edges. Note that important internal edges are missing, while edges due to wrinkles and nails confound scene structure. (c) Depth edges obtained with our multi-flash technique

the interaction between deaf and hearing people. Extensive research has been done in both word level and fingerspelling components.

Previous approaches to word level sign recognition rely heavily on statistical models such as Hidden Markov Models (HMMs) [17, 18, 4]. Excellent recognition rates were obtained for small word lexicons, but scalability is still an issue for glove-free sign recognition. For fingerspelling recognition, most successful approaches are based on instrumented gloves [8, 14], which provide information about finger positions.

In general, non-intrusive vision-based methods, while useful for recognizing a small subset of convenient hand configurations [7, 1], are limited to discriminate configurations with high amounts of finger occlusions – a common scenario in most fingerspelling alphabets. In such cases, traditional edge detectors or segmentation algorithms fail to detect important internal edges along the hand shape (due to the low intensity variation in skin-color), while keeping edges due to nails and wrinkles, which may confound scene structure and the recognition process (see Fig. 1b). Also, some signs might look very similar to each other, with small differences on finger positions, thus posing a problem for appearance-based approaches [7].

We address this problem by using a technique we have recently proposed for conveying shape in non-photorealistic rendering [13]. Our approach is based on a simple and inexpensive modification of the capture setup: a multi-flash camera is used with flashes strategically positioned to cast shadows along depth discontinuities in the scene, allowing efficient and accurate hand shape extraction, as shown in Fig. 1c. Our method was also extended to handle dynamic scenes, being suitable for real-time processing.

We show that depth discontinuities (also known as depth edges) may be used as a signature to reliably discriminate among complex hand configurations in the ASL alphabet, which would be difficult with current glove-free vision methods. For classification, we have used a shape descriptor similar in spirit to shape context matching [2], which is invariant with respect to image translation and scaling.

The remainder of this chapter is organized as follows: we discuss related work in Sect. 2 and describe our multi-flash technique for extraction of depth edges in Sect. 3. Section 4 covers our shape descriptor and classification method. We report our experimental results in Sect. 5 and discuss issues and perspectives of our technique in Sect. 6. Finally, conclusions and future work are addressed in Sect. 7.

2 Related Work

Regarding word level sign recognition, most successful approaches are based on statistical, generative models. Starner and Pentland [17] presented a video-based system for the recognition of short sequences of American Sign Language (ASL) based on HMMs. Using a 40 word lexicon, they achieved 92% word accuracy with a desk mounted camera and 98% accuracy with a camera mounted in a cap worn by the user. Vogler and Metaxas [18] described an HMM-based system for continuous ASL recognition, using three video cameras with an electromagnetic tracking system for obtaining 3D motion. They achieved 90% word accuracy on a 53 word lexicon. More recently, Chen et al. [4] proposed a system to handle a large vocabulary of the Chinese Sign Language (5113 signs). Using CyberGloves and a method based on a fuzzy decision tree and HMMs, they reported a recognition rate of 91.6%. On the other hand, scalability is still an issue for glove-free word level sign recognition.

For fingerspelling recognition, most proposed methods rely on instrumented gloves, due to the hard problem of discriminating complex hand configurations with vision-based methods. Lamar and Bhuiyant [8] achieved letter recognition rates ranging from 70% to 93%, using colored gloves and neural networks. More recently, Rebollar et al. [14] used a more sophisticated glove to classify 21 out of 26 letters with 100% accuracy. The worst case, letter 'U', achieved 78% accuracy.

Shadows, the main cue used in our work, have already been exploited for gesture recognition and interactive applications. Segen and Kumar [15] describes a system which uses shadow information to track the user's hand in 3D. They demonstrated applications in object manipulation and computer games. Leibe et al. [9] presented the concept of a *perceptive workbench*, where shadows are exploited to estimate 3D hand position and pointing direction. Their method used infrared lighting and was demonstrated in augmented reality gaming and terrain navigation applications. In this book, Kale, Kwan, and Jaynes, demonstrate an interesting method for user pushbutton selection in projected interfaces.

These approaches consider light sources far away from the camera center of projection and casted shadows are separated from the objects. In contrast, our approach consider light sources with small baseline distance from the camera, allowing them to be built in a self-contained device, no larger than existing digital cameras.

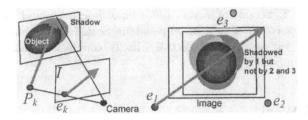

Fig. 2. Imaging geometry. Shadows of the gray object are created along the epipolar ray. We ensure that depth edges of all orientations create shadow in at least one image while the same shadowed points are lit in some other image

3 Multi-Flash Imaging

The technique for detecting shape features in images was recently described in [13], for non-photorealistic rendering. For completeness we review the basic idea here.

The method is motivated by the observation that when a flashbulb (*close* to the camera) illuminates a scene during image capture, thin slivers of cast shadow are created at depth discontinuities. Moreover, the position of the shadows is determined by the relative position of the camera and the flashbulb: when the flashbulb is on the right, the shadows are created on the left, and so on. Thus, if we can shoot a sequence of images in which different light sources illuminate the subject from various positions, we can use the shadows in each image to assemble a depth edge map using the shadow images.

3.1 Imaging Geometry

In order to capture the intuitive notion of how the position of the cast shadows are dependent on the relative position of the camera and light source, we examine the imaging geometry, illustrated in Fig. 2. Adopting a pinhole camera model, the projection of the point light source at P_k is at pixel e_k on the imaging sensor. We call this *image* of the light source the *light epipole*. The images of (the infinite set of) light rays originating at P_k are in turn called the *epipolar rays*, originating at e_k. We use the terms depth discontinuities and depth edges interchangeably here.

There are two simple observations that can be made about cast shadows:

- A shadow of a depth edge pixel is constrained to lie along the epipolar ray passing through that pixel.
- When a shadow is induced at a depth discontinuity, the shadow and the light epipole will be at opposite sides of the depth edge.

These two observations suggest that if we can detect shadow regions in an image, then depth edges can be localized by traversing the epipolar rays

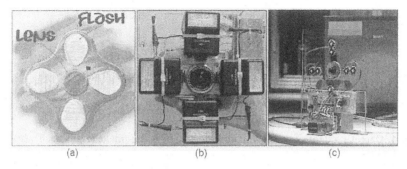

(a)   (b)   (c)

Fig. 3. (a) Our prototype to capture depth discontinuities. (b) Setup for static scenes. (c) Setup for dynamic scenes

starting at the light epipole and identifying the points in the image where the shadows are first encountered.

3.2 Removing and Detecting Shadows

Our approach for reliably removing and detecting shadows in the images is to position lights so that every point in the scene that is shadowed in some image is also captured without being shadowed in at least one other image. This can be achieved by placing lights strategically so that for every light, there is another on the opposite side of the camera to ensure that all depth edges are illuminated from two sides. Also, by placing the lights close to the camera, we minimize changes across images due to effects other than shadows.

To detect shadows in each image, we first compute a *shadow-free image*, which can be approximated with the MAX composite image, which is an image assembled by choosing at each pixel the maximum intensity value among the image set. The shadow-free image is then compared with the individual shadowed images. In particular, for each shadowed image, we compute the *ratio image* by performing a pixel-wise division of the intensity of the shadowed image by the intensity of the MAX image. The ratio image is close to 1 at pixels that are not shadowed, and close to 0 at pixels that are shadowed. This serves to accentuate the shadows and remove intensity transitions due to surface material changes.

3.3 Algorithm

Codifying the ideas discussed we arrive at the following algorithm:

Given n light sources positioned at $P_1, P_2, \ldots, P_n$,
- Capture n pictures I_k, $k = 1, \ldots, n$ with a light source at P_k
- For all pixels x, $I_{\max}(x) = \max_k(I_k(x))$, $k = 1, \ldots, n$

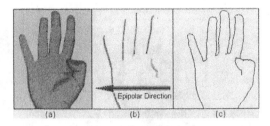

Fig. 4. Detecting depth edges. (a) Hand image. (b) Ratio image (right flash). (c) Detected edges

- For each image k,
  - ▷ Create a ratio image, R_k, where
    $R_k(x) = I_k(x)/I_{\max}(x)$
- For each image R_k
  - ▷ Traverse each epipolar ray from epipole e_k
  - ▷ Find pixels y with step edges with negative transition
  - ▷ Mark the pixel y as a depth edge

3.4 Building Multi-Flash Cameras

We propose using the following configuration of light sources: four flashes at left, right, top and bottom positions (Fig. 3). This setup makes the epipolar ray traversal efficient. For the left-right pair, the ray traversal is along horizontal scan lines and for the top-bottom pair, the traversal is along vertical direction. Figure 4 illustrates depth edge detection using this setup.

We have also extended our method to dynamic scenes. As in the static case, we bypass the hard problem of finding the rich per-pixel motion representation and focus directly on finding the discontinuities, i.e., depth edges in motion. We refer to [13] for a description of the algorithm. The setup is similar to the static case with flashes around the camera, but triggered in a rapid cyclic sequence, one flash per frame (see Fig. 3c).

Our basic prototype for static scenes (Fig. 3b) makes use of a 4 MegaPixel Canon Powershot G3 digital camera. The four booster (slaved Quantarray MS-1) 4 ms duration flashes are triggered by optically coupled LEDs turned on sequentially by a PIC microcontroller, which in turn is interrupted by the hot-shoe of the camera. For dynamic scenes, our video camera (Fig. 3c) is a PointGrey DragonFly camera at 1024×768 pixel resolution, 15 fps which drives the attached 5W LumiLeds LED flashes in sequence. Another alternative setup for dynamic scenes based on colored lights, which we are currently investigating, will be discussed in Sect. 6.1.

4 Shape Descriptor and Classification

In this section, we present a shape descriptor for depth edges which is invariant with respect to image translation and scale. Our approach is simple and yet very effective. It has been recently evaluated on a large dataset for content-based image retrieval [11].

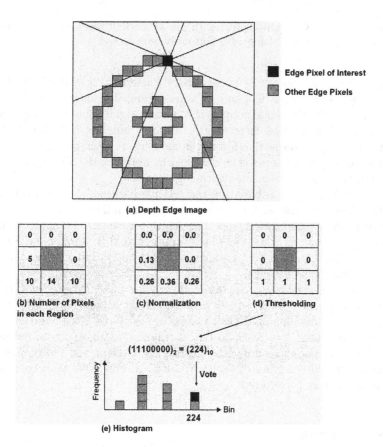

Fig. 5. Shape descriptor used for classification

The basic idea is illustrated in Fig. 5. For each edge pixel of interest, we first analyze its context by counting the number of other edge pixels in eight neighboring regions, as shown in Fig. 5a. This gives us a vector of eight elements C_i, $1 \leq i \leq 8$ (Fig. 5b). We then normalize each element for scale invariance (Fig. 5c) by denoting $S_i = C_i/C$, where $C = \sum_i^8 C_i$. Finally, thresholding is applied (Fig. 5d), so that each element encodes the information of either high or low density of edge pixels along a specific direction of the pixel of interest. The threshold value 0.15 is obtained empirically.

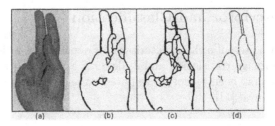

Fig. 6. (a) Letter 'K' of ASL alphabet. (b),(c) Mean Shift segmentation algorithm with different parameter settings. (d) Output of our method

Inspired by the concept of Local Binary Patterns [12] in the field of texture analysis, the values "0"s and "1"s are arranged counter-clockwise from a reference region (in our example, the bottom-right region) to express an 8-bit binary number. The correspondent decimal number d, $0 \leq d \leq 255$ is used to vote for the respective bin in the histogram shown in Fig. 5e. A 256-dimensional feature vector is then obtained by applying the above mentioned process to all edge pixels in the depth edge image.

Since the descriptor is based on the relative position of edge pixels, it is clear that it is invariant with respect to image translation. Scale invariance is obtained in the normalization step. The descriptor can also be made rotation invariant [11]. However, this may not be appropriated for some fingerspelling alphabets (e.g., Japanese Sign Language), which might have letters that are rotated versions of the others.

We have used a nearest-neighbor technique for classification. Initially, supervised learning is carried out by acquiring a set of images for each letter in the fingerspelling alphabet. Depth edges are then extracted and the shape descriptor technique is applied, so that a training database comprised of labeled 256-dimensional feature vectors is formed. Given a test image, features are extracted and the class of the best match training sample according to Euclidean distance is reported.

5 Experiments

We compared the hand contours obtained using our technique with the output of a traditional Canny edge detector [3] and a state-of-the-art Mean Shift segmentation algorithm [5]. We refer to Fig. 1 for a comparison of our method with Canny edges. Changing parameter settings in the Canny algorithm could reduce the amount of clutter, but important edges along the hand shape would still not be detected. Figure 6 shows a comparison with Mean Shift algorithm. Clearly, due to the low intensity skin-color variation in the inner hand region, the segmentation method is not able to detect important boundaries along depth discontinuities. Our method accurately locates depth edges and also offers the advantage that no parameter settings are required.

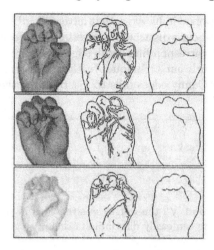

Fig. 7. From left to right: input image, Canny edges and depth edges. Note that our method misses finger boundaries due to the absence of depth discontinuities. This turns out to be helpful to provide unique signatures for each letter

We realized that depth edges are good features to discriminate among signs of fingerspelling alphabets. Even when the signs look very similar (e.g., letters 'E', 'S' and 'O' in ASL alphabet), the depth edge signature is quite discriminative (see Fig. 7). This poses an advantage over vision methods that rely on appearance or edge-based representations. Note that our method does not detect edges in finger boundaries with no depth discontinuity. It turns out that this is helpful to provide more unique signatures for each letter.

In order to quantitatively evaluate the advantages of using depth edges as features for fingerspelling recognition, we considered an experiment with the complete ASL alphabet, except letters 'J' and 'Z', which require motion analysis to be discriminated. We collected a small set of 72 images using our multi-flash camera (three images per letter, taken at different times, with resolution 640×480). The images showed variations in scale, translation and slight variations in rotation. The background was plain, with no clutter, since our main objective is to show the importance of obtaining clean edges in the interior of the hand. It is worth mentioning that textured but flat/smooth backgrounds would not affect our method, but would make an edge detection approach (used for comparison) much more difficult.

For each image, features were extracted as described in Sects. 3 and 4. For sake of comparison, we also considered shape descriptors based on Canny edges. Recognition rate was obtained using a leave-one-out scheme in the collected dataset. Our approach achieved 96% of correct matches, compared with 88% when using Canny edges.

Rebollar [14] mentioned in his work that letters 'R', 'U' and 'V' represented the worst cases, as their class distributions overlap significantly. Figure 8 shows these letters and their corresponding depth edge signatures. Note that they are easily discriminated with our technique. In the experiment described above, the method based on Canny edges fails to discriminate them.

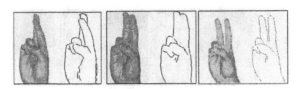

Fig. 8. Letters 'R', 'U' and 'V', the worst cases reported in [14]. Note that the use of a depth edge signature can easily discriminate them

Figure 9 shows a difficult case for traditional methods, where our method also fails to discriminate between letters 'G' and 'H'. In this particular case, we could make use of additional information, such as the intensity variation that happens between the index and the middle finger in letter 'H' and not 'G'.

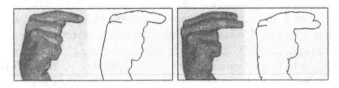

Fig. 9. A difficult case for traditional algorithms (letters 'G' and 'H'), where our method may also fail

All the images in our experiment were collected from the same person. We plan to build a more complete database with different signers. We believe that our method will better scale in this case, due to the fact that texture edges (e.g., wrinkles, freckles, veins) vary from person to person and are eliminated in our approach. Also, shape context descriptors [2] have proven useful for handling hand shape variation from different people. For cluttered scenes, our method would also offer the advantage of eliminating all texture edges, thus considerably reducing clutter (see Fig. 10)

For segmented hand images with resolution 96×180, the computational time required to detect depth edges is 4 ms on a 3 GHz Pentium IV. The shape descriptor computation requires on average 16 ms. Thus, our method is suitable for real-time processing. For improving hand segmentation, depth edges could be computed in the entire image. In this case, the processing time for 640×480 images is 77 ms.

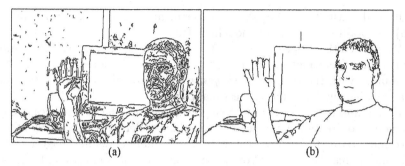

(a)   (b)

Fig. 10. (a) Canny edges (b) Depth edges. Note that our method considerably reduces the amount of clutter, while keeping important detail in the hand shape

We intend to adapt our method for continuous sign recognition in video. Demonstration of detection of depth edges in motion are showed in our previous work [13]. We are currently exploiting a frequency division multiplexing scheme, where flashes with different colors (wavelength) are triggered simultaneously (see Sect. 6.1). We hope this will allow for efficient online tracking of depth edges in sign language analysis.

6 Discussion

In this section, we discuss issues related to our method and propose ways to overcome failure situations. Then we follow with a brief discussion on related work.

There is a tradeoff in choosing the baseline distance between camera and light sources. A larger baseline is better to cast a wider detectable shadow in the internal edges of the hand, but a smaller baseline is needed to avoid separation of shadow from the fingers (shadow detachment) when the background is far away. The width of the abutting shadow in the image is $d = fB(z_2 - z_1)/(z_1z_2)$, where f is the focal length, B is baseline in mm, and z_1, z_2 are depths, in mm, to the shadowing and shadowed edge. Shadow detachment occurs when the width, T, of the object is smaller than $(z_2 - z_1)B/z_2$. Fortunately, with rapid miniaturization and sophistication of digital cameras, we can choose a small baseline while increasing the pixel resolution (proportional to f), so that the product fB remains constant.

What if there is no cast shadows due to lack of background? In these cases only the outermost depth edge, the edge shared by foreground and distant background, is missed in our method. This could be detected with a foreground-background estimation technique. The ratio of $I_0/I_{\max}$ (where I_0 is the image acquired with no flash and $I_{\max}$ is the max composite of flash images), is near 1 in background and close to zero in interior of the foreground.

Another solution for both problems cited above is to consider a larger baseline and explore it to detect only internal edges in the hand, while using traditional methods (such as skin-color segmentation or background subtraction) to obtain the external hand silhouette.

We noticed that depth edges might appear or disappear with small changes in viewpoint (rotations in depth). This was in fact explored in the graphics community with the concept of *suggestive contours* [6]. We believe this may be a valuable cue for hand pose estimation [1].

A common thread in recent research on pose estimation involves using a 3D model to create a large set of exemplars undergoing variation in pose, as training data [16, 1]. Pose estimation is formulated as an image retrieval problem in this dataset. We could use a similar approach to handle out-of-plane hand rotations. In this case, a 3D hand model would be used to store a large set of depth edge signatures of hand configurations under different views.

We have not seen any previous technique that is able to precisely acquire depth discontinuities in complex hand configurations. In fact, stereo methods for 3D reconstruction would fail in such scenarios, due to the textureless skin-color regions as well as low intensity variation along occluding edges.

Many exemplar-based [1] and model-based [10] approaches rely on edge features for hand analysis. We believe that the use of depth edges would lead to significant improvements in these methods. Word level sign language recognition could also benefit from our technique, due to the high amounts of occlusions involved. Flashes in our setup could be replaced by infrared lighting for user interactive applications.

6.1 Perspectives: Variable Wavelength

In real-world scenarios, our method would require a high speed camera, with flashes triggered in a rapid cyclic sequence, to account for the fast gesture motion in sign language analysis. However, current off-the-shelf high speed cameras are still expensive and limited to store just a few seconds of data because of the huge bandwidths involved in high speed video.

We are currently exploring a different approach for video-based gesture recognition that could be used with standard inexpensive cameras. The idea is to use light sources with different colors, so that we can trigger them all in the same time, in one single shot, and then exploit the colored shadows to extract depth edges.

Figure 11 shows a preliminary result using a camera with three lights of different color: red, green, and blue. Details about our algorithm using colored lights will be described in another article.

7 Conclusions

We have introduced the use of depth edges as features for reliable, vision-based fingerspelling recognition. We basically bypass dense 3D scene reconstruction

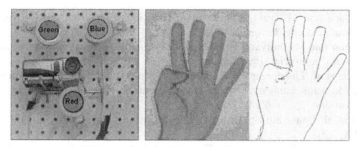

Fig. 11. (a) Our setup for dynamic scenes with different wavelength light sources. (b) Input image. The shadows appear with different colors. (c) Depth edge detection

and exploit only depth discontinuities, which is a valuable information to recognize hand postures with high amounts of finger occlusions, without making use of instrumented gloves.

Our method is simple, efficient and requires no parameter settings. We demonstrated preliminary but very promising experimental results, showing that the use of depth edges outperforms traditional Canny edges even considering simple scenarios with uncluttered background. In more complex scenarios, our technique significantly reduces clutter by eliminating texture edges and keeping only contours due to depth discontinuities.

Evaluating our method in a large database with different signers and addressing the problem of continuous signing in dynamic scenes are topics of future work.

Acknowledgments

This work was partially supported under the auspices of the U.S. Department of Energy by the Lawrence Livermore National Laboratory under contract No. W-7405-ENG-48.

References

1. V Athitsos and S Sclaroff. Estimating 3D hand pose from a cluttered image. *Proc CVPR*, 2003.
2. S Belongie et al. Shape matching and object recognition using shape contexts. *IEEE Trans PAMI*, pp 509–522, 2002.
3. J Canny. A computational approach to edge detection. *IEEE Trans PAMI*, pp 679–698, 1986.
4. Y Chen et al. CSLDS: Chinese sign language dialog system. *Proc Int Workshop on Analysis and Modeling of Faces and Gestures*, 2003.
5. C Christoudias et al. Synergism in low level vision. *Proc ICPR*, 2002.
6. D DeCarlo et al. Suggestive contours for conveying shape. *ACM Transactions on Graphics*, pp 848–855, 2003.

7. M Kölsch and M Turk. Robust hand detection. *Proc Int Conf on Automatic Face and Gesture Recognition,* 2004.
8. M Lamar and M Bhuiyant. Hand alphabet recognition using morphological PCA and neural networks. *Proc Int Joint Conf on Neural Networks,* 1999.
9. B Leibe et al. The perceptive workbench: Toward spontaneous and natural interaction in semi-immersive virtual environments. *IEEE Computer Graphics and Applications,* pp 54–65, 2000.
10. S Lu et al. Using multiple cues for hand tracking and model refinement. *Proc CVPR,* 2003.
11. G Ohashi and Y Shimodaira. Edge-based feature extraction method and its application to image retrieval. *Proc World Multi-Conf on Systemics, Cybernetics and Informatics,* 2003.
12. T Ojala et al. A comparative study of texture measures with classification based on feature distributions. *Pattern Recognition,* pp 51–59, 1996.
13. R Raskar et al. A non-photorealistic camera: Depth edge detection and stylized rendering with multi-flash imaging. *Proc SIGGRAPH,* 2004.
14. J Rebollar et al. A multi-class pattern recognition system for practical finger-spelling translation. *Proc Int Conf on Multimodal Interfaces,* 2002.
15. J Segen and S Kumar. Shadow gestures: 3D hand pose estimation using a single camera. *Proc CVPR,* 1999.
16. G Shakhnarovich et al. Fast pose estimation with parameter sensitive hashing. *Proc ICCV,* 2003.
17. T Starner et al. Real-time American sign language recognition using desk and wearable computer-based video. *IEEE Trans PAMI,* pp 1371–1375, 1998.
18. C Vogler and D Metaxas. ASL recognition based on a coupling between HMMs and 3D motion analysis. *Proc ICCV,* 1998.

Appearance-Based Real-Time Understanding of Gestures Using Projected Euler Angles

Sharat Chandran and Abhineet Sawa

Indian Institute of Technology
sharat@cse.iitb.ac.in
abhineet.sawa@gmail.com

Over the years gesture recognition with a static camera has become a well studied problem in computer vision. Many current methods use complex 3D model of non-rigid hands and involved paradigms in solving the general problem. The problem of representing or recognizing motion captured by *moving camera with a moving actor* is particularly non-trivial.

We believe that an appearance based scheme has significant advantages for real-time scenarios. In this chapter we look at a subproblem of sign language alphabet recognition where gestures are made with protruded fingers. In contrast to the more intricate schemes, we propose a simple, fast classification algorithm using two-dimensional projection of Euler angles.

1 Introduction

Apart from language, the use of hands and fingers in gesturing is a hallmark of information transfer in social conversations. It is no wonder therefore that significant research in human-computer interaction seeks to replicate understanding hand gestures much the way we humans do in our day to day tasks. This chapter focuses on an *appearance* based scheme in the computer vision problem of gesture recognition.

The general problem appears difficult for several non-mutually exclusive reasons as outlined below

- The notions on what a gesture means is not unambiguous.
- Gestures might be made with either hand. The size, shape, and orientation of the palm and the fingers are not standard across the "actors."
- Computer vision algorithms are sensitive to lighting changes, occlusion, and viewpoint changes, especially as they try to track three-dimensional gestures in video sequences.

When we take into account that in day-to-day activities, both the camera (the eye of the listener) and the actor (the speaker) move, the problem the visual understanding problem seems intractable. Possibly as a result, many of the current work use a fairly complicated model of the hand, and follow it up by a fairly involved solution paradigm. Our main result in this work is that by making certain mild assumptions on the nature of the problem (see below in Sect. 2), we can use projected Euler angles to recover English "alphabets" in sign language (see Fig. 1). The result is a much simpler and direct algorithm.

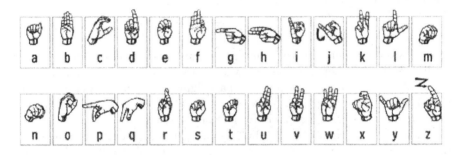

Fig. 1. Gestured alphabets

The rest of this chapter is organized as follows. In the next section, we discuss related work, and our contributions. An overview of our scheme is given in Sect. 3. In Sect. 4, we provide empirical results based on our implementation to support our approach. The input data for many of these results come from a publicly available database on the Internet. Some concluding remarks are made in Sect. 5, where we refer the general problem in the context of this chapter.

2 Related Research

A short survey of general issues in vision-based gesture recognition has been given in [18]. We direct the interested reader to this and similar [11, 5] work for various aspects of gesture research such as the application to user interface, types of gestures, the features for gesture recognition, and the temporal aspect of gesture understanding.

This chapter is related to sign languages but is different from other reported work. In [4] a recognition system for French sign sentences has been used. This work, however, uses a data glove. In [7] also, a dataglove is used to recognize Taiwanese sign language. In [14], a video-based system is used for recognizing short sentences in the American sign language (ASL). In [17] three video cameras are used along with an electromagnetic tracking system for obtaining 3D movement parameters. All the above use the Hidden Markov Model paradigm. Indeed, since different applications demand different levels of accuracy, it is natural that there are systems that use a combination of non-vision based and vision based ideas.

Our focus is in what might be termed as *isolated* gestures as opposed to the continuous gestures. We assume that a key frame in a video sequence has isolated an image containing a "hand" under fronto-parallel camera with uniform lighting, and the palm in the hand occupies a significant portion of the image. Similar assumptions are made in [10] where a neural network scheme is used in a three dimensional model of a hand consisting of cylinders, and prisms. A neural network scheme is also employed in [9]. The method in [2] is also appearance-based, but attempts to solve a more general problem, that of recovering the three-dimensional shape. The methods also use different similarity measures (edge information, and geometric moments) whereas we use projected angles. A graph based scheme for representing objects using skeletons is described in [15], and in this sense overlaps with the way our angles are computed.

A "bunch graph" [16] based model has also been suggested earlier and contains one of the best (in terms of recognition) results on complex background. The authors in this work state that real-time performance is not their focus; indeed, no computational times have been reported in their work.

2.1 Our Contributions

We list our main contributions here

- Our method (see Sect. 3) is simpler than many of the above schemes. As a result it lends itself to real-time implementation; our unoptimized naive approach using standard Linux tools runs in 30 milliseconds or less on an unbranded P4 Linux workstation with 256 MB main memory. To our knowledge, this particular idea of projected Euler angles has not been demonstrated earlier.
- Our method has been tested experimentally with about 40% of our input coming from a public Internet available database [16]. Many of these have cluttered background. The rest of our results are on our homegrown database which contain postures in the American sign language *not* present in [16].

3 Details of Our Proposal

Our algorithm is made up of
the following steps. It is in-
structive to look at the example input image (Fig. 2) ideally
on a color monitor to follow the
sequence of steps.

Fig. 2. An input, depicted to describe the algorithm. No assumption is made that a typical input
should be as clean

1. A color model (Fig. 3) of skin is employed to detect areas which potentially
   correspond to the hand. The Gaussian model [13] used (shown below) is

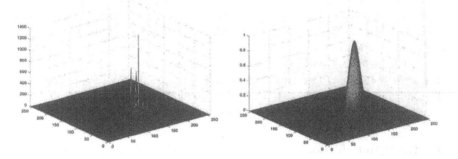

Fig. 3. Building a color model

reasonably resilient to skins of various colors (lighting appears to be a
bigger factor than skin color). There is no assumption made that 'skin' is
present in only a single portion of the image. Therefore we first compute
the probability that a pixel is 'skin' (shown as higher intensity in the left
of Fig. 4).

A connected component analysis on the binarized image leads us to the
hand, defined to be the largest component that has skin color.

Fig. 4. Connected components to identify the hand

2. A contour building algorithm is employed to trace the outline of the hand.

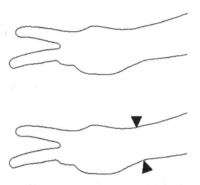

Fig. 5. Identifying the carpo-metacarpal joint

3. The extremities of the finger are detected (Fig. 5 and Fig. 6) based on the curvature. The method used for this is similar to the contour following idea in [6] except that the goal is to come up with a polygon representing the palm. To achieve this either the carpo-metacarpal joints are detected (again by contour following) or by performing a flood fill followed by-erosion. An approximate "centroid" is computed and deemed to be the center of the palm.

Fig. 6. Arrows represent significant detected points

4. The steps mentioned above enable the computation of projected Euler angles. Some angles are shown in Fig. 7; this represents a typical situation. The angles are then used as points in a low-dimensional space; the dimension depends on the number of protruded fingers.

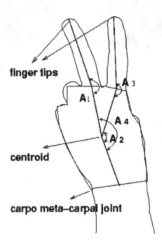

Fig. 7. Projected Euler angles

5. Classification can be done provided prior offline training has been performed. In the training stage, a database of 3 images per gesture is used to learn the gesture. More specifically, for each gesture we calculate $2n + 1$ angles where n is the number of protruded fingers. An example of $n = 2$ appears in Fig. 7 where 4 angles are shown. The $2n + 1$th (last) angle corresponds to the angle between the skeleton of the leftmost protruding finger (if any) with the vertical. This enables us to distinguish, for instance, the letter d from g in Fig. 9. The features corresponding to these are stored as points in feature space. For a query input, we first use the dimension of the space to identify the number of protruded fingers. Given this, a second step is used to find the closest gesture and thus a letter classification (as in Fig. 1) is made. We have used the Euclidean distance here.

4 Experimental Results

We tested our program on a self-collected database and a (different) publicly available database (the file BochumGestures1998.tgz at http://cloudbreak. ucsd.edu/~triesch/data) on the Internet. The running time (including all the steps) was about 30 milliseconds suggesting a real-time classification. A few representative results have been shown in Fig. 9 where the gestures have been correctly identified. Some of these figures (best viewed in color) illustrate the cluttered background that could potentially distract the algorithm. The

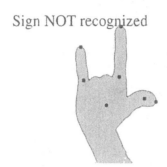

Sign NOT recognized

Fig. 8. A "rejected" gesture

algorithm is also capable of rejecting characters (based on threshold values) that do not fall within the gambit of its database, thereby preventing false positives. An example appears in Fig. 8.

Although the public database contained more than 1000 images, not all of the gestures containing protruded fingers in Fig. 1 were available. Further, many of the images have been taken (possibly deliberately) in poorly illuminated areas where the palm has no skin color regions. These two facts, and the fact that segmentation of the hand was not our main focus, necessitated the capture of about 60 images in our database. In all, 60 assorted person-independent gestures (several on complex backgrounds) in our database, and 45 images in the public database were tried. Some of the results on the latter appear in Fig. 10.

Our success rate was about 91% which compares well with some of the recent [16] results given that our approach

• Is considerably faster
• Has no manual intervention in the training phase or the testing phase
• Does not require any choice of weighting parameters of the type of filters used.

Unlike [16] our focus is not on the segmentation problem; sometimes the segmentation module provides poor clustering which leads our algorithm astray.

In summary, when all the protruded fingers are available, classification is worth attempting using projected angles.

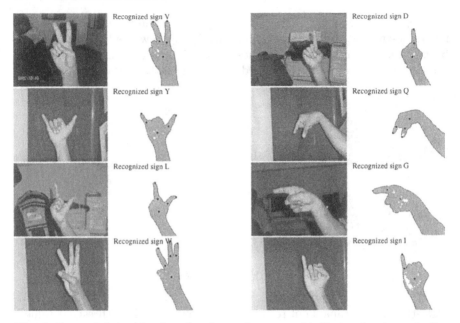

Fig. 9. Successful classification of v, d, y, q, l, g, w, and i. Notice the clutter in the background of several images

5 Final Remarks

The shape of the human hand is useful in a variety of applications such as human-computer interaction, sign language recognition, gestural communication, and multimedia transmission. The nature of the application dictates the use of electromagnetic and non-vision based techniques. In this chapter, we looked at the low level alphabet recognition problem in isolated person-independent gestures using a single camera.

Even at this level, many of the current algorithms [2, 12] generalize the problem, and create a three-dimensional model of the hand resulting in a state space of high dimensions. Appearance based classification schemes [2, 8, 1, 3] are attractive, but we need to experiment with different similarity measures in order to achieve better results. In this work, we have used projected Euler angles as the basis for classification. To get to these angles from an image, we have described and used a skin color model to detect the hand, and a contour algorithm to determine salient points. While the hand orientation could be obtained using other means such as the principal component analysis [8], a simple geometric model seems to be efficient, when the hand is assumed to be approximately upright, an assumption made by several authors. Our results on our self-collected database, and other person independent *public* databases are encouraging; they demonstrate that there is enough information in Euler angles for classification.

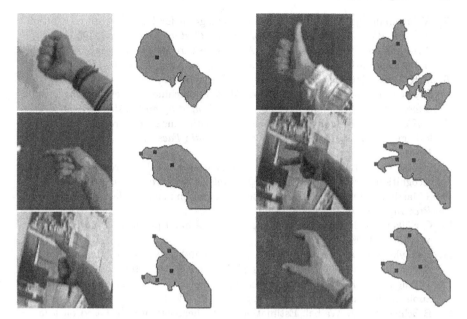

Fig. 10. Successful classification of gestures available from a public database. Improper segmentation as in the top right does not distract the algorithm

An image of a scene at a given time represents a projection of the scene which depends on the position of the camera. There are eight possibilities for the dynamic nature of the camera, actor, and world setup. However since all this processing is done in the reference frame of the camera, they can classified into the following categories:

- Stationary camera and stationary Region Of Interest (ROI). This is the case that has been considered in the bulk of the chapter above.
- Stationary camera and moving ROI. This is a generalization of the above step.
- Moving camera and stationary ROI. This is similar to stereo vision, and techniques explored from stereo can be used here.
- Moving camera and moving ROI. An appearance based scheme would be quite useful here.

References

1. M J Black and A D Jepson. Eigentracking: Robust matching and tracking of articulated objects using a view-based representation. *Proc ECCV*, 1996.
2. I A Essa et al. A unified approach for physical and geometric modeling for graphics and animation. *Proc Eurographics*, 1992.

3. W Freeman and M Roth. Orientation histogram for hand gesture recognition. *Proc Int Workshop on Automatic Face and Gesture Recognition*, 1995.

4. P Harling and E Edwards. ARGo: An architecture for sign language recognition and interpretation. *Progress in Gestural Interaction*, pp 17–30, 1996.

5. M Krueger. *Artificial Reality*. Addison-Wesley, 1991.

6. S Kumar and J Segen. Gesture-based 3D man-machine interaction using a single camera. *Proc IEEE Conf on Multimedia Computing and Systems*, 1999.

7. R H Liang and M Ouhyoung. A real-time continuous gesture recognition system for sign language. *Proc Int Conf on Automatic Face and Gesture Recognition*, 1998.

8. J Martin and J L Crowley. An appearance-based approach to gesture-recognition. *Proc Int Conf on Image Analysis and Processing*, 1997.

9. S Martin and O Bernier. Hand posture recognition in a body-face centered space. *Proc Int Gesture Workshop*, 1999.

10. C Nölker and H Ritter. Visual recognition of hand postures. *Proc Int Gesture Workshop*, 1999.

11. V Pavlović et al. Visual interpretation of hand gestures for human-computer interaction: A review. *IEEE Trans PAMI*, pp 677–695, 1997.

12. J Rehg and T Kanade. Visual tracking of high DOF articulated structures: An application to human hand tracking. *Proc ECCV*, 1994.

13. B Schiele and A Waibel. Estimation of the head orientation based on a face–color–intensifier. *Proc Int Symp on Intelligent Robotic Systems*, 1995.

14. T Starner et al. Real-time American sign language recognition using desk and wearable computer based video. *IEEE Trans PAMI*, pp 1371–1375, 1998.

15. H Sundar et al. Skeleton based shape matching and retrieval. *Shape Modeling International*, pp 130–142, 2003.

16. J Triesch and C von der Malsburg. A system for person-independent hand posture recognition against complex backgrounds. *IEEE Trans PAMI*, pp 1449–1453, 2001.

17. C Vogler and D Metaxas. Adapting Hidden Markov Models for ASL recognition by using three-dimensional computer vision methods. *Proc IEEE Int Conf on Systems, Man, and Cybernetics*, 1997.

18. Y Wu and T S Huang. Vision-based gesture recognition: A review. *Proc Int Gesture Workshop*, 1999.

Flocks of Features for Tracking Articulated Objects

Mathias Kölsch[1] and Matthew Turk[2]

[1] Computer Science Department, Naval Postgraduate School, Monterey
   kolsch@nps.edu
[2] Computer Science Department, University of California, Santa Barbara
   mturk@cs.ucsb.edu

Tracking non-rigid and articulated objects in live video is a challenging task, particularly because object geometry and appearance can undergo rapid changes between video frames. Color-based trackers do not rely on geometry, yet they have to make assumptions on the background's color as to avoid confusion with the foreground object. This chapter presents "Flocks of Features," a tracking method that combines motion cues and a learned foreground color distribution for fast and robust 2D tracking of highly articulated objects. Many independent image artifacts are tracked from one frame to the next, adhering only to local constraints. This concept is borrowed from nature since these tracks mimic the flight of flocking birds – exhibiting local individualism and variability while maintaining a clustered entirety. The method's benefits lie in its ability to track objects that undergo vast and rapid deformations, its ability to overcome failure modes from the motion cue as well as the color cue, its speed, and its robustness against background noise. Tracker performance is demonstrated on hand tracking with a non-stationary camera in unconstrained indoor and outdoor environments. When compared to a CamShift tracker on the highly varied test data, Flocks of Features tracking yields a threefold improvement in terms of the number of frames of successful target tracking.

1 Introduction

Flocks of Features is a fast method for tracking the 2D location of highly articulated objects from monocular views, for example, human hands. By integrating image cues obtained from optical flow and a color probability distribution, a flock of features is able to follow rapid hand movements despite arbitrary finger configuration changes (postures). It can deal with dynamic backgrounds, gradual lighting changes, and significant camera motion such as experienced with a hand-held camera during walking. It does not require a geometry model or a shape model of the target, thus it is in principle applicable to tracking any deformable or articulated object. Tracking performance increases with a more distinct and more uniform object color. The Flocks of Features method was first presented at the IEEE Workshop on Real-Time Vision for Human-Computer Interaction [13].

1.1 Flocking Behavior

The method's core idea was motivated by the seemingly chaotic clustering behavior of a school of fish or a flock of birds, for example, pigeons. While no single bird has any global control, the entire flock still stays tightly together. This decentralized organization has been found to mostly hinge upon two simple constraints that can be evaluated on a local basis: birds like to maintain a minimum safe flying distance to the other birds, but they also desire not to be separated from the flock by more than a certain maximum distance [19].

A Flocks of Features tracker utilizes a set of small image areas, or features, that move from frame to frame in a way similar to a flock of birds. The features' "flight paths" are determined by optical flow, resulting in independent feature movements. Thereafter, every feature's location is constrained to observe a minimum distance from all other features, and to not exceed a maximum distance from the feature median. If one or both of these conditions are violated, the feature is repositioned to a new location that is in compliance again. In addition, an attempt is made to select new locations with a high skin color probability. This consultation of a second image cue counters the drift of features onto nearby background artifacts as it might happen if these exhibit strong gray-level gradients.

Fig. 1. Hand tracking despite a moving camera, hand rotations and articulations, changing lighting conditions and backgrounds. (The images are selected frames from sequence #5, see Table 1)

The speed of pyramid-based KLT feature tracking (see Sect. 3.1 and references [4, 17, 22]) allows Flocks of Features to overcome the computational limitations of model-based approaches to tracking, easily achieving the real-time performance that is required for vision-based interfaces. The flocking behavior in combination with the color cue integration is responsible for the quality of the results: in experiments (see Sect. 4), hands were tracked repeatedly for more than a minute, despite all efforts to distract the tracker. Several examples are shown in the video clip that is associated with the book and is available from the first author's web page.[3] A few frame snapshots are also shown in Fig. 1. Section 5 covers extensive experiments with hands, demonstrating significant performance improvement over another popular tracking method, called CamShift [2].

1.2 HandVu

Human-computer interfaces that observe and utilize hand gestures have the potential to open new realms of applications and functionalities, especially for non-traditional computing environments such as augmented reality and mobile and worn computing devices. Recognizing hand motions and configurations by means of computer vision is a particularly promising approach as it allows a maximum of versatility without encumbering the user. The tracker described here is an integral part of *HandVu*,[4] the first vision-based hand gesture interface that is publicly available and that allows quick and easy interface deployment (see [12]). For example, *HandVu* is used to operate a mobile computer [15] solely through hand gesture recognition. A head-worn camera provides the input, and a head-worn display in the same physical unit is responsible for the visual output. All other components need not be accessed and are stowed away in a conventional backpack.

In *HandVu*, robust hand detection (see [14]) initializes the vision system which then tracks the hand with the method described here. Key postures are recognized and, along with the 2D hand location, drive input to the applications. Posture recognition also serves as re-initialization of the tracking, reducing feature drift and accommodating for lighting changes. Key aspects of the vision components are user independence, their robustness to arbitrary environments, and their computational efficiency as they must run in concert on a laptop computer, providing real-time and low-latency responses to user actions.

2 Related Work

Rigid objects with a known shape can be tracked reliably before arbitrary backgrounds in gray-level images [1, 8]. However, when the object's shape varies vastly over time such as with gesturing hands, most approaches resort to

---

[3] Currently at http://www.cs.ucsb.edu/~matz/RTV4HCI.wmv
[4] Currently at http://www.cs.ucsb.edu/~matz/HGI/HandVu.html

shape-free color information or background differencing [5, 16, 20]. This makes assumptions about the background color or requires a stationary camera and a fixed background, respectively. Violation of just one of these assumptions has to be considered a unimodal failure mode. The Flocks of Features method, on the other hand, uses a multimodal technique to overcome these vulnerabilities. Other multi-cue approaches integrate, for example, texture and color information and can then recognize and track a small number of fixed shapes despite arbitrary backgrounds [3]. A flock of features tracks without a priori knowledge of possible postures and can handle any number of them. However, it makes no attempt at estimating the articulation of the hand's phalanges or finger configurations, this is left for subsequent processing (for example, see [25, 23, 15]).

Object segmentation based on optical flow can produce good results for tracking objects that exhibit a limited amount of deformations during global motions and thus have a fairly uniform flow [18, 5]. Flocks of Features relaxes this constraint and can track despite concurrent articulation and location changes (see Fig. 3). Depth information combined with color also yields a robust hand tracker [6], yet stereo approaches have their own limitations and are more expensive than the single imaging device required for monocular approaches.

The Flocks of Features approach is different from Monte Carlo methods (often called particle filters, condensation, or particle swarm optimization) [21, 7, 11]. The features in a flock react to local observations only and do not have global knowledge as the samples or particles in Monte Carlo methods do. The features' realm is the two-dimensional image data (optical flow), not a higher-level model space. But most of all, they move in a deterministic way, rather than probabilistically sampling their state space. Having said that, the repositioning of features that have violated the flocking conditions could be interpreted as an attempt to probabilistically model a global "distribution" of the tracked object (for example, the hand), with feature distance and color as its two marginalizations.

3 Method

The motivation for this approach stems from the difficulty of tracking highly articulated objects such as hands during rapid movements. This is particularly challenging when real-time constraints have to be met and only a monocular view in the visible light spectrum is available. If the environment can not be constrained, for example, to a static or uniformly colored background, single-modality methods fail if only one assumption is violated. The approach that Flocks of Features takes integrates two image cues in a very natural manner.

The first image cue exploits the fact that object artifacts can be followed reliably if their appearance remains fairly constant between frames. The method of choice is a popular tracking method that was conceived by Kanade, Lucas, and Tomasi [17, 22], frequently referred to as pyramid-based KLT feature tracking. It delivers good accuracy on quickly moving rigid objects and it can be computed very efficiently. The flocking feature behavior was introduced to allow for tracking of objects whose appearance changes over time, to make up for features that are "lost" from one frame to another because the image mark they were tracking disappeared.

The second image cue is color: mere feature re-introduction within proximity of the flock can not provide any guarantees on whether it will be located on the object of interest or some background artifact. Placing these features at image locations that exhibit a color similar to the hand's color, however, increases the chances of features being located on hand artifacts. An overview of the entire algorithm is given in Fig. 2.

```
input:
   bound_box  - rectangular area containing hand
   hand_mask  - probability of every pixel in bound_box to be hand
   min_dist   - minimum pixel distance between features
   n          - number of features to track
   winsize    - size of feature search windows

initialization:
   learn foreground color histogram based on bound_box and hand_mask,
      and background color histogram based on remaining image areas
   find n*k good-features-to-track with min_dist
   rank them based on color and fixed hand_mask
   pick the n highest-ranked features

tracking:
   update KLT feature locations with image pyramids
   compute median feature
   for each feature
      if less than min_dist from any other feature
         or outside bound_box, centered at median
         or low between-frames appearance match correlation
      then relocate feature onto good color spot
         that meets the flocking conditions

output:
   the average feature location
```

Fig. 2. The Flocks of Features tracking algorithm. Good-features-to-track [22] are those that have a strong gray-level image gradient in two or more directions, that is, corners. k is an empirical value, chosen so that enough features end up on good colors; $k = 3$ was found to be sufficient. The offline-learned hand mask is a spatial distribution for pixels belonging to some part of the hand in the initial posture

3.1 KLT Features and Tracking Initialization

KLT features are named after Kanade, Lucas, and Tomasi who found that a steep brightness gradient along at least two directions makes for a promising feature candidate to be tracked over time ("good features to track," see [22]). In combination with image pyramids (a series of progressively smaller-resolution interpolations of the original image [4, 17]), a feature's image area can be matched efficiently to the most similar area within a search window in the following video frame. The feature size determines the amount of context knowledge that is used for matching. If the feature match correlation between two consecutive frames is below a threshold, the feature is considered "lost."

In the mentioned *HandVu* system [12], a hand detection method [14] supplies both a rectangular bounding box and a probability distribution to initialize tracking. The probability mask is learned offline and contains for every pixel in the bounding box the likelihood that it belongs to the hand. Next, approximately 100 features are selected within the bounding box according to the goodness criterion and observing a pairwise minimum distance. These features are then ranked according to the combined probability of their locations' mask- and color probabilities. The *target number* highest-ranked features form the subset that is chosen for tracking. This cardinality will be maintained throughout tracking by replacing lost features with new ones.

Each feature is tracked individually from frame to frame. That is, its new location becomes the area with the highest match correlation between the two frame's areas. The features will not move in a uniform direction; some might be lost and others will venture far from the flock.

3.2 Flocks of Features

As one of the method's key characteristics, fast-moving and articulating objects can be tracked without the need for an object model.[5] Flocking is a way of enforcing a loose global constraint on the feature locations that keeps them spatially confined. During tracking, the feature locations are first updated like regular KLT features as described in the previous subsection and their median is computed. Then, two conditions are enforced: no two features must be closer to each other than a threshold distance, and no feature must be further from the median than a second threshold distance. Unlike birds that will gradually change their flight paths if these "flocking conditions" are not met, affected features are abruptly relocated to a new location that fulfills the conditions. The flock of features can be seen in Fig. 3 as clouds of little dots.

The effect of this method is that individual features can latch on to arbitrary artifacts of the object being tracked, such as the fingers of a hand.

---

[5] The color distribution can be seen as a model, yet it is not known a priori but learned on the fly.

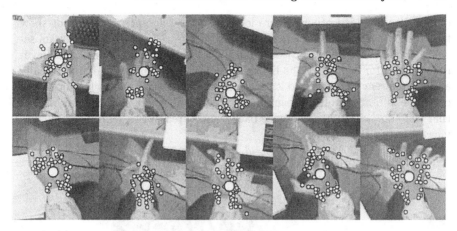

Fig. 3. These images are taken from individual frames of the video with highly articulated hand motions, sequence #3. Areas with 200×230 pixel were cropped from the 720×480-sized frames. The cloud of little dots represents the flock of features, the big dot is their mean. Note the change in size of the hand appearance between the first and fifth image and its effect on the feature cloud

They can then move independently along with the artifact, without disturbing most other features and without requiring the explicit updates of model-based approaches, resulting in flexibility and speed. Too dense concentrations of features that would ignore other object parts are avoided because of the minimum-distance constraint. Similarly, stray features that are likely to be too far from the object of interest are brought back into the flock with the help of the maximum-distance constraint.

Choosing the *median* over the mean location to enforce the maximum-distance constraint is advantageous because of its robustness towards spatial outliers. In fact, the furthest 15% of features are also skipped for the median computation to achieve temporally more stable results. However, the location of the tracked object as a whole is considered to be the *mean* of all features since this measure changes more smoothly over time than the median. The gained precision is important for the vision-based interface's usability.

3.3 Color Modality and Multi-Cue Integration

When the hand is first detected, the observed hand color is learned in a normalized-RGB histogram and contrasted to the background color. The background color is sampled from a horseshoe-shaped area around the location where the hand was detected (see Fig. 4). This assumes that no other exposed skin body parts of the same person who's hand is to be tracked is within that background reference area. Since most applications for *HandVu* assume a forward- and downward-facing head-worn camera, this assumption is reasonable. It was ensured that in the initialization frames of the test videos (which also included other camera locations) the reference area did not show the tracked person's skin. The color distribution was not restricted in subsequent frames. The segmentation quality that this dynamic learning achieves is very good for as long as the lighting conditions do not change dramatically and the reference background is representative for the actual background. The color cue is not a good fall-back method in cases where skin-colored objects that were not within the reference background area during learning come into view shortly thereafter.

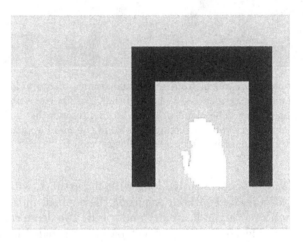

Fig. 4. The areas for learning the skin color model: The color in the hand-masked area (white) is learned in the foreground color histogram. The pixelized look stems from scaling the 30×20 sized hand mask to the detected hand's size. The background color histogram is learned from the horseshoe-shaped area around the hand (black); it is presumed to contain only background. The gray area is not used

The color information is used as a probability map (of a pixel's color belonging to the hand) in three places. First, the CamShift method – which Flocks of Features was compared to – solely operates on this modality. Second, at tracker initialization time, the KLT features are placed preferably onto locations with a high skin color probability. This is true even for the two tracking styles that did not use color information in subsequent tracking steps, see Sect. 4.

Third, the new location of a relocated feature (due to low match correlation or violation of the flocking conditions) is chosen to have a high color probability, currently above a fixed 50 percent threshold. If this is not possible without repeated violation of the flocking conditions, it is chosen randomly. A change in lighting conditions that results in poor color classification causes gracefully degrading tracking performance: only relocated features suffer while most features will continue to follow gray-level artifacts.

Feature relocation does not take the gray-level gradient information, the goodness-to-track, into account to save processing time. However, this is presumed to not significantly improve tracking because in application the features automatically move to those locations after a few frames.

The described consultation of the color cue leads to a very natural multimodal integration, combining cues from feature movement based on gray-level image texture with cues from texture-less skin color probability. The relative contribution of the modalities can be controlled by changing the threshold of when a KLT features is considered lost between frames. If this threshold is low, features are relocated more frequently, raising the importance of the color modality, and vice versa.

4 Experiments

The main objective of the experiments described in the following is to assess Flocks of Features' performance in comparison to a frequently used, state of the art tracking method. A CamShift tracker [2] was chosen because it is widely available and because it is representative of single-cue approaches. The contribution of both the flocking behavior and of the multi-cue integration to the overall performance was also of interest. Therefore, five tracking styles were compared:

- **1 – CamShift:** The OpenCV implementation of CamShift [2] was supplied with the learned color distribution. A pilot study using a fixed HSV histogram yielded inferior results.
- **2 – KLT features only:** The KLT features were initialized on the detected hand and subject to no restrictions during subsequent frames. If their match quality from one to the next frame was below a threshold, they were reinitialized randomly within proximity of the feature median.
- **3 – KLT features with flocking behavior:** As style 2, but the constraints on minimum pairwise feature distance and maximum distance from the median were enforced (see Sect. 3.2).
- **4 – KLT features with color:** As style 2, but resurrected features were placed onto pixels with high skin-color probabilities (see Sect. 3.3).
- **5 – Combined flocking and color cue:** The actual Flocks of Features, this tracker combines styles 3 and 4 as described in Sect. 3.

All styles used color information that was obtained in identical ways. All KLT-based styles used the same feature initialization technique, based on a combination of known hand area locations and learned hand color. This guaranteed equal starting conditions to all styles.

Feature tracking was performed with three-level pyramids in 720×480 video, which arrived at the tracking method at approximately 13 fps. The tracking results were available after 2–18 ms processing time, depending on search window size and the number of features tracked.

Aside from comparing different tracking styles, some of the experiments investigated different parameterizations of the Flocks of Features method. In particular, the the following independent variables were studied: the number features tracked, the minimum pairwise feature distance, and the feature search window size.

4.1 Video Sequences

A total of 518 seconds of video footage was recorded in seven sequences. Each sequence follows the motions of the right hand of one of two people, some filmed from the performer's point of view, some from an observer's point of view. For 387 seconds (or 4979 frames) at least one of the styles successfully tracked the hand. Table 1 details the sequences' main characteristics. The videos were shot in an indoor laboratory environment and at various outdoor locations, the backgrounds including walkways, random vegetation, bike racks, building walls, etc. The videos were recorded with a hand-held DV camcorder, then streamed with firewire to a 3 GHz desktop computer and processed in real-time. The hand was detected automatically when in a certain "initialization" posture with a robust hand detection method [14]. Excerpts of the sequences can be found in the video associated with this chapter (see Introduction).

Table 1. The video sequences and their characteristics: three sequences were taken indoors, four in the outdoors. In the first one, the hand was held in a mostly rigid posture (fixed finger flexion and orientation), all other sequences contained posture changes. The videos had varying amounts of skin-colored background within the hand's proximity. Their full length is given in seconds, counting from the frame in which the hand was detected and tracking began. The maximum time in seconds and the maximum number of frames that the best method tracked a given sequence are stated in the last two columns

id	outdoors	posture changes	skin background	total length	max tracked	
1	no	no	yes	95s	79.3s	1032f
2	no	yes	yes	76s	75.9s	996f
3	no	lots	little	32s	18.5s	226f
4	yes	yes	little	72s	71.8s	923f
5	yes	yes	yes	70s	69.9s	907f
6	yes	yes	yes	74s	31.4s	382f
7	yes	yes	yes	99s	40.1s	513f

5 Results

Tracking was defined to be lost when the mean location is not on the hand anymore, with extremely concave postures being an exception. The tracking

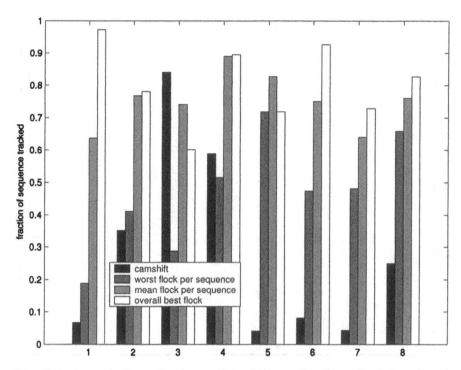

Fig. 5. This graph shows the time until tracking was lost for each of the different tracking styles, normalized to the best style's performance for each video sequence. Groups 1-7 are the seven video sequences. Group 8 is the sum of all sequences, normalized to the sum of each sequence's best style's performance. The Flocks of Features method tracks the hand much longer than the comparison tracker

for the sequence was stopped then, even though the hand might later have coincidentally "caught" the tracker again due to the hand's path intersecting the erroneously tracked location. Since the average feature location can not be guaranteed to be on the center of the hand or any other particular part, merely measuring the distance between the tracked location and some ground truth data can not be an accurate measure for determining tracking loss. Thus, the tracking results were visually inspected and manually annotated.

5.1 General Performance

Figure 5 illustrates the method's performance in comparison to the CamShift tracker that is purely based on color. The leftmost bar for each of the seven sequences shows that CamShift performs well on sequences three and four due to the limited amount of other skin-colored objects nearby the tracked hand. In all other sequences, however, the search region and the area tracked quickly expand too far and lose the hand in the process.

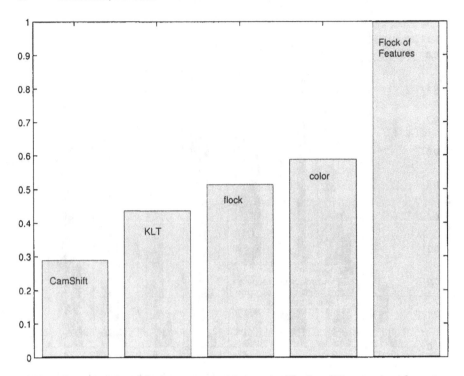

Fig. 6. Contribution of flocking versus color to the Flocks of Features' performance which combines both flocking and color information. Shown is the normalized sum of the number of frames tracked with each tracker style, similar to the eighth group in Fig. 5. Tracking with the Flocks of Features method distinctively shows synergy effects over the other methods' performances

The other bars are from twelve Flocks of Features trackers with 20–100 features and search window sizes between 5 and 17 pixels squared. Out of these twelve trackers, the worst and mean tracker for the respective sequence is shown. In all but two sequences, even the worst tracker outperforms CamShift, while the best tracker frequently achieves an order of magnitude better performance (each sequence's best tracker is normalized to 1 on the y-axis and not explicitly shown). The rightmost bar in each group represents a single tracker's performance: the overall best tracker which had 15×15 search windows, 50 features and a minimum pairwise feature distance of 3 pixels.

Next, the relative contributions of the flocking behavior and the color cue integration on the combined tracker's performance were investigated. Figure 6 indicates that adding color as an additional image cue contributes more to the combined tracker's good performance than the flocking behavior in isolation. The combination of both techniques achieves the vast improvements over the CamShift tracker across the board.

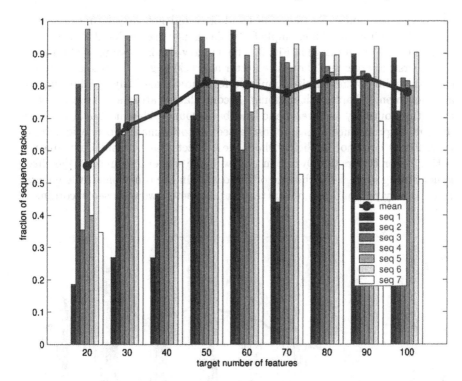

Fig. 7. How varying the number of features influences the performance for each of the video sequences. The KLT features were updated within an 11×11 search window and a pairwise distance of 2.0 pixels was enforced. The bars are normalized for each sequence's best tracker, of which only one (40 features, sequence #6) is shown here

5.2 Parameter Optimizations

Figure 7 presents the tracking results after varying the target number of features that the flocking method maintains. The mean fraction's plateau suggests that 50 features are able to cover the hand area equally well as 100 features. The search window size of 11×11 pixels allows for overlap of the individual feature areas, making this a plausible explanation for no further performance gains after 50 features.

In a related result (not shown), no significant effect related to the minimum pairwise feature distance was observed in the range between two and four. Smaller threshold values however (especially the degenerative case of zero) allow very dense feature clouds that retract to a confined part on the tracked hand, decreasing robustness significantly.

Just as the previous two parameters, the search window size should ideally depend on the size of the hand and possibly on the size of its articulations. These values were constants in the experiments since they were conducted exclusively on hands. Further, the hand sizes did not vary by more than a factor of roughly two. An example for scale change are the hand appearances in the first and fifth image in Fig. 3. The window size has two related implications. First, a larger size should be better at tracking global motions (position changes), while a smaller size should perform advantageously at following finger movements (hand articulations). Second, larger areas are more likely to cross the boundary between hand and background. Thus it should be more difficult to pronounce a feature lost based on to its match correlation. However, Fig. 8 does not explicitly show these effects. One possible explanation is that other factors play a role in how well the sequences fared, or the effect is not strong enough for the size of the data. On the other hand, the general trend is very pronounced and the tracker parameters were chosen accordingly.

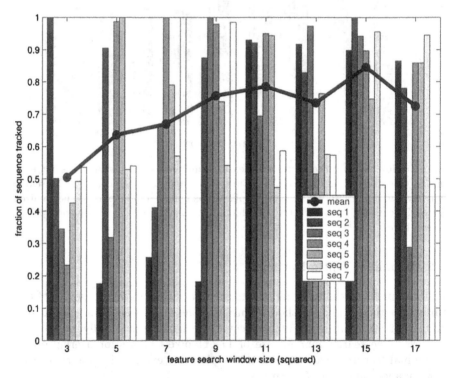

Fig. 8. How tracker performance is affected by search window size (square, side length given on x−axis). Larger window sizes improve tracking dramatically for sequences with very rapid hand location changes (sequences 3, 4, 5), but tracking of fast or complicated configuration variations suffer with too large windows (sequences 3, 7)

6 Discussion

The experiments showed that the performance improvement must be attributed to two factors. First, the purely texture-based and thus within-modality technique of flocking behavior contributes about 20 percent increase over KLT, as witnessed by comparing KLT features with and without flocking (see Fig. 6). Second, the cross-modality integration adds to the performance, visible in improvements from flocking-only and color-only to the combined approach.

A perfect integration technique for multiple image cues would reduce the failure modes to simultaneous violations of *all* modalities' assumptions. To achieve this for the presented method and its on-demand consultation of the color cue, a failure in the KLT/flocking modality would have to be detectable autonomously (without help from the color cue). To the best of our knowledge, this cannot be achieved theoretically. In practice, however, each feature's match quality between frames is a good indicator for when the modality might not be reliable. This was confirmed by the experiments as the features flocked towards the center of the hand (and its fairly stable appearance there) as opposed to the borders to the background where rapid appearance changes are frequent.

The presented method's limitations can thus be attributed to two causes, undetected failure of the KLT tracking and simultaneous violation of both modalities' assumptions. The first case occurs when features gradually drift off to background areas without being considered lost nor violating flocking constraints. The second case occurs if the background has a high skin-color probability, has high gray-level gradients to attract and capture features, and the tracked hand undergoes transformations that require many features to reinitialize.

Flocks of features frequently track the hand successfully despite partial occlusions. Full object occlusions can be impossible to handle at the image level and are better dealt with at a higher level, such as with physical and probabilistic object models [9, 24]. The Flocks' output improves the input to these models, providing them with better image observations that will in turn result in better model parameter estimates. Enforcing temporal consistency by applying a Kalman filter [10] or Monte Carlo methods (see Sect. 2) is another way to improve tracking robustness.

There is a performance correlation between the target number of features, the minimum distance between features, and the search window size. The optimal parameters also depend on the size of the hand, which is assumed to vary after initialization with no more than approximately a factor of two in each dimension. It is left for further investigation to quantify these relationships and to derive optimal parameters for different object sizes.

The Flocks of Features approach was conceived for coarse hand tracking for a time span in the order of ten seconds. It is to provide 2D position estimates to an appearance-based posture recognition method that does not require an overly precise bounding box on the hand area. Thus, it was sufficient to obtain the location of some hand area, versus that of a particular spot such as the index finger's tip. In *HandVu*, the complete vision-based gesture interface (see [15, 12]), every successful posture classification re-initializes tracking and thus extends the tracking period into the long-term range.

The reported frame rate was limited by the image acquisition and transmission hardware and not by the tracking algorithm. During a second set of experiments with live video capture and processing, consistent frame rates of 30 Hz were achieved (color firewire camera in 640×480 resolution). Higher frame rates allow "superlinear" performance improvements because KLT feature tracking becomes increasingly faster and less error prone with less between-frame object motion.

7 Conclusions

Flocks of Features is a new 2D tracking method for articulated objects such as hands. The method integrates two image cues, motion and color, to surpass the robustness of unimodal trackers towards lighting changes, background artifacts, and articulations. It operates indoors and outdoors, with different people, and despite dynamic backgrounds and camera motion. The method does not utilize a geometric object model, but, instead, enforces a loose global constraint on otherwise independently moving features. It is very fast (2–18 ms computation time per 720×480 RGB frame), resulting in high frame rates (typical 30 Hz on a 3 GHz Xeon), but also leaving CPU cycles for other computation. For example, the vision-based hand gesture interface *HandVu* combines Flocks of Features with hand posture recognition methods in order to tap more than just the location of the hand for human-computer interaction. These novel interfaces point the way for natural, intuitive communication with machines in non-traditional environments such as wearable computing and augmented reality.

Acknowledgments

This work was partially supported under the auspices of the U.S. Department of Energy by the Lawrence Livermore National Laboratory under contract No. W-7405-ENG-48.

References

1. S Birchfield. Elliptical head tracking using intensity gradients and color histograms. *Proc CVPR*, 1998.

2. G R Bradski. Real-time face and object tracking as a component of a perceptual user interface. *Proc IEEE Workshop on Applications of Computer Vision*, 1998.
3. L Bretzner et al. Hand gesture recognition using multi-scale colour features, hierarchical models, and particle filtering. *Proc IEEE Int Conf on Automatic Face and Gesture Recognition*, 2002.
4. P J Burt and E H Adelson. The Laplacian pyramid as a compact image code. *IEEE Trans Comm*, pp 532–540, 1983.
5. R Cutler and M Turk. View-based interpretation of real-time optical flow for gesture recognition. *Proc IEEE Int Conf on Automatic Face and Gesture Recognition*, 1998.
6. S Grange et al. Vision-based sensor fusion for human-computer interaction. *Proc Int Conf on Intelligent Robots and Systems*, 2002.
7. M Isard and A Blake. Condensation – Conditional density propagation for visual tracking. *Int J Computer Vision*, 1998.
8. M Isard and A Blake. A mixed-state CONDENSATION tracker with automatic model-switching. *Proc ICCV*, 1998.
9. N Jojić et al. Tracking self-occluding articulated object in dense disparity maps. *Proc ICCV*, 1999.
10. R E Kalman. A new approach to linear filtering and prediction problems. *ASME J of Basic Engineering*, pp 34–45, 1960.
11. J Kennedy and R Eberhart. Particle swarm optimization. *Proc IEEE Int Conf on Neural Networks*, 1995.
12. M Kölsch. Vision based hand gesture interfaces for wearable computing and virtual environments. PhD Thesis, University of California, Santa Barbara, 2004.
13. M Kölsch and M Turk. Fast 2D hand tracking with flocks of features and multi-cue integration. *Proc IEEE Workshop on Real-Time Vision for Human-Computer Interaction*, 2004.
14. M Kölsch and M Turk. Robust hand detection. *Proc IEEE Intl Conf on Automatic Face and Gesture Recognition*, 2004.
15. M Kölsch et al. Vision-Based interfaces for mobility. *Proc Int Conf on Mobile and Ubiquitous Systems*, 2004.
16. T Kurata et al. The Hand Mouse: GMM hand-color classification and mean-shift tracking. *Proc Int Workshop on Recognition, Analysis, and Tracking of Faces and Gestures in Real-Time Systems*, 2001.
17. B D Lucas and T Kanade. An iterative image registration technique with an application to stereo vision. *Proc Imaging Understanding Workshop*, 1981.
18. F Quek. Unencumbered gestural interaction. *IEEE Multimedia*, pp 36–47, 1996.
19. C W Reynolds. Flocks, herds, and schools: A distributed behavioral model. *ACM Trans on Graphics*, pp 25–34, 1987.
20. J Segen and S Kumar. GestureVR: Vision-based 3D hand interface for spatial interaction. *Proc ACM Int Multimedia Conference*, 1998.
21. C Shan et al. Real-time hand tracking by combining particle filtering and mean-shift. *Proc IEEE Int Conf on Automatic Face and Gesture Recognition*, 2004.
22. J Shi and C Tomasi. Good features to track. *Proc CVPR*, 1994.
23. B Stenger et al. Filtering using a tree-based estimator. *Proc ICCV*, 2003.
24. C R Wren and A P Pentland. Dynamic models of human motion. *Proc IEEE Int Conf on Automatic Face and Gesture Recognition*, 1998.
25. Y Wu and T S Huang. Hand modeling, analysis, and recognition. *IEEE Signal Proc Mag*, pp 51–60, 2001.

Static Hand Posture Recognition Based on Okapi-Chamfer Matching

Hanning Zhou, Dennis J. Lin, and Thomas S. Huang

ECE Department
University of Illinois at Urbana-Champaign
hzhou@ifp.uiuc.edu
djlin@ifp.uiuc.edu
huang@ifp.uiuc.edu

Recent years have witnessed the rise of many effective text information retrieval systems. By treating local visual features as terms, training images as documents and input images as queries, we formulate the problem of posture recognition into that of text retrieval. Our formulation opens up the opportunity to integrate some powerful text retrieval tools with computer vision techniques. In this chapter, we propose to improve the efficiency of hand posture recognition by an Okapi-Chamfer matching algorithm. The algorithm is based on the inverted index technique.

The inverted index is used to effectively organize a collection of text documents. With the inverted index, only documents that contain query terms are accessed and used for matching. To enable inverted indexing in an image database, we build a lexicon of local visual features by clustering the features extracted from the training images. Given a query image, we extract visual features and quantize them based on the lexicon, and then look up the inverted index to identify the subset of training images with non-zero matching score. To evaluate the matching scores in the subset, we combined the modified Okapi weighting formula with the Chamfer distance. The performance of the Okapi-Chamfer matching algorithm is evaluated on a hand posture recognition system. We test the system with both synthesized and real-world images. Quantitative results demonstrate the accuracy and efficiency our system.

1 Introduction

Hand posture recognition is an important task for many human-computer interaction (HCI) applications. The problem of hand posture recognition can be considered as a special case of object recognition. There are two types of approaches for object recognition. One is 3D-model-based, the other is appearance-based. Appearance-based object recognition typically involves matching an input image with an image of the object from a database including several characteristic views. According to the matching criterion, the appearance-based approaches can be categorized into two kinds. The first is based on matching salient local features [27, 37, 17, 9, 15, 24]. This kind of approach detects salient points and uses local invariant feature descriptors to represent the object class. They have been very successful in recognizing rigid objects under partial occlusion and slight pose variation. They usually require the object to have consistent and distinct texture. The second kind of appearance-based approaches rely on global-shape descriptors, such as moment invariants, Fourier descriptor or shape context [4, 35, 2]. They can handle objects of little texture, but usually require clean segmentation.

The object classes we are interested in are postures of articulated objects, e.g., the human hand. Their deformations have many degrees of freedom. It requires a large image database to cover all the characteristic shapes under different views. Matching a query image with all training images in the database is time-consuming unless one uses a PC cluster [11]. To improve the efficiency, [1] proposes to embed the manifold of hand shapes into a lower-dimensional Euclidean space. [28] proposes to use parameter sensitive hashing. [34] proposes tree-based filtering. Most of these approaches are based on global-shape matching, because there is very little salient texture on the hand, and the traditional local feature based approaches are not directly applicable.

This chapter takes a different approach to improve the efficiency in recognizing postures of hand. We formulate the problem of posture recognition as that of text retrieval. A training image is treated as a document; a test image is treated as a query. This formulation enables us to accelerate the database matching with the inverted index. The inverted index is a widely used technique to effectively organize a collection of text documents. A brief description of the inverted index can be found in Sect. 4.4. Based on the inverted index, we can identify the subset of training images that share at least one quantized visual feature with the query image at constant computational cost. This technique significantly improves the efficiency of image retrieval, because we only have to match with training images in the subset.

Another effective tool in text retrieval systems is the Okapi weighting formula. It matches a query with a document based on a weighted sum of the terms that appears in both the document and the query. However the Okapi weighting formula is not sufficient for matching images, because it disregards the location of a term in the document. In the case of image retrieval, the image positions of local features are very important. Therefore, we propose to combine the Okapi weighting formula with the Chamfer distance. We assign to each local feature a spatial tag recording its relative image position, and use this tag to calculate the Chamfer distance.

From a computer vision point of view, the Okapi-Chamfer matching algorithm integrates local features into a global shape matching algorithm. The local features are extracted from the binary patches along the boundary between foreground and background. The geometry of the boundary is modeled by the spatial tags.

The rest of the chapter is organized as follows. Section 2 briefly reviews the related work. Section 3 describes visual feature extraction and quantization. Section 4 introduces the vector space model and the Okapi-Chamfer matching algorithm based on the inverted index. Section 5 provides experimental results in both quantitative and visual forms. Section 6 summaries our work and points out future directions.

2 Related Work

In the content-based image retrieval community, the idea of indexing low-level features has been proposed [25, 31]. For instance, [32] uses a N-depth binary tree to index N-dimensional binary features; [19] indexes the image database with a code book for color features; [26] uses the ratio between the two dimensions of an image as the index. However, to our best knowledge, there has not been any image retrieval system that takes advantage of the inverted index technique.

In terms of combining local feature with global matching, the proposed Okapi-Chamfer algorithm is related to the idea of connecting local invariant features with a deformable geometrical model [5, 20], but our method does not require manual specification of the geometric model. Therefore it can accommodate a wide range of deformations of articulated objects.

In terms of quantizing local feature descriptors, our work bears some similarity with [30]. The difference is that [30] uses the original SIFT descriptor [16] to characterize textured regions, while our method simplifies SIFT and use a group of local features to describe the silhouette of low texture objects. In the signal processing community, contourlet [6] and ridgelet are investigated to give a sparse representation of images. They usually specify a general set of directional filters to model the local patterns, while our method trains the pattern from the image database.

Another line of research that links visual primitives with text information is [7], which complements image retrieval with its associated text annotation. In our case, there is no text annotation. The image itself is treated as a text document.

The problem of articulated posture estimation (of hand or human body) has been investigated in the context of tracking. One category of tracking algorithms [13, 21, 38, 33, 18] searches the configuration space of a 3D kinematic model, and estimates the posture with an analysis-by-synthesis approach. The second category [29, 2], which this chapter belongs to, uses the segmented hand region as a query image to retrieve similar images in database of labeled training images. Tomasi et al. [36] pointed out the link between tracking and sequential recognition.

3 Extracting and Quantizing Visual Features

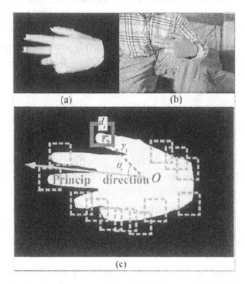

Fig. 1. (a) An example of training image. (b) An example of test image. (c) Illustration of the feature extraction process

For a query image of the hand (Fig. 1b), the basic steps for feature extraction are:

- Segment the hand region based on the skin-color histograms.
- Find discriminative patches along the boundary between the hand region and the background.
- Extract local orientation histogram feature from each patch.
- Quantize the local feature based on a pre-trained lexicon.

For a training image generated with computer graphics (Fig. 1a), we can get the hand region directly. The next two steps are the same as those for a query image. The lexicon is trained by clustering the local features extracted from all the training images. The details of each step are given in the following subsections.

3.1 Skin Color Histogram Based Segmentation

For a query image, we convert it into HSI (hue, saturation and intensity) color space. The HSI image is mapped to a likelihood ratio image L. The value of pixel (u, v) in L is defined as:

$$L(u,v) = \frac{p(H(u,v)|\text{skin})}{p(H(u,v)|\text{nonskin})} \tag{1}$$

where $H(u, v)$ is the hue and saturation value of pixel (u, v). We train the likelihood $p(H(u, v)|\text{skin})$ and $p(H(u, v)|\text{nonskin})$ by collecting color histogram from manually segmented images of the hand and the background regions. We segment the hand region by thresholding L [12]. In contrast to traditional matching algorithms based on global measurements (e.g., Chamfer distance between two sets of contour points), our matching algorithm collectively matches local features. Therefore it is more robust against mis-segmentation. We can use a low threshold (so that more pixels are segmented into the hand region) which fits the general scenarios.

3.2 Local Orientation Histogram Feature Descriptor

Figure 1c illustrates the visual feature extraction. The local features are generated from a binary image of the segmented hand. We do not use salient point detector such as Harris corner detector or difference of Gaussian detector, because there is no reliable texture in a query image. On the binary image, 24×24 subwindows (denoted by d_i, $i = 1, \ldots, n$) are selected if at least 20% but no more than 80% of the pixels in the subwindow belongs to the hand region. The thresholds are set to eliminate subwindows that are almost entirely within the hand region or in the background.

We characterize the shape in the subwindow with a local orientation histogram feature descriptor as described in [16]. The histogram covers from 0 degree to 360 degrees, with 8 bins. The difference is that we do not subdivide the subwindow into smaller blocks, because cascading features from the subdivided blocks in the same subwindow will make the feature descriptor orientation dependent. The final descriptor for each subwindow is an 8-dimensional vector f_i.

To ensure the descriptor is invariant with respect to the rigid motion of the hand (including in-plane rotation, scaling and 2D translation), we take the following steps (the notations are illustrated in Fig. 1):

1. Find the centroid O of the hand region.
2. Measure the radius γ_i between O and the center of each subwindow d_i.
3. Normalize γ_i by dividing it with the median of all γ_i ($i = 1, \ldots, n$).
4. Measure the angle θ_i.
5. Take the mode among all θ_i ($i = 1, \ldots, n$), and define it as the principal angle $\theta_{\text{principal}}$.
6. Calculate relative angle $\theta_i^{\text{rel}} = \theta_i - \theta_{\text{principal}}$. Since we are mapping from Manifold S_1 to R, we have to handle the problem of sudden jump between 0 degree and 360 degrees[1].

---

[1] We apply the following mapping to make sure θ_i^{rel} is always positive: $\theta_i^{\text{rel}} = \theta_i^{\text{rel}} + 360$, if $\theta_i^{\text{rel}} < 0$. When measuring distance between two angles θ_i^{rel} and θ_j^{rel} inside $\text{Dist}_{\text{Chamfer}}$ in (5), we first ensure $\theta_i^{\text{rel}} < \theta_j^{\text{rel}}$ and then define $\text{dist}(\theta_i^{\text{rel}}, \theta_j^{\text{rel}}) = \min\{(\theta_j^{\text{rel}} - \theta_i^{\text{rel}}), (\theta_i^{\text{rel}} - \theta_j^{\text{rel}} + 360)\}$

Each 8-dimensional feature vector is assigned a tag of its relative spatial information, denoted by $s_i = (\gamma_i, \theta_i)$. At this stage, an image d can be represented by a list $\{f_i, s_i\}_{i=1,\ldots,n}$.

3.3 Building the Lexicon and Quantizing the Image

Given a collection of training images, we can generate a large number[2] of feature vectors denoted by f_i $(i = 1, \ldots, D)$. To build a lexicon for the feature vectors, we used the EM algorithm [10] to find $|V|$ clusters, where $|V|$ is the pre-specified lexicon size. We run EM clustering with increasing $|V|$, until the average quantization error is smaller than a threshold. The center c_j $(j = 1, \ldots, |V|)$ of each cluster represents a unique term in the lexicon. Figure 2 shows some examples of the patches in a cluster.

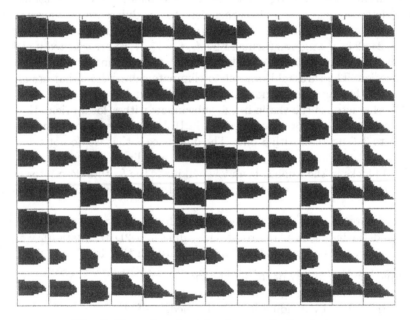

Fig. 2. Examples of patches in a particular cluster

The majority of the patches in this cluster correspond to the angular shape between the proximal phalanges of two adjacent fingers. Given the lexicon, a feature vector f_i can be quantized into a term

$$t_i = \underset{j=1,\ldots,|V|}{\arg\min} \ \mathbf{Dist}(f_i, c_j) \tag{2}$$

where **Dist** is Euclidean distance.

---

[2] In our case, D = 11,647,966.

In building the lexicon, we only use the feature descriptor part f_i (but not the spatial tag s_i), so multiple occurrences of the same term with different spatial tags are not distinguished.

With the lexicon, a training image of n local features can be represented by a list $\{t_i, s_i\}_{i=1,...,n}$. This is similar to a document consisting of n terms. The difference is that in most text retrieval systems, the spatial information of one occurrence of one term is not recorded[3], while in our image retrieval system, each term t_i has a 2D spatial tag s_i. The spatial tags are used for evaluating Chamfer distance in (5).

The local features in the test image are also quantized using (2).

4 Matching with the Okapi-Chamfer Weighting Formula

Having defined the lexicon in Sect. 3.3, we can formulate the problem of posture recognition as that of text retrieval. In the following subsections a training image is called a document; an image database is called a collection of documents; a test image is called a query. Both a document and a query are a list of terms. The following subsections give the details on the Okapi-Chamfer matching algorithm.

4.1 Vector Space Model

Assuming the size of the lexicon is $|V|$, a document (or query) can be represented by a vector $\mathbf{x} = [x_1, \ldots, x_{|V|}]$, where x_i is an importance weight of a term w_i in the document (or query). The vector space of $\mathbf{x}$ is denoted by Π. Typically $x_i = 0$, if w_i does not appear in the document (or query). Therefore the vector $\mathbf{x}$ is very sparse.

The similarity score between the query $\mathbf{q}$ and document $\mathbf{d}$ can be measured by an inner product $\mathbf{Sim}(\mathbf{q}, \mathbf{d}) = \sum_{i=1}^{|V|} q_i d_i$, which can be evaluated on co-occurring terms in both the document and the query, as (3) shows.

$$\mathbf{Sim}(\mathbf{q}, \mathbf{d}) = \sum_{w \in \mathbf{q} \cap \mathbf{d}} W(w) \tag{3}$$

The function W is a weighting function that is typically defined on the basis of two popular heuristics: term frequency (TF) and inverse document frequency (IDF).

TF $= c(w, \mathbf{d})$ counts the number of occurrences of a term w in document $\mathbf{d}$. The intuition is that w is more important if it occurs more frequently in a document/query. IDF $= \ln \frac{N+1}{f_d(w)}$, where $f_d(w)$ is the number of documents that include term w, and N is the total number of documents in the collection. The intuition is w is more discriminative if it only appears in a few documents.

---

[3] In other words, multiple occurrences of the same term are not distinguished among each other. Only the term frequency within the document matters.

The vector space model is so general that many similarity measurements originally deducted from probabilistic model [23] or language model [14] can be implemented as (3) with different weighting function W. In some sense, one can think of W as a kernel function that transforms the vector space Π into a higher-dimensional feature space. Therefore the linear function in (3) can approximate various matching functions.

4.2 The Modified Okapi Weighting

This chapter uses the modified Okapi weighting, because it satisfies a set of prescribed constraints and performances among the best in extensive text information retrieval experiments [8].

In the original Okapi formula, a negative IDF occurs when the a query term has very high document frequency (e.g., a verbose query[4]). When the IDF part of the original Okapi formula is negative, it will give a misleading importance weight, because a higher TF will only push the weight further to the negative side, and this defeats the purpose of the TF heuristic.

In the case of posture recognition, the query image is verbose. From an arbitrary input query image, many non-disseminative local features will be extracted and included in the query. Therefore we need to adopt the modification suggested in [8]. The modified version changes the IDF part so that it is always positive, as in the following equation.

$$\mathrm{Sim}(\mathbf{q},\mathbf{d}) = \sum_{w \in \mathbf{q} \cap \mathbf{d}} \frac{(k_1+1)\,c(w,\mathbf{d})}{k_1\left(1-b+b\frac{|\mathbf{d}|}{a}\right)+c(w,\mathbf{d})} \frac{(k_3+1)\,c(w,\mathbf{q})}{k_3+c(w,\mathbf{q})} \ln\frac{N+1}{f_d(w)} \quad (4)$$

where $|\mathbf{d}|$ denotes the length of document $\mathbf{d}$ and a is the average length of documents in the collection. k_1, k_2 and b are the same parameters as defined in the original Okapi weighting formula [22].

4.3 Okapi-Chamfer Matching

The original Okapi weighting formula considers the content of a document invariant under permutation of terms. However, the image position of the local features will affect the label of an image. Therefore we need to model the spatial distribution of the local features and integrate it to the weighting formula.

To record the spatial information, we use the spatial tag s_i, which records the relative spatial location that term t_i occurs in the document, as defined in Sect. 3.2.

To match the spatial tags in the query with those in the document, we use the Chamfer distance, which has proved to be an effective way of matching spatial distributions of silhouette points [1]. It is computationally expensive

---

[4] As opposed to a key-word query, which only include discriminative terms.

to compute the Chamfer distance between two point-sets. Fortunately, in our case, we are computing the Chamfer distance between two sets of local features. The number of elements in each set is much smaller.

Combining the modified Okapi with the Chamfer distance, we define the similarity measure as follows.

$$\mathbf{Sim}(\mathbf{q}, \mathbf{d}) = \sum_{w \in \mathbf{q} \cap \mathbf{d}} \frac{(k_1 + 1)\, c(w, \mathbf{d})}{k_1 \left(1 - b + b\frac{|\mathbf{d}|}{a}\right) + c(w, \mathbf{d})} \frac{(k_3 + 1)\, c(w, \mathbf{q})}{k_3 + c(w, \mathbf{q})} \ln \frac{N + 1}{f_d(w)} +$$

$$+ \mu\, \mathbf{Dist}_{\mathrm{Chamfer}}(S_{\mathbf{q}, w}, S_{\mathbf{d}, w}) \qquad (5)$$

where μ is the coefficient that decides how much effect the spatial distribution has upon the matching score. $\mathbf{Dist}_{\mathrm{Chamfer}}$ denotes the Chamfer distance between two sets of spatial tags. They are defined as follows.

$$\begin{aligned} S_{\mathbf{q}, w} &= \{s_i \in \mathbf{q} | t_i = w\} \\ S_{\mathbf{d}, w} &= \{s_i \in \mathbf{d} | t_i = w\} \end{aligned} \qquad (6)$$

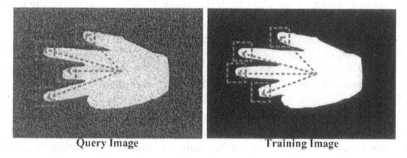

Query Image   Training Image

Fig. 3. An illustration of Chamfer distance between matched terms in a query image and a training image. The red boxes indicates the locations where the matched term w appears in the two images

The pair-wise distance between individual spatial tags is Euclidean. Figure 3 illustrates the Chamfer distance between a query image and a training image according to a particular term w. In Fig. 3 the matched term w happens to represent the arch pattern of the finger tips. In practice, w can be any matched shape pattern.

4.4 Fast Matching with the Inverted Index

Formulating the image retrieval problem as that of text retrieval based on a vector space model, we are ready to use a powerful tool in the area of text retrieval: the inverted index.

An inverted index includes two components: a lexicon of distinct terms and for each term, a list of documents that contain the term. Consider the following two documents:

$D1$: This is an interesting paper.

$D2$: That is a boring paper.

The inverted index for these two documents would be:

$$\text{This} \rightarrow \{D1\}$$
$$\text{is} \rightarrow \{D1, D2\}$$
$$\text{an} \rightarrow \{D1\}$$
$$\text{interesting} \rightarrow \{D1\}$$
$$\text{paper} \rightarrow \{D1, D2\}$$
$$\text{That} \rightarrow \{D2\}$$
$$\text{a} \rightarrow \{D2\}$$
$$\text{boring} \rightarrow \{D2\}$$

With the inverted index, only documents that contain at least one query term are accessed and matched with the query, in order to retrieve the matching results.

In a collection of N documents, the computational cost of matching with inverted index is $O(B|V_q|)$, where B is the average number of training documents in which a query term appears. $|V_q|$ is the vocabulary size of a query. In comparison, the cost of matching with every documents in the collection is $O(N|V_q|)$.

To take advantage of the inverted index, B should be as small as possible. One typical way to reduce B is to eliminate the stop words from the lexicon. Stop words are terms that appear in many documents. According to the IDF heuristic, stop words are not very discriminative and will give low weight in the Okapi formula. For details, please refer to [3].

By organizing the database of training images with the inverted index and eliminating stop words from the lexicon of visual features, we accelerate the speed of processing one query by a factor of 82.2 on average.

5 Experimental Results

To evaluate the performance of the Okapi-Chamfer matching algorithm, we test it on a database of 16,384 images of hand at different postures. We use a 3D kinematic mesh model to generate 1024 hand shapes. Each shape is rendered from 16 different view angles. We follow a similar procedure as [11] in choosing the 1024 hand shapes and the 16 view angles.

Assuming all three flexing joint angles in one finger are linearly related and the abduction angles are fixed, we parameterize the finger configuration with $\theta = [\theta_{\text{thumb}} \ \theta_{\text{index}} \ \theta_{\text{middle}} \ \theta_{\text{ring}} \ \theta_{\text{pinky}}]$. Each component of θ determines the three flexing joint angles of one finger. We take four different values for each of the five components, which are 8, 26, 48, and 75 degrees.

The 16 view angles are the combinations of 4 discrete rotations along x−axis and 4 discrete rotations along y−axis. The rotation angles are 0, 20, 40, and 60. We do not need to generate multiple images of the same hand shape under different in-plane rotations (i.e., rotation along z−axis), because the local visual feature is invariant to in-plane rotations.

During testing, we used two kinds of query images. One kind of query images are generated with a 3D kinematic hand model from several view points. The rotation angles along x−axis and y−axis range from 0 to 60 degrees. The angle along z−axis range from 0 to 360 degrees. We also added Gaussian noise the synthesized query images to imitate the segmentation error due to sensor noise. We tested only 500 synthesized query images and their finger configurations are randomly sampled.

The second kind is real-world images. The real hand geometry is slightly different from the 3D computer graphics model used to generate the image database. The finger configurations are manually labeled.

Figure 4 shows some samples of retrieval results of synthesized query images without in-plane rotation. The left most column is the query image and the other columns

Figure 5 shows some samples of retrieval results of synthesized query images with in-plane rotations. This demonstrates that our local feature is invariant to in-plane rotations.

Figure 6 shows some samples of retrieval results of real-world query images. This demonstrates that our matching algorithm is robust against clutter background and variation in the geometry of the hand.

The goal of our recognition system is to recover the finger configurations (i.e., the joint angles) from an input image. We take the label of rank one retrieval result as the estimation result for a query image. In the quantitative evaluations, instead of showing a precision-recall curve, we measure the root mean square error between the estimated parameter $\hat{\theta}$ and the ground truth parameter θ which is defined as $\sqrt{E\{\|\hat{\theta} - \theta\|^2\}}$, where $\| \cdot \|$ is L^2-norm.

In Fig. 7, the vertical axis is the root mean square error (RMSE). The horizontal axis is the variance of Gaussian noises that are added to the synthesized input image. The figure demonstrates that using the modified Okapi or the Chamfer distance alone will give larger errors. With a proper coefficient μ the Okapi-Chamfer matching algorithm (the curve labeled with '$\diamond$') gives much smaller errors. When μ is set too large, using the Okapi-Chamfer matching (the curve labeled with 'o') will be almost equivalent to using the Chamfer distance alone (the curve labeled with '+'). The recognition error when using the modified Okapi alone is not very sensitive to image noise. This is because the modified Okapi disregards the position of the local features. The image noise only affects the TF part of the weighting formula, but will not affect the

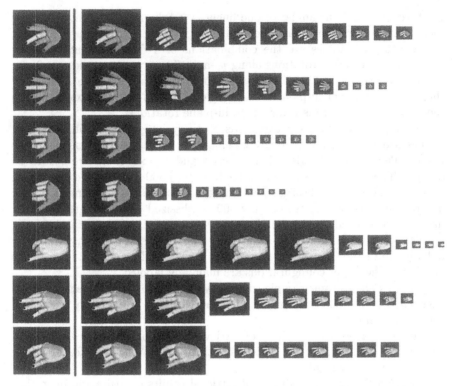

Fig. 4. Some samples of retrieval results of synthesized query images without in-plane rotation. The left most column is the query image and the other columns are the retrieval results. The size of the retrieved images are proportional to their matching scores

IDF part of the weighting, as long as at least one of the previously detected local feature survives the noise.

The four curves are different only in terms of matching algorithm. The same inverted index is used for all four curves.

The speed of our posture recognition system is around 3 seconds/query on a 1 GHz Pentium III PC in a database of 16384 training images. Although the current Matlab implementation is meant to validate the framework and is not optimized for speed, its speed is comparable to the state of the art. [11] reported 3.7 seconds/query and [1] reported 2.3 seconds/query. Both are in a comparable setup as that of our experiments. After optimizing the implementation and porting the code to C/C++, we can reach the goal of real-time posture recognition.

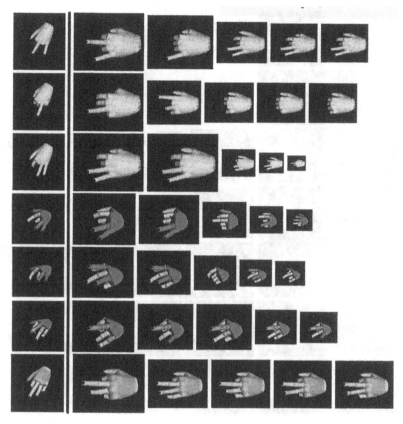

Fig. 5. Some samples of retrieval results of synthesized query images with in-plane rotation. The retrieval results are ordered according to their matching score. The size of the retrieved images are proportional to their matching scores

6 Conclusions

The main contributions of our work are:

- Formulated the problem of posture recognition as that of text retrieval.
- Introduced the inverted index technique to organize an image database.
- Proposed and implemented a matching algorithm that combines the modified-Okapi weighting formula with the Chamfer distance.

The current framework of posture recognition is briefly summarized into the following steps:

1. Extract and quantize local features from a query image.
2. For each local feature in the test image, find a subset of training images that contains at least one local feature in the query.

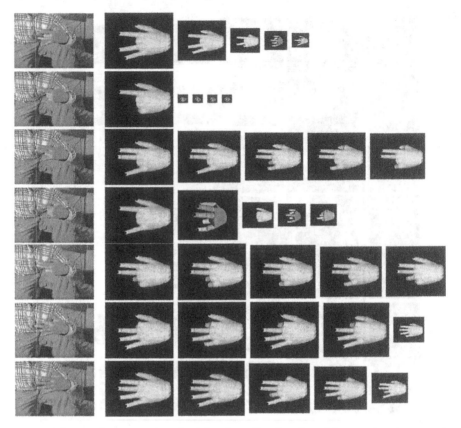

Fig. 6. Some samples of retrieval results of real-world query images

3. Within the subset, match the Chamfer distance between the two sets of spatial tags that are associated with a mutual local feature.
4. Combine the Chamfer distance with the modified Okapi formula to get the weight of current local feature.
5. Sum up the weights of all local features as the final matching score.

There are many possible improvements that we are still investigating. For example, in Step 3, we could obtain more accurate matching score by incorporating the original visual feature into the Chamfer distance. This can reduce the effect of quantization error in building the lexicon. On the other hand, we chose linear combination of Okapi weighting and Chamfer distance, because it is the most simple form and involves only one coefficient. However other ways of combining the two measurements might further improve the accuracy. More specifically, we can put Chamfer distance inside the Okapi weight formula by discounting the TF part according to the Chamfer distance.

In order to integrate the current algorithm into a real-time HCI system, we need to solve the problem of temporal segmentation, that is, detecting

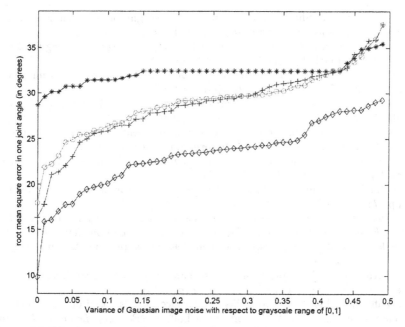

Fig. 7. RMSE of parameter θ. The curve labeled with '$*$' corresponds to results by using modified Okapi only, i.e., $\mu = 0$ in (4). The curve labeled with '$+$' corresponds to results by using Chamfer distance only. The curve labeled with 'o' is corresponds to results by using Okapi-Chamfer matching with $\mu = 15$. The curve labeled with '$\diamond$' is corresponds to results by using Okapi-Chamfer matching with $\mu = 5$

the event that a user is signaling to the computer and activating the recognition algorithm. This could involve defining a dedicated region to activate the system as the EyeToy game in PlayStation2.

Acknowledgments

This work was supported in part by National Science Foundation Grant IIS 01-38965.

References

1. V Athitsos et al. Boostmap: A method for efficient approximate similarity rankings. *Proc CVPR*, 2004.
2. V Athitsos and S Sclaroff. Estimating 3D hand pose from a cluttered image. *Proc CVPR*, 2003.
3. R Baeza-Yates and B Ribeiro-Neto. *Modern Information Retrieval*. Addison-Wesley, 2000.

4. S Belongie et al. Shape matching and object recognition using shape contexts. Technical Report UCB//CSD00-1128, UC Berkeley, 2001.
5. M C Burl et al. A probabilistic approach to object recognition using local photometry and global geometry. *Proc CVPR*, 1998.
6. M N Do and M Vetterli. Contourlets: A directional multiresolution image representation. *Proc Int Conf on Image Proc*, 2002.
7. J Edwards et al. Words and pictures in the news. *Proc Workshop on Learning Word Meaning from Non-Linguistic Data*, 2003.
8. H Fang et al. A formal study of information retrieval heuristics. *Proc Int Conf on Research and Development in Information Retrieval*, 2004.
9. V Ferrari et al. Simultaneous object recognition and segmentation by image exploration. *Proc ECCV*, 2004.
10. H Hartley. Maximum likelihood estimation from incomplete data. *Biometrics*, pp 174–194, 1958.
11. A Imai et al. 3D hand posture recognition by training contour variantion. *Proc IEEE Int Conf on Automatic Face and Gesture Recognition*, 2004.
12. M Jones and J Rehg. Statistical color models with application to skin detection. *Proc CVPR*, 1999.
13. J J Kuch and T S Huang. Vision-based hand modeling and tracking for virtual teleconferencing and telecollaboration. *Proc ICCV*, 1995.
14. J Lafferty and C Zhai. Probabilistic relevance models based on document and query generation. In: W B Croft and J Lafferty (Editors). *Language Modeling and Information Retrieval*. Kluwer, 2003.
15. S Lazebnik et al. Semi-local affine parts for object recognition. *Proc British Machine Vision Conference*, 2004.
16. David Lowe. Object recognition from local scale-invariant features. *Proc ICCV*, 1999.
17. David Lowe. Distinctive image features from scale-invariant keypoints. *Int J Computer Vision*, pp 91–110, 2004.
18. Shan Lu et al. Using multiple cues for hand tracking and model refinement. *Proc CVPR*, 2003.
19. A Mojsilović et al. Matching and retrieval based on the vocabulary and grammar of color patterns. *IEEE Trans Image Proc*, pp 38–54, 2000.
20. D Ramanan and D A Forsyth. Using temporal coherence to build models of animals. *Proc ICCV*, 2003.
21. J Rehg and T Kanade. Model-based tracking of self-occluding articulated objects. *Proc ICCV*, 1995.
22. S E Robertson and S Walker. Some simple effective approximations to the 2-Poisson model for probabilistic weighted retrieval. *Proc Int Conf on Research and Development in Information Retrieval*, 1994.
23. S E Robertson et al. Probabilistic models of indexing and searching. In: R N Oddy et al (Editors). *Information Retrieval Research*. Butterworths, 1981.
24. F Rothganger et al. Learning methods for generic object recognition with invariance to pose and lighting. *Proc CVPR*, 2004.
25. Y Rui et al. Image retrieval: Current techniques, promising directions, and open issues. *J Visual Communication and Image Representation*, pp 1–23, 1999.
26. R Schettini et al. Quick look system. http://www.ivl.disco.unimib.it/Activities/Quicklook.html
27. C Schmid and R Mohr. Local grayvalue invariants for image retrieval. *IEEE Trans PAMI*, pp 530–535, 1997.

28. G Shakhnarovich et al. Fast pose estimation with parameter sensitive hashing. *Proc ICCV*, 2003.
29. N Shimada et al. Real-time 3D hand posture estimation based on 2D appearance retrieval using monocular camera. *Proc Int Workshop on Recognition, Analysis, and Tracking of Faces and Gestures in Real-Time Systems*, 2001.
30. J Sivic and A Zisserman. Video data mining using configurations of viewpoint invariant regions. *Proc CVPR*, 2004.
31. A W M Smeulders et al. Content-based image retrieval at the end of the early years. *IEEE Trans PAMI*, pp 1349–1380, 2000.
32. J R Smith and S F Chang. Automated binary feature sets for image retrieval. *Proc ICASSP*, 1996.
33. B Stenger et al. Model based 3D tracking of an articulated hand. *Proc CVPR*, 2001.
34. B Stenger et al. Filtering using a tree-based estimator. *Proc ICCV*, 2003.
35. A Thayananthan et al. Shape context and chamfer matching in cluttered scenes. *Proc CVPR*, 2003.
36. C Tomasi et al. 3D tracking = classification + interpolation. *Proc ICCV*, 2003.
37. T Tuytelaars and L J Van Gool. Content-based image retrieval based on local affinely invariant regions. *Proc Int Conf on Visual Information and Information Systems*, 1999.
38. Y Wu et al. Capturing natural hand articulation. *Proc ICCV*, 2001.

Visual Modeling of Dynamic Gestures Using 3D Appearance and Motion Features

Guangqi Ye, Jason J. Corso, and Gregory D. Hager

Computational Interaction and Robotics Laboratory
The Johns Hopkins University
grant@cs.jhu.edu
jcorso@cs.jhu.edu
hager@cs.jhu.edu

We present a novel 3D gesture recognition scheme that combines the 3D appearance of the hand and the motion dynamics of the gesture to classify manipulative and controlling gestures. Our method does not directly track the hand. Instead, we take an object-centered approach that efficiently computes 3D appearance using a region-based coarse stereo matching algorithm. Motion cues are captured by differentiating the appearance feature with respect to time. An unsupervised learning scheme is carried out to capture the cluster structure of these features. Then, the image sequence of a gesture is converted to a series of symbols that indicate the cluster identities of each image pair. Two schemes, i.e., forward HMMs and neural networks, are used to model the dynamics of the gestures. We implemented a real-time system and performed gesture recognition experiments to analyze the performance with different combinations of the appearance and motion features. The system achieves recognition accuracy of over 96% using both the appearance and motion cues.

1 Introduction

Gestures have been one of the important interaction media in current human-computer interaction (HCI) systems [3, 4, 11, 12, 14, 16, 18, 22, 25, 26, 28]. Furthermore, for 3D virtual environments (VE) in which the user manipulates 3D objects, gestures are more appropriate and potentially powerful than traditional interaction media, such as a mouse or a joystick. Vision-based gesture processing also provides more convenience and immersiveness than those based on mechanical devices.

We are interested in modeling manipulative and controlling gestures [14] for direct manipulation and natural interaction. These gestures have a temporal nature that involves complex changes of hand configurations. Furthermore, human hands and arms are highly articulate and deformable objects. As a result, gestures normally consist of complex 3D global and local motion of the hands and arms. The complex spatial properties and dynamics of such gestures render the problem extremely difficult for pure 2D (e.g., template matching) methods. Ideally, we would capture the full 3D information of the hands to model the gestures [11]. However, the difficulty and computational complexity of visual 3D localization [19] prompts us to question the necessity of doing so for gesture recognition.

Most reported gesture recognition work in the literature (see Sect. 1.1) relies heavily on visual tracking and template recognition algorithms. However, general human motion tracking is well-known to be a complex and difficult problem [8, 17]. Additionally, while template matching may be suitable for static gestures, its ability to capture the spatio-temporal nature of dynamic gestures is in doubt.

To that end, we present a novel scheme to model and recognize 3D temporal gestures using 3D appearance and motion cues without tracking and explicit localization of the hands. Instead, we follow the site-centered computation fashion of Visual Interaction Cues (VICs) paradigm [3, 25].

We propose that interaction gestures can be captured in a local neighborhood around the manipulated object based on the fact that the user only initiates manipulative gestures when his or her hands are close enough to the objects. The advantages of this scheme are its efficiency and flexibility. The dimension of the volume of the local neighborhood around the manipulated object can be adjusted conveniently according to the nature of the particular interaction environment and the applicable gestures. For example, in a desktop interaction environment, the interaction elements are represented as small icons on a flat panel. Manipulative gestures are only initiated when the user's hand is near the surface of the panel, so we only need to observe a small volume above the panel with the icon sitting at the center of the bottom. The height and diameter of the volume is also limited to be able to capture enough visual cues to carry out successful gesture recognition.

The remainder of this chapter is structured as follows. In Sect. 2 we present a novel method to efficiently capture the 3D spatial information of the gesture without carrying out a full-scale disparity computation. We discuss how to learn the cluster structure of the appearance and motion features via an unsupervised learning process in Sect. 3. Two ways to model the dynamics of the gestures — forward Hidden Markov Models (HMMs) [10, 20] and multilayer neural networks [6] — are also presented. In Sect. 4 we demonstrate our real-time system that implements the proposed method and present the results of gesture recognition. Section 5 concludes the chapter.

1.1 Related Work

In [23], Wu and Huang presented a general overview of the state of the art in gesture analysis for vision-based human-computer interaction. Robust hand localization and tracking, modeling the constraints of hand motion and recognizing temporal gesture patterns are among the most difficult and active research areas. Compared to other techniques, such as neural network and rule-based methods [14], HMMs [24, 25] and its extensions [2] are a popular scheme to model temporal gestures.

Many HCI systems [12, 14, 16, 22, 23] have been reported that enable the user to use gestures as a controlling or communicative media to manipulate interaction objects. The hand or fingertips are detected based on such cues as visual appearance, shape, and human body temperature via infrared cameras. A variety of algorithms have been applied to track the hand [23], such as the Kalman filter and particle filter [5].

With a model-based approach [1, 13], it is possible to capture the gesture in higher dimensionality than 2D. In [1] the 3D hand model is represented as a set of synthetic images of the hand with different configurations of the fingers under different viewpoints. Image-to-model matching is carried out using a Chamfer distance-based computation. One of the difficulties of this approach is constructing a good 3D model of the hand that can deal with variance between different users. Furthermore, efficient algorithms are necessary to handle the matching between models and input images. Another approach to capture 3D data is to use special cameras [11], such as 3D cameras or other range sensors. However, the hardware requirement limits its application to general HCI systems.

2 Capturing 3D Features of Manipulative Gestures

Manipulative and controlling gestures have a temporal 3D nature involving the interaction between human hands and other objects. Example subjects include the tools and toys in a VE, interaction elements in an HCI interface, and so forth. One of the most difficult problems in visual modeling of gestures is data collection and feature representation [23]. We propose an efficient scheme to capture 3D gesture appearance and motion in an object-centered fashion. We use the Visual Interaction Cues (VICs) [27] paradigm in this work. We provide a brief summary of the paradigm in Sect. 2.1. Under the VICs paradigm, we are able to make the assumption that the content of a manipulative gesture can be captured in a local region around the manipulated object. This assumption is valid in many HCI scenarios [27], such as a WIMP-style interface [21].

2.1 The Visual Interaction Cues Paradigm

As we discussed earlier, manipulative and controlling gestures involve the interaction between human hands and objects in the environment. Typical methods for vision-based interaction attempt to perform continuous, global user tracking to model the interaction. Such techniques are computationally expensive, prone to error and the re-initialization problem, prohibit the inclusion of arbitrary numbers of users, and often require a complex gesture-language the user must learn.

However, under the VICs paradigm [27], we focus on the components of the interface itself instead of on the user. The VICs paradigm is a methodology for vision-based interaction operating on the fundamental premise that, in general vision-based human-computer interaction settings, global user modeling and tracking are not necessary. There are essentially two parts to the VICs paradigm.

First, we define and maintain a mapping between the interface components and their respective projections in the images (Fig. 1). Let $\mathcal{I}$ be an image defined by a set of pixel locations (points in $\mathbf{R}^2$). Let $\mathcal{W}$ be the space in which the components of the interface reside. In general, $\mathcal{W}$ is the 3D Euclidean space $\mathbf{R}^3$ but it can be the Projective plane $\mathbf{P}^2$ or the Euclidean plane $\mathbf{R}^2$. Define an interface component mapping $M : \mathcal{C} \to \mathcal{X}$, where $\mathcal{C} \subset \mathcal{W}$ and $\mathcal{X} \subset \mathcal{I}$. In Fig. 1, we show an example of this concept for stereo cameras. In this case, two mappings are required with one for each image. Intuitively, the mapping defines a region in the image to which an interface component projects.

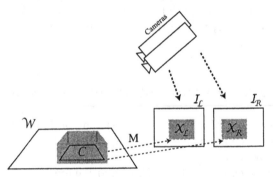

Fig. 1. Schematic explaining the principle of local image analysis for the VICs paradigm: M is the component mapping that yields a region of interest in the stereo images $\mathcal{I}_{\mathcal{L}}$ and $\mathcal{I}_{\mathcal{R}}$ for analyzing actions on component $\mathcal{C}$

Second, if, for each interface component and the current images, a map is known, detecting a user action reduces to analyzing a local region in the image. This is a fairly general statement and the subject of this chapter. We provide a simple example here for expository purposes. Let the interface component be a standard push-button. Then, to detect a button-press by a user, we expect a certain sequence of *interaction cues* to occur in the image region. An example of such cues might be *motion → skin-color → finger-shape → finger pauses → motion and absence of skin-color*. Such cues may be heuristically defined or learned as in this chapter.

2.2 3D Gesture Volume

Given a pair of stereo images of a scene, a disparity map can be computed using a standard correspondence search algorithm. Since we only care about the local neighborhood around the object, we can constrain the stereo search to a limited 3D space around the object. This brings about two advantages: first, we only care about the small patch of the image centered at the object; second, we only need to search through a small number of disparities (depths), which is a limited range around the depth of the object. To simplify the computation, we carry out the stereo matching process for a discrete number of image patches, not for each pixel position.

Formally, let I_l and I_r be a pair of images of the scene. We split the images into tiles of equal size of $w \times h$. Here w and h refer to the width and height of the tile, respectively. Suppose we only consider a local area of size of $m \times n$ tiles, starting at patch (x_0, y_0). Define SIM as a similarity measurement between two image tiles. Example measurements include the sum of absolute differences and sum of squared differences. Given a discrete parallax search range of $[0, (p-1) \times w]$, we can characterize the scene using a $m \times n \times p$ volume V as:

$$V_{x,y,z} = \text{SIM}(I_{l(x_0+x,y_0+y)}, I_{r(x_0+x+z,y_0+y)}) \tag{1}$$

where $x \in \{0,\ldots,m-1\}$, $y \in \{0,\ldots,n-1\}$, and $z \in \{0,\ldots,p-1\}$. Note that in (1) the image index indicates a tile of the image, not a particular pixel.

We convert the color images into hue images to reduce the impact of changes in lighting intensity because hue is a good color-invariant model [9]. Furthermore, we perform a comprehensive color normalization process [7] on each image to overcome the variance of illumination and lighting geometry across different interaction sessions. These techniques ensure the relative stability of the appearance feature under different imaging conditions.

Following this scheme, we can extract the features of the image as a very simple vector with the size of $m \times n \times p$. The typical size of the extracted appearance vector is from 125 to 1000. In contrast, the size of the original image is 640×480 and the size of the local image around a typical object in our experiments is approximately 150×150. Thus, this feature extraction scheme significantly reduces the size of the the input data.

Figure 2 shows examples of the stereo image pair and the extracted 3D features of the scene. It can be seen that the extracted feature volume characterizes the different configuration of the user's hand with respect to the target interaction subject.

2.3 Motion by Differencing

Since we represent the 3D appearance of the gesture images using feature vectors, one simple way to capture the motion information of the gestures is

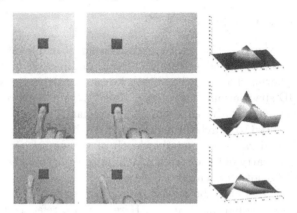

Fig. 2. Examples of the image pair and extracted appearance feature. The left and middle columns display left images and right images of the scene, respectively. The right column shows the bottom layer of the feature volume (i.e., $V_{x,y,z}$ with $z = 0$)

to compute the displacement in this feature space. In our real-time system, the change between consecutive frames is normally very small because of the high frame rate. Thus we compute the difference between the appearance feature of the current frame and that of several frames before.

$$\text{Motion}_i = V_i - V_{i-k} \quad (i = k + 1, \ldots, M) \tag{2}$$

One way to combine the appearance feature and the motion feature is to concatenate the two vectors to form a larger vector. This new vector contains both the static and temporal information of the gesture.

2.4 Analysis of the 3D Features

Given an image sequence that contains a particular manipulative gesture, we convert the sequence into a series of vectors, or points in the appearance or motion space. Thus, the gesture can be conceptualized as a directed path connecting these points in the appropriate order. Intuitively we can model the gesture by learning the parameters of such a path. However, this appearance or motion space is still a relatively high-dimensional space, making the learning and recognition difficult to handle.

Furthermore, for a set of a 3D appearance or motion feature points that are extracted from a dataset of gesture sequences, we can expect that there will be much redundancy of information. The reason is that the training set contains repeatable gestures and there are only a limited number of gestures in the set. To analyze the data redundancy, we use principal components analysis (PCA) technique on a dataset that consists of 622 gesture sequences. We experiment with representing the 125-dimensional appearance feature space using different numbers of principal components. Figure 3 shows the relationship between the average reconstruction error and the number of principal components. It can be seen that, using the first 25 principal components, we can achieve an average reconstruction error of less than 5%. Therefore, we expect to be able to characterize the appearance or motion feature of the gestures using data of much lower dimensionality without losing the capability to discriminate between them.

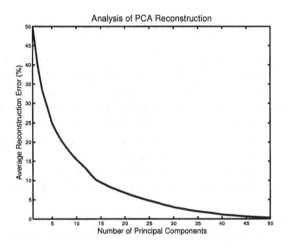

Fig. 3. PCA analysis on the 125-dimensional appearance feature space

In Sect. 3, we will discuss the techniques to learn the cluster structures of the 3D features and to model the dynamics of the temporal gestures in a feature space of reduced dimensionality.

3 Learning the Gesture Structure

In this section, we address the problem about how to efficiently reduce the dimensionality of these features for statistical modeling of dynamic gestures.

3.1 Unsupervised Learning of the Cluster Structures of 3D Features

One of the popular ways to model temporal signals is to learn a statistical model [6]. However, the size of training data needed for statistical learning normally increases exponentially with the dimensionality of input features. This curse of dimensionality is one of the reasons that visual modeling of gestures is difficult. Thus we propose to reduce the dimensionality of the 3D feature by learning its cluster configuration.

We propose an unsupervised method to learn the cluster structure of the high-dimensional raw feature. Basically, we implement a K-means algorithm to learn the centroid of each of the clusters of the feature set. Then, the feature vectors are clustered using a Vector Quantization (VQ) [10] algorithm. We represent each feature v_i with one of the k clusters $\mathcal{C} = \{C_1, C_2, \ldots, C_k\}$ based on nearest-neighbor criterion.

$$VQ(v_i) = \arg\min_{C_j \in \mathcal{C}} \text{Dist}(C_j, v_i) \tag{3}$$

Here, $Dist$ is computed as the Euclidean distance between two feature points.

The choice of the number of clusters to initialize the VQ algorithm is a difficult model selection problem. We handle this problem based on the analysis of the average representation error. The representation error is defined as the distance between feature point v_i and its corresponding cluster centroid $VQ(v_i)$. In theory, as the number of clusters k increases, the average representation error decreases. On the other hand, our aim of feature dimensionality reduction prefers smaller k. A trade-off is achieved by increasing the number of clusters until the average representation error only decreases slightly as k grows larger.

Figure 4 shows an example of the relationship between k and the representation error for a dataset of 125D appearance features. We can see that, when the cluster number is larger than 8, increasing the cluster number can only slightly reduce the average error. Thus, we can select the number of clusters to be 8. In Sect. 4, we include an experimental validation of this analysis.

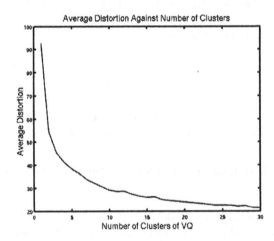

Fig. 4. The average representation error against number of clusters

This learning scheme allows different ways of combining appearance and motion cues. Let V^{appr} and V^{mot} denote the extracted appearance and motion feature, respectively. The first way is to normalize each visual feature to the same scale and then concatenate the feature vectors to form a new feature $(V^{\text{appr}}, V^{\text{mot}})$. The dimensionality of this new feature space is the sum of the dimensionality of the individual feature spaces. Then we can carry out VQ on this new feature space. The second way to combine these two visual cues is to carry out VQ on each feature space separately. Let VQ_{appr} and VQ_{mot} denote the VQ projection in the appearance and motion feature space, respectively. The overall representation of the visual features thus can be expressed as a discrete vector $(VQ_{\text{appr}}(V^{\text{appr}}), VQ_{\text{mot}}(V^{\text{mot}}))$. Furthermore, since we know the number of clusters in each feature space, which is equivalent to the dimensionality of corresponding element of the 2D discrete vector, we can further convert the 2D vector into a scalar.

3.2 Gesture Modeling Using HMMs

We use typical forward HMMs to model the dynamics of the temporal gestures. The input to the HMMs is the gesture sequence represented as a series of symbols with each symbol indicating the cluster identity of current frame. The basic idea is to construct a HMM for each gesture and learn the parameters of the HMM from the training sequences that belong to this gesture using the Baum-Welch algorithm [10, 15]. The probability that each HMM generates the given sequence is the criterion of recognition. The gesture sequence is recognized as the class with the highest probability. Rejection of invalid gestures is based on the thresholding of the best probability. If the highest probability that a sequence achieves on all HMMs is lower than a threshold, the sequence will be rejected. This threshold is chosen to be smaller than the lowest probability that each HMM generates the sequences that belong to that class in the training set.

In our experiment, we use a 6-state forward HMM to model each of the six manipulative gestures. Figure 5 shows the topology of the HMMs.

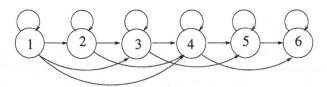

Fig. 5. HMM structure for the interaction gestures

The choice of the number of the states in the forward HMM is based on the intuitive analysis of the temporal properties of the gestures to be modeled. In our current experiment, each of the gestures can be decomposed into less than 6 distinct stages. For example, if we use 3 spatial layers to represent the vicinity of a manipulated object, the gesture of swiping an icon to the left can be viewed as such a configuration sequence of the hand: (1) entering the outer layer of the vicinity of the icon, (2) entering the inner layer (3) touching the icon to select it and (4) swiping the icon by moving the finger to the left side of the icon. Ideally, each of the distinct stages can be modeled by a certain state of the forward HMM. The parameter sets of the trained HMMs verify our expectation, in which the observation probability of each symbol of a gesture is high in one of the states and very small in the other states. Generally speaking, a dynamic process with n stages can be modeled using an n-state forward HMM with similar topology. For example, in [20], four-state HMMs are used to recognize American Sign Language.

3.3 Gesture Modeling Using a Multilayer Neural Network

Another way to learn gestures is to use multilayer neural networks. The input to the neural network is the entire gesture sequence, which is now a sequence of symbols. The output is the identity of the gesture. To meet the requirement of the neural network, we need to fix the length of each input sequence. We align each sequence to a fixed length by carrying out sub-sampling on those sequences that are longer than the predefined length and interpolation on those that are shorter. The parameters of the network are also learned from training data using the standard backpropagation algorithm [6].

In our current system, the neural network consists of 3 layers, i.e., the input and output layer and the hidden layer. The number of nodes in the hidden layer is chosen to be 50.

4 Experimental Results

To test the efficiency and efficacy of the proposed scheme for gesture modeling, we present our experimental setup and some results in this section.

4.1 Experimental Setup

We use the 4D Touchpad [3, 27] as our experimental platform. It is based on the 3D-2D projection-based mode of the VICs framework (see Sect. 2.1). We use a pair of color cameras to observe the interaction desktop which is presented as a flat panel on which the interaction elements are rendered. The system is calibrated using a pair of homographies thereby defining the required interface component mappings between the rendered image and the images captured from the cameras. The user interacts with the objects on the panel using manipulative and controlling gestures. Figure 6 shows the configuration of our experiment platform.

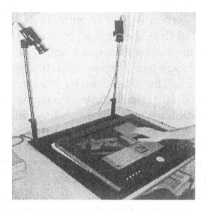

Fig. 6. The 4D Touchpad HCI platform

In our current experiments, we collect gesture sequences consisting of 6 interactive gestures, i.e., pushing a button, twisting a dial clockwise, twisting a dial anti-clockwise, toggling a switch, swiping an icon to the left and swiping an icon to the right. Table 1 shows several snapshots of the typical image sequences of the gestures.

Table 1. Example images of the gestures

Gesture	Push	Twist	Twist Anti	Toggle	Swipe Left	Swipe Right
Stage 1						
Stage 2						
Stage 3						
Stage 4						
Stage 5						

We implement the system on a PC with dual Pentium III processors. The system achieves real-time speed; the processing is limited by the cameras (30 Hz). The system processes the continuous video in the following fashion. For each captured image pair, the appropriate appearance and/or motion features are extracted and the corresponding cluster identity of current features is computed based on trained cluster centroids. We define an "empty scene" as the configuration without the user's hand in the vicinity of the object. We can check whether current frame is an empty scene by comparing the cluster identity of the current frame with that of an empty configuration. We begin the processing of a sequence when the system observes a non-empty scene, which means the hand has entered the vicinity of the object. We carry out the recognition of the current sequence and notify the user when a valid gesture is recognized. The recording of the current sequence is then terminated and the system enters a new cycle. Another case for ending the current sequence is that the system continuously observes the empty configuration for several frames.

4.2 Gesture Recognition Results

To perform training of the HMMs and the neural network, we record over 100 gesture sequences for each of the 6 gestures. A separate test set contains over 70 sequences of each gesture.

We carry out the training and testing on several feature sets. These different sets are characterized by the dimensionality of our 3D gesture volume described in Sect. 2 and different combination of the appearance and motion cues.

In our experiment, we record the data as subimages around the manipulated object. The size of the area is 220×210 pixels. When computing the appearance volume using (1), we split this local area into tiles of appropriate dimension according to the choice of the dimensionality of the appearance volume, i.e., m and n. The dimension is calculated as $w = 220/m$ and $h = 210/n$. For example, in the first appearance dataset, we choose $m = n = 5$. So the dimensionality of the image tiles is 44×42. For convenience, in all the datasets, we set $m = n = p$.

1. **Appearance Only** (125D)
   In this set, we only use the appearance feature. We set $m = m = p = 5$ and thus the dimensionality is $5 \times 5 \times 5 = 125$.
2. **Appearance Only** (1000D)
   Similar to the first set, except that the dimensionality of the appearance feature is $10 \times 10 \times 10 = 1000$.
3. **Motion Only** (1000D)
   We compute the motion feature by taking the difference between two 1000D appearance vectors.

4. **Concatenation of Appearance and Motion**
   In this set, we concatenate the 125D appearance feature with the 1000D motion vector to form a 1125D vector.
5. **Combination of Appearance (125D) and Motion**
   We carry out K-means on the 125D appearance feature and 1000D motion features separately. Then each frame is represented as a 2D discrete vector containing both the appearance cluster identity and motion cluster character.
6. **Combination of Appearance (1000D) and Motion**
   Similar to the previous setting except that we use the 1000D appearance feature.

We perform the training and testing on these sets for the HMM models and the neural network. For the neural network, we align each gesture sequence to the fixed length of 20. For the HMM models, we also carry out comparison experiments between using the same aligned sequences as the neural network and applying the raw unaligned sequence. Table 2 shows the gesture recognition results for all the feature sets and both gesture models. For each model we report both the recognition accuracy on the training set (left) and on the test set (right). We also present the number of clusters used to carry out the VQ.

Table 2. Gesture recognition results for different feature spaces

Set	Clusters	HMM		NN		Unaligned	
Appearance(125D)	8	99.5	99.5	100.0	98.8	99.4	99.4
Appearance(1000D)	8	99.5	100.0	98.4	94.4	98.4	98.0
Motion(1000D)	15	98.4	98.1	97.7	86.3	97.9	98.8
Concatenation	18	98.9	99.0	98.9	87.7	96.7	96.1
Combination 1	120	100.0	100.0	100.0	96.6	98.2	97.3
Combination 2	120	99.8	99.8	99.8	97.1	99.2	99.5

The results show that aligning the sequences to the same length improves the recognition accuracy. It can also be seen that the motion feature alone seems to perform slightly worse than those with appearance cues. However, combining appearance features with the motion features achieves the best recognition accuracy for our current gesture set.

Another interesting comparison between the HMM model and neural network shows that our multilayer neural network tends to over-train on the feature sets. The neural network model achieves equivalent or higher accuracy on the training set as the HMM model, but performs worse on the test set. During the training of the HMMs, the Baum-Welch algorithm runs for less than 5 iterations before the overall system entropy reaches a local minimum. During the neural network training process, the backpropagation algorithm typically runs for over 1000 iterations. We stop the the procedure when the decrease of the output error between consecutive runs is lower than a threshold, which is typically a very small number such as 0.00001.

Alternatively, one could stop the backpropagation algorithm interactively by measuring the performance on a validation set after each iteration and halting the training process if the classification on this validation set degenerates. However, we choose a fixed threshold to preserve the generality of the method and keep the training process automatic.

We also compare the gesture modeling using HMMs based on the raw sequences and those using collapsed sequences. Each raw sequence containing a gesture is packed in such a way that we only record a symbol if it is different from its previous one. In essence, we only record the order of the appearance of each feature, excluding the duration in the original temporal sequence. This is similar to the rule-based and state-based gesture modeling [2, 23]. Table 3 shows the gesture recognition results based on the datasets of collapsed sequences.

Table 3. Gesture recognition results for collapsed sequences

Feature Sets	Training	Test
Appearance(125D)	89.3%	88.8%
Appearance(1000D)	88.3%	86.1%
Motion(1000D)	98.4%	96.6%
Concatenation	90.8%	89.0%
Combination 1	94.2%	96.8%
Combination 2	99.8%	98.8%

Compared to the results using raw sequences, the gesture recognition using collapsed sequences performs slightly worse. Still, for the combination of the appearance and the motion features, this scheme of gesture modeling based only on key frames achieves very good recognition performance.

We also carry out the HMM recognition experiments using different numbers of clusters for the VQ algorithm. Figures 7 and 8 summarize the training and testing results for the first four datasets. For the two datasets where we combine the clustering result of appearance and motion into a 2D vector, we present the experimental results in Fig. 9.

It can be seen that, the recognition accuracy generally increases with the growth of the number of clusters. The reason is that gestures are represented by trajectories in a feature space of higher dimensionality, so that more characteristic detail of the gestures will be modeled. However, when the number of clusters increases beyond a certain limit, the HMMs tend to overtrain on the training data and the accuracy on the test set deteriorates. A trade-off between training and testing accuracy must be made.

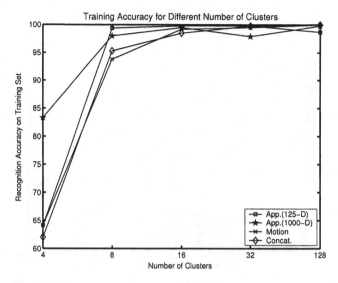

Fig. 7. Training accuracy using different number of clusters

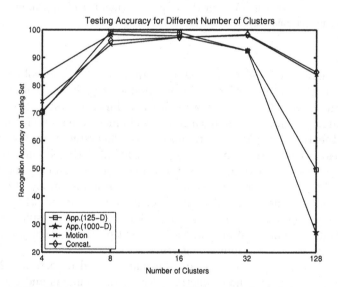

Fig. 8. Testing accuracy using different number of clusters

5 Conclusions

In this chapter, we present a novel real-time 3D gesture recognition system that combines the 3D appearance of the hand and the motion dynamics of the gesture to classify manipulative and controlling gestures. Instead of tracking

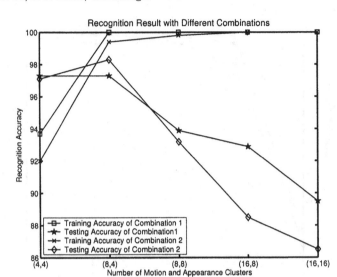

Fig. 9. Training and testing result for different combinations of appearance and motion features. The label on the x–axis represents the number of clusters for the appearance and motion features in the format of (number of appearance clusters, number of motion clusters)

the user's hand, we capture the 3D appearance of the local volume around the manipulation subject. Motion is computed as the difference of the appearance features between frames. We reduce the dimensionality of the 3D feature by employing unsupervised learning. We implemented a real-time system based on the 4D Touchpad platform and tested the system using two different approaches to model the temporal gestures, forward HMMs and multilayer neural networks. By combining the appearance and motion cues, both HMM models and the neural network achieved a recognition accuracy of over 96%. The proposed scheme is a flexible and efficient way to capture 3D visual cues in a local neighborhood around an object. The experiment results show that these local appearance and motion features capture the necessary visual cues to recognize different manipulative gestures.

In our current experiment setup, the manipulated objects are 2D icons that lie on a 2D plane. The geometry between the cameras and each object is similar and relatively fixed. The proposed appearance feature is not invariant to geometric transforms, such as rotation and translation. For general VEs, the interaction subjects can occupy a relatively large space, such that the geometry of each object with respect to the cameras can vary greatly. To overcome this variance, improvement to the feature extraction scheme is necessary.

The gesture vocabulary in our current experiment only consists of six dynamic gestures. In the future, we intend to address more complex gestures and a larger gesture vocabulary. We also plan to investigate other ways to model the gesture dynamics, such as HMMs that achieve minimal classification errors.

Acknowledgments

We are grateful to Darius Burschka for help with the Visual Interaction Cues project. This material is based upon work supported by the National Science Foundation under Grant No. 0112882. Any opinions, findings, and conclusions or recommendations expressed in this material are those of the author(s) and do not necessarily reflect the views of the National Science Foundation.

References

1. V Athitsos and S Sclaroff. Estimating 3D hand pose from a cluttered image. *Proc CVPR*, 2003.
2. A Bobick and A Wilson. A State-based approach to the representation and recognition of gesture. *IEEE Trans PAMI*, pp 1325–1337, 1997.
3. J J Corso et al. The 4DT: Unencumbered HCI with VICs. *Proc Workshop on CVPRHCI*, 2003.
4. J Davis and A Bobick. The representation and recognition of action using temporal templates. *Proc CVPR*, 1997.
5. J Deutscher et al. Articulated body motion capture by annealed particle filtering. *Proc CVPR*, 2000.
6. R Duda et al. *Pattern Classification*. John Wiley and Sons, 2001.
7. G D Finlayson et al. Comprehensive colour image normalization. *Proc ECCV*, 1998.
8. D Gavrila. The visual analysis of human movement: A survey. *Computer Vision and Image Understanding*, pp 82–98, 1999.
9. T Gevers. Color based object recognition. *Pattern Recognition*, pp 453–464, 1999.
10. F Jelinek. *Statistical Methods for Speech Recognition*. MIT Press, 1999.
11. S Malassiotis et al. A gesture recognition system using 3D data. *Proc Int Symp on 3D Data Processing Visualization and Transmission*, 2002.
12. K Oka et al. Real-time fingertip tracking and gesture recognition. *IEEE Computer Graphics and Applications*, pp 64–71, 2002.
13. V Parameswaran and R Chellappa. View invariants for human action recognition. *Proc CVPR*, 2003.
14. F Quek. Unencumbered gesture interaction. *IEEE Multimedia*, pp 36–47, 1996.
15. L Rabiner. A tutorial on Hidden Markov Models and selected applications in speech recognition. *Proceedings of the IEEE*, pp 257–286, 1989.
16. A Ramamoorthy et al. Recognition of dynamic hand gestures. *Pattern Recognition*, pp 2069–2081, 2003.

17. J M Rehg and T Kanade. Visual tracking of high DOF articulated structures: An application to human hand tracking. *Proc ECCV*, 1994.
18. C Wren et al. Pfinder: Real-time tracking of the human body. *IEEE Trans PAMI*, pp 780–784, 1997.
19. D Scharstein and R Szeliski A taxonomy and evaluation of dense two-frame stereo correspondence algorithms. *Int J Computer Vision*, pp 7–42, 2002.
20. T Starner and A Pentland. Real-time ASL recognition from video using Hidden Markov Models. Technical Report TR-375, MIT Media Lab, 1996.
21. A van Dam. Post-wimp user interfaces. *Comm ACM*, pp 63–67, 1997.
22. C von Hardenberg and F Berard. Bare-hand human-computer interaction. *Proc Workshop on Perceptive User Interfaces*, 2001.
23. Y Wu and T S Huang. Hand modeling, analysis, and recognition. *IEEE Signal Proc Mag*, pp 51–60, 2001.
24. J Yamato et al. Recognizing human actions in time-sequential images using Hidden Markov Model. *Proc CVPR*, 1992.
25. G Ye et al. VICs: A modular vision-based HCI framework. *Proc Int Conf on Computer Vision Systems*, 2003.
26. G Ye and G D Hager. Appearance-based visual interaction. Technical report. CIRL Lab, The Johns Hopkins University, 2002.
27. G Ye et al. VICs: A modular HCI framework using spatio-temporal dynamics. *Machine Vision and Applications*, pp 13–20, 2004.
28. Z Zhang et al. Visual Panel: Virtual mouse keyboard and 3D controller with an ordinary piece of paper. *Proc Workshop on Perceptive User Interfaces*, 2001.

Head and Facial Animation Tracking Using Appearance-Adaptive Models and Particle Filters

Franck Davoine and Fadi Dornaika

HEUDIASYC Mixed Research Unit
CNRS / Compiegne University of Technology, FRANCE
franck.davoine@hds.utc.fr
dornaika@cvc.uab.es

In this chapter, we address the problem of tracking a face and its actions in real video sequences, considering two approaches. The first approach is based on a particle filter tracker capable of tracking the 3D head pose of a person. In this case, the distribution of observations is derived from an eigenspace decomposition. The second approach introduces an appearance-adaptive tracker capable of tracking both the 3D head pose and facial animations. It consists of an online adapted observation model of the face texture, together with adaptive dynamics in the sense that they are guided by a deterministic search in a state space. This approach extends the concept of online appearance models to the case of tracking 3D non-rigid face motion (3D head pose and facial animations). Experiments on real video sequences show the effectiveness of the developed methods. Accurate tracking was obtained even in the presence of perturbing factors such as significant head pose or local facial occlusions.

1 Introduction

This chapter addresses the problem of tracking in a single video the global motion of a face as well as the local motion of its inner features, due to expressions, for instance, or other facial behaviors. This task is required in many emerging applications, like surveillance, teleconferencing, emotional computer interfaces, motion capture for video synthesis, automated lipreading, driver drowsiness monitoring, etc. Face tracking poses challenging problems because of the variability of facial appearance within a video sequence, most notably due to changes in head pose, expressions, lighting or occlusions. Much research has thus been devoted to the problem of face tracking, as a specially difficult case of non-rigid object tracking.

In the object tracking literature, the following formulation of the tracking problem is conveniently used: at each time step t, the goal is to infer the unobserved state of the object, denoted $\mathbf{b}_t \in \mathcal{B}$, given all the observed data until time t, denoted $\mathbf{y}_{1:t} \equiv \{\mathbf{y}_1, \ldots, \mathbf{y}_t\}$. When tracking a face in 3D, the unobserved state $\mathbf{b}_t$ includes motion or pose parameters like the position, scale and orientation of the face; when facial features are also tracked, the unobserved state should contain parameters describing their independent motion. The observed data $\mathbf{y}_t$ consists of measurements derived from the current video frame, such as gray-level patches, edges, or color histograms. In order to evaluate a hypothesized state, the measurements are actually only considered in the image area corresponding to the hypothesized location. For instance, the most natural measurement consists of the pixel gray-level values themselves. Basically, a given state $\mathbf{b}_t$ (motion parameters) is then evaluated by comparing the motion-compensated gray-level image patch $\mathbf{x}(\mathbf{b}_t)$ with a gray-level template face patch $\mathbf{g}_{\text{model}}$.

The tracking task then essentially consists in searching the current state $\hat{\mathbf{b}}_t \in \mathcal{B}$ that matches at best the measurements $\mathbf{y}_t$ in the current image. The tracking history $\hat{\mathbf{b}}_{1:(t-1)}$ is mainly used as a prior knowledge in order to search only a small subset of the state space $\mathcal{B}$. More specifically, for a hypothesized state $\mathbf{b}_t$, measurements $\mathbf{x}(\mathbf{b}_t)$ are extracted from the image patch at the hypothesized location, and those measurements are matched against some model of the object. The various tracking methods can be categorized according to the considered class of measurements, joint model of state and measurements and induced matching criterion (error functional to minimize or probability to maximize), and inference technique (deterministic or stochastic). According to this classification, a brief and non-exhaustive survey of tracking approaches is given below.

In a non-probabilistic formulation of the tracking problem, the state $\mathbf{b}_t$ is usually sought so as to minimize an error functional $d\,[\mathbf{x}(\mathbf{b}_t); \mathbf{g}_{\text{model}}]$, e.g., an Euclidean or robust distance. Actually, in a tracking setting, the state is supposed to evolve little between consecutive time steps. The solution is thus inferred from the previous frame estimation: $\hat{\mathbf{b}}_t = \hat{\mathbf{b}}_{t-1} + \widehat{\Delta \mathbf{b}_t}$. The optimal displacement is typically obtained by a gradient-like descent method. The well-known Lucas-Kanade algorithm [12] is a particular case of such a formulation, and has been recently generalized in [2]. Instead of being specified by a single face gray-level template $\mathbf{g}_{\text{model}}$, the face model can span a subspace of gray-level patches, learnt by principal component analysis from a face training set. The error functional is then a distance from the image patch $\mathbf{x}(\mathbf{b}_t)$ to the face subspace, usually taken to be the distance to the projection in face subspace. The subspace modeling allows to account for some variability of the global face appearance. The eigentracking method is based on such a principle [3]. Using also principal component analysis, the Active Appearance Models (AAMs) encode the variations of face appearance by learning the shape and texture variations [5]. They enable thus the tracking of both global motion and inner features. In the case of AAMs, the gradient matrix (Jacobian matrix) is pre-computed in order to reduce the processing time. In practice, tracking using the deterministic AAM search appears to work well while the lighting conditions remain stable and only small occlusions are present. However, large occlusions often make the AAM search converge to incorrect positions and loose track of the face.

In probabilistic formulations, the hidden state and the observations are linked by a joint distribution; this statistical framework offers rich modeling possibilities. A Markovian dynamic model describes how the state evolves through time. An observation model specifies the likelihood of each hypothesized state, i.e., the probability that the considered state may generate the observed data. Such generative models can represent the variability in the motion and appearance of the object to track. Note that even the non-probabilistic minimization of an error functional can be recast as the maximization of a likelihood:

$$p(\mathbf{x}_t|\mathbf{b}_t) \propto \exp\left(-d\left[\mathbf{x}(\mathbf{b}_t); \mathbf{g}_{\text{model}}\right]\right).$$

Based on such a generative model, Bayesian filtering methods recursively evaluate the posterior density of the target state at each time step conditionally to the history of observations until the current time.

Stochastic implementations of Bayesian filtering are generally based on sequential Monte Carlo estimation, also known as particle filtering [8]. When compared with the analytical solution provided by the well-known Kalman filter, particle filtering has two advantages: it is not restricted to the case of linear and Gaussian models, and it can maintain multiple hypotheses of the current state, a desirable property when the background is complex and contains distracting clutter.

For video tracking, the CONDENSATION algorithm was first proposed in conjunction with edge measurements produced by an edge detector [10]. Since then, this algorithm has attracted much interest, and other kinds of measurements have given valuable variants. For instance, tracking based on color histograms has gained recent interest due to the development of efficient search techniques, whether based on the deterministic mean-shift search paradigm [4] or the stochastic particle filtering framework [15]. In the case of particle filtering, motion is used as an additional information in order remove ambiguities due to color used alone. However, since color histograms are global, they do not allow to track the motion of internal facial features as is the goal here. A gray-level patch is used as measurement vector by Zhou et al. [16]. In order to cope with the changing appearance of the face, the likelihood is taken to be a mixture of three appearance templates, and the parameters of the mixture are re-estimated during the tracking. They consider a modified version of the online appearance model (OAM) proposed by Jepson et al. [11]. Their model considers global inter-frame face motion and appearance templates in the likelihood, and global motion parameters in the state vector. In order to track the local motion of facial features, De la Torre et al. [6] model the face appearance as a set of image patches taken at feature points.

This chapter has two main contributions. The first one consists in combining a modified version of the AAM as developed in [1] with the CONDENSATION stochastic search in order to augment its robustness to occlusions and strong out-of-plane face rotations. This approach uses a 3D wireframe model of a human face. It is developed to track the global 3D head pose of a person. The second contribution consists in combining a modified version of the OAM as proposed in [16, 11] with the 3D parameterized wireframe model deformed by Animation Units (AUs) that describe deformations that are possible to perform by a human face. This second contribution extends the concept of OAM to the case of tracking 3D non-rigid face motion (3D head pose and facial animations).

The chapter is organized as follows. Section 2 describes the deformable 3D face model that we use to create shape-free facial patches from input images. Section 3 describes the condensation-based 3D head tracking. Section 4 describes the head and facial animation tracking using an adaptive facial appearance model and an adaptive transition model. In Sects. 3 and 4 we also present some experimental results and conclude this chapter with Sect. 5.

2 Modeling Faces

In this section, we introduce a deformable 3D face model and briefly discuss the shape-free facial patches.

2.1 A Deformable 3D Model

We introduce here the 3D face model *Candide*. This 3D deformable wireframe model was first developed for the purpose of model-based image coding and computer animation. The 3D shape of this wireframe model is directly recorded in coordinate form. It is given by the coordinates of the 3D vertices $\mathbf{P}_i$ $(i = 1, \ldots, n)$ where n is the number of vertices. Thus, the shape up to a global scale can be fully described by the $3n$-vector $\mathbf{g}$; the concatenation of the 3D coordinates of all vertices $\mathbf{P}_i$. The vector $\mathbf{g}$ is written as:

$$\mathbf{g} = \overline{\mathbf{g}} + \mathbf{S}\tau_{\mathbf{s}} + \mathbf{A}\tau_{\mathbf{a}} \tag{1}$$

where $\overline{\mathbf{g}}$ is the standard shape of the model, τ_s and τ_a are shape and animation control vectors, respectively, and the columns of $\mathbf{S}$ and $\mathbf{A}$ are the Shape and Animation Units. A Shape Unit provides a way to deform the 3D wireframe such as to adapt the eye width, the head width, the eye separation distance etc. Thus, the term $\mathbf{S}\tau_{\mathbf{s}}$ accounts for shape variability (inter-person variability) while the term $\mathbf{A}\tau_{\mathbf{a}}$ accounts for the facial animation (intra-person variability). The shape and animation variabilities can be approximated well enough for practical purposes by this linear relation. Also, we assume that the two kinds of variability are independent.

In this study, we use twelve modes for the Shape Units matrix and six modes for the Animation Units matrix. Without loss of generality, we have chosen the six following AUs: jaw drop, lip stretcher, lip corner depressor, upper lip raiser, eyebrow lowerer and outer eyebrow raiser. These AUs are enough to cover most common facial animations (mouth and eyebrow movements).

In (1) the 3D shape is expressed in a local coordinate system. However, one should relate the 3D coordinates to the image coordinate system. To this end, we adopt the weak perspective projection model. We neglect the perspective effects since the depth variation of the face can be considered as small compared to its absolute depth. Therefore, the mapping between the 3D face model and the image is given by a 2×4 matrix, $\mathbf{M}$, encapsulating both the 3D head pose and the camera parameters.

Thus, a 3D vertex $\mathbf{P}_i = (X_i, Y_i, Z_i)^T \subset \mathbf{g}$ will be projected onto the image point $\mathbf{p}_i = (u_i, v_i)^T$ given by:

$$(u_i, v_i)^T = \mathbf{M} (X_i, Y_i, Z_i, 1)^T \qquad (2)$$

For a given person, τ_s is constant. Estimating τ_s can be carried out using either feature-based or featureless approaches. Thus, the state of the 3D wireframe model is given by the 3D head pose parameters (three rotations and three translations) and the internal face animation control vector $\tau_\mathbf{a}$. This is given by the 12-dimensional state vector $\mathbf{b}$:

$$\mathbf{b} = \begin{bmatrix} \theta_x & \theta_y & \theta_z & t_x & t_y & t_z & \tau_\mathbf{a}^T \end{bmatrix}^T \qquad (3)$$

2.2 Shape-Free Facial Patches

A face texture is represented as a shape-free texture (geometrically normalized image). The geometry of this image is obtained by projecting the standard shape $\overline{\mathbf{g}}$ using a centered frontal 3D pose onto an image with a given resolution. The texture of this geometrically normalized image is obtained by texture mapping from the triangular 2D mesh in the input image (see Fig. 1) using a piece-wise affine transform, $\mathcal{W}$. The warping process applied to an input image $\mathbf{y}$ is denoted by:

$$\mathbf{x}(\mathbf{b}) = \mathcal{W}(\mathbf{y}, \mathbf{b}) \qquad (4)$$

where $\mathbf{x}$ denotes the shape-free texture patch and $\mathbf{b}$ denotes the geometrical parameters. Two resolution levels have been considered for the shape-free textures, encoded by 1310 or 5392 pixels. Regarding photometric transformations, a zero-mean unit-variance normalization is used to partially compensate for contrast variations. The complete image transformation is implemented as follows: (i) transfer the texture $\mathbf{y}$ using the piece-wise affine transform associated with the vector $\mathbf{b}$, and (ii) perform the gray-level normalization of the obtained patch.

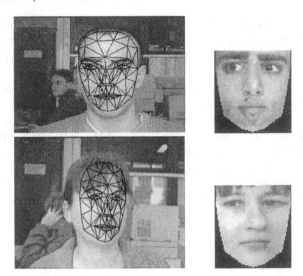

Fig. 1. Left column: two input images with correct adaptation. Right column: the corresponding shape-free facial patches

3 Condensation-Based Head Pose Tracking

Given a video sequence depicting a moving face, the tracking consists in estimating, for each frame, the head pose as well as the facial animations encoded by the control vector $\tau_\mathbf{a}$ [7]. In other words, one would like to estimate the vector $\mathbf{b}_t$, defined in (3) at time t. In a tracking context, the model parameters associated with the current frame will be handed over to the next frame.

In this section, we are interested in tracking the global 3D head pose. Therefore, the state vector $\mathbf{b}$ is given by $\mathbf{b} = [\theta_x\ \theta_y\ \theta_z\ t_x\ t_y\ t_z]^T$. In this particular case, the animation parameters $\tau_\mathbf{a}$ are set to zero. We propose a CONDENSATION-based method for tracking the six degrees of freedom associated with the head motion where the face model is given by the *Candide* model.

Particle filtering approximates the posterior state density $p(\mathbf{b}_t|\mathbf{y}_{1:t})$ by a set of J weighted samples (particles) at each time step. The CONDENSATION algorithm consists in propagating this sample set $\{\mathbf{b}_t^{(j)}, w_t^{(j)}\}_{j=1}^{J}$ through time using a dynamic model and in weighting each sample proportionally to its likelihood function value [10] (the particles explore the state space following independent realizations from a state evolution model, and are redistributed according to their consistency with the observations). Finally, the state estimate $\hat{\mathbf{b}}_t$ at time t can be set to the maximum *a posteriori*:

$$\hat{\mathbf{b}}_t = \arg\max_{\mathbf{b}_t} p(\mathbf{b}_t|\mathbf{y}_{1:t}) \approx \arg\max_{\mathbf{b}_t} w_t^{(j)} \qquad (5)$$

In this work, we use the following simple state evolution model:

$$\mathbf{b}_t = \hat{\mathbf{b}}_{t-1} + \mathbf{U}_t \qquad (6)$$

$\mathbf{U}_t$ is a random vector having a centered normal distribution, $\mathbf{N}(\mathbf{0}, \Sigma)$. The covariance matrix Σ is learned offline from the state vector differences $\mathbf{b}_t - \mathbf{b}_{t-1}$ associated with previously tracked video sequences.

Since image data $\mathbf{y}$ are represented as shape-free texture patches $\mathbf{x}$, we can set the observation likelihood $p(\mathbf{y}_t|\mathbf{b}_t)$ to $p(\mathbf{x}_t|\mathbf{b}_t)$. It quantifies the consistence of the texture $\mathbf{x}(\mathbf{b}_t)$ with the statistical texture model represented by texture modes (eigenvectors). For this purpose, we use a likelihood measure such as the one proposed in [13]:

$$p(\mathbf{x}_t|\mathbf{b}_t) = c \exp\left(-\frac{1}{2}\sum_{i=1}^{M}\frac{\xi_i^2}{\lambda_i}\right) \exp\left(-\frac{e^2(\mathbf{x}_t)}{2\rho^\star}\right) \qquad (7)$$

where $e^2(\mathbf{x}_t)$ is the "distance-from-feature-space," λ_is are the eigenvalues associated with the first M eigenvectors, ξ_is are the first M principal components, and $\rho^\star$ is the arithmetic average of the remaining eigenvalues.

---

1. Initialization $t = 0$: Generate J state samples $\mathbf{a}_0^{(1)}, \ldots, \mathbf{a}_0^{(J)}$ according to some prior density $p(\mathbf{b}_0)$ and assign them identical weights, $w_0^{(1)} = \ldots = w_0^{(J)} = 1/J$
2. At time step t, we have J weighted particles $(\mathbf{a}_{t-1}^{(j)}, w_{t-1}^{(j)})$ that approximate the posterior distribution of the state $p(\mathbf{b}_{t-1}|\mathbf{x}_{1:(t-1)})$ at previous time step
   a) Resample the particles proportionally to their weights, i.e., keep only particles with high weights and remove particles with small ones. Resampled particles have the same weights
   b) Draw J particles according to the dynamic model $p(\mathbf{b}_t|\mathbf{b}_{t-1} = \mathbf{a}_{t-1}^{(j)})$
      These particles approximate the predicted distribution $p(\mathbf{b}_t|\mathbf{x}_{1:(t-1)})$
   c) Compute the geometrically normalized texture $\mathbf{x}(\mathbf{b}_t)$ according to (4)
   d) Weight each new particle proportionally to its likelihood:

   $$w_t^{(j)} = \frac{p(\mathbf{x}_t|\mathbf{b}_t = \mathbf{a}_{t-1}^{(j)})}{\sum_{m=1}^{J} p(\mathbf{x}_t|\mathbf{b}_t = \mathbf{a}_{t-1}^{(m)})}$$

   The set of weighted particles approximates the posterior $p(\mathbf{b}_t|\mathbf{x}_{1:t})$
   e) Give an estimate of the state $\hat{\mathbf{b}}_t$ as the MAP:

   $$\hat{\mathbf{b}}_t = \arg\max_{\mathbf{b}_t} p(\mathbf{b}_t|\mathbf{y}_{1:t}) \approx \arg\max_{\mathbf{a}_t^{(j)}} w_t^{(j)}$$

Fig. 2. CONDENSATION algorithm

The sketch of the CONDENSATION algorithm is recalled in Fig. 2. For a good introduction to the algorithm, the reader is referred to the seminal paper of Isard and Blake [10].

During a filtering iteration, due to the resampling step, samples with a high weight may be chosen several times while others with relatively low weights may not be chosen at all. Note that the initial distribution $p(\mathbf{b}_0)$ can be either a Dirac or Gaussian distribution centered on a solution provided by a detector algorithm or manually specified.

3.1 Experiments

Figure 3 displays the tracking results associated with several frames of a long test sequence. It corresponds to the CONDENSATION-based tracking algorithm using a statistical texture model. The number of particles is set to 300. For each frame in this figure, only the MAP solution is displayed. The statistical facial texture is built with 330 training face images and the number of the principal eigenvectors is 20. Figure 4 displays the weights associated with the bottom-right image.

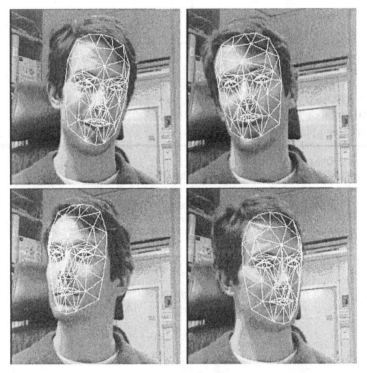

Fig. 3. CONDENSATION-based 3D head tracking with a statistical facial texture model

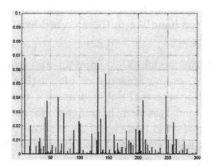

Fig. 4. Drawing of the 300 particle weights associated to the bottom-right image of Fig. 3

4 Head and Facial Animation Tracking Using an Adaptive Appearance Model

In this section, we consider now the 3D head pose as well as the facial animations, that is, the state vector **b** is given by $\mathbf{b} = [\theta_x \ \theta_y \ \theta_z \ t_x \ t_y \ t_z \ \tau_\mathbf{a}^T]^T$.

4.1 Motivation

The efficiency of the stochastic tracking algorithm presented in Sect. 3 depends on different factors. However, the main factor which limits the efficiency of stochastic tracking algorithms is the lack of a suitable state evolution model. Indeed, there are two ways for handling the transition model. (i) the first is to learn state transition models directly from training video sequences. For example, in [14] the authors use Expectation-Maximization combined with the CONDENSATION algorithm to learn multiclass dynamics associated with a juggled ball. However, such models may not necessarily succeed when presented with testing videos featuring different types of motions. (ii) the second is to use a fixed model with fixed noise variance for simplicity, that is, the predicted state is simply the previous state (or a shifted version of it) to which a random noise with fixed variance is added (this methodology was adopted in Sect. 3). If the variance is very small, it is hard to model rapid movements; if the variance is large, it is computationally inefficient since many more particles are needed to accommodate large noise variance.

In addition to the problems associated with the state transition model, the observation model has its own limitations. For example, if the observation model (observation likelihood) is built upon a statistical texture model, any significant change in the imaging conditions will make the corresponding learned observation model useless and one should build a new observation model based on a new statistical texture model.

For all these factors, we develop a new tracking framework capable of coping with the limitations mentioned above. Our approach is to make both observation and state transition models adaptive in the framework of a particle filter, with provisions for handling outliers embedded. The main features of the developed approach are:

- Adaptive observation model. We adopt an appearance-based approach, using the concept of online appearance model (OAM) developed in [11] and modified in [16], where the appearance is learned online from the tracked video sequence. However, in our case, we extend this paradigm to the case of tracking the 3D non-rigid face motion (3D head pose together with facial animations). Therefore, the observation model is adaptive as the appearance of the texture.
- Adaptive state transition model. Instead of using a fixed state transition model, we use an adaptive model, where the motion velocity is predicted using a registration technique between the incoming observation and the current appearance configuration. We also use an adaptive noise component whose magnitude is a function of the registration error. We vary the number of particles based on the noise component.
- Handling occlusion. Occlusion and large image variations are handled using robust statistics. We improve the robustness of the likelihood measurement and the motion estimate by downweighting the outlier pixels.

4.2 Adaptive Observation Model

The appearance model at time t, A_t, is a time-varying on that it models the appearances present in all observations $\mathbf{x}$ up to time $(t-1)$. For each frame, the observation is simply the warped texture patch associated with the computed geometric parameters $\mathbf{b}_t$. We use the HAT symbol for the tracked parameters and textures. For a given frame t, $\hat{\mathbf{b}}_t$ represents the computed geometric parameters and $\hat{\mathbf{x}}_t$ the corresponding texture patch, that is,

$$\hat{\mathbf{x}}_t = \mathbf{x}(\hat{\mathbf{b}}_t) = \mathcal{W}(\mathbf{y}_t, \hat{\mathbf{b}}_t) \tag{8}$$

The appearance model A_t obeys a Gaussian with a center μ and a variance σ. Notice that μ and σ are vectors consisting of d pixels (d is the size of $\mathbf{x}$) that are assumed to be independent of each other. In summary, the observation likelihood is written as

$$p(\mathbf{y}_t|\mathbf{b}_t) = p(\mathbf{x}_t|\mathbf{b}_t) = \prod_{i=1}^{d} \mathbf{N}(x_i; \mu_i, \sigma_i) \tag{9}$$

where $\mathbf{N}(x; \mu_i, \sigma_i)$ is the normal density:

$$\mathbf{N}(x; \mu_i, \sigma_i) = (2\pi\sigma_i^2)^{-1/2} \exp\left[-\frac{1}{2}\left(\frac{x - \mu_i}{\sigma_i}\right)^2\right] \tag{10}$$

We assume that A_t summarizes the past observations under an exponential envelop with a forgetting factor α. When the appearance is tracked for the current input image, i.e., the texture $\hat{\mathbf{x}}_t$ is available, we can compute the updated appearance and use it to track in the next frame.

It can be shown that the appearance model parameters, i.e., μ and σ can be updated using the following equations (see [11] for more details on OAMs):

$$\mu_{t+1} = \alpha \, \mu_t + (1 - \alpha) \, \hat{\mathbf{x}}_t \qquad (11)$$

$$\sigma_{t+1}^2 = \alpha \, \sigma_t^2 + (1 - \alpha) \, (\hat{\mathbf{x}}_t - \mu_t)^2 \qquad (12)$$

In the above equations, all μs and σ^2s are vectorized and the operation is element-wise. This technique, also called recursive filtering, is simple, time-efficient and therefore, suitable for real-time applications.

Note that μ is initialized with the first patch $\mathbf{x}$. However, (12) is not used until the number of frames reaches a certain value (e.g., the first 40 frames). For these frames, the classical variance is used, i.e., (12) is utilized with α being set to $1 - \frac{1}{t}$.

4.3 Adaptive Transition Model

Instead of using a fixed function to predict the transition state from time $(t - 1)$ to time t, we use the following adaptive transition model:

$$\mathbf{b}_t = \hat{\mathbf{b}}_{t-1} + \Delta \mathbf{b}_t + \mathbf{U}_t \qquad (13)$$

where $\Delta \mathbf{b}_t$ is the shift in the geometric parameters and $\mathbf{U}_t$ is the random noise. Our basic idea allowing to recover the solution $\mathbf{b}_t$ or equivalently the deterministic part of (13) is to use region-based registration techniques. In other words, the current input image $\mathbf{y}_t$ is registered with the current appearance model A_t. For this purpose, we minimize an error measure between the warped texture and the current appearance mean,

$$\min_{\mathbf{b}_t} e(\mathbf{b}_t) = \min_{\mathbf{b}_t} d \left[\mathbf{x}(\mathbf{b}_t), \mu_t \right] = \sum_{i=1}^{d} \left(\frac{x_i - \mu_i}{\sigma_i} \right)^2 \qquad (14)$$

Note the appearance parameters μ_t and σ_t are known. The above criterion can be minimized using iterative first-order linear approximation.

Gradient-descent registration

We assume that there exists a $\mathbf{b}_t = \hat{\mathbf{b}}_{t-1} + \Delta \mathbf{b}_t$ such that the warped texture will be very close to the appearance mean, i.e.,

$$\mathcal{W}(\mathbf{y}_t, \mathbf{b}_t) = \mathbf{x}(\mathbf{b}_t) \simeq \mu_t$$

Approximating $\mathbf{x}(\mathbf{b}_t)$ via a first-order Taylor series expansion around $\hat{\mathbf{b}}_{t-1}$ yields

$$\mathbf{x}(\mathbf{b}_t) \simeq \mathbf{x}(\hat{\mathbf{b}}_{t-1}) + \mathbf{G}_t \varDelta \mathbf{b}_t$$

where $\mathbf{G}_t$ is the gradient matrix, and $\mathbf{G}_t^+$ its pseudo-inverse. By combining the above two equations we have:

$$\mu_t = \mathbf{x}(\hat{\mathbf{b}}_{t-1}) + \mathbf{G}_t \varDelta \mathbf{b}_t$$

Therefore, the shift in the parameter space is given by:

$$\varDelta \mathbf{b}_t = \mathbf{b}_t - \hat{\mathbf{b}}_{t-1} = -\mathbf{G}_t^+ \left(\mathbf{x}(\hat{\mathbf{b}}_{t-1}) - \mu_t \right) \tag{15}$$

In practice, the solution $\mathbf{b}_t$ (or equivalently the shift $\varDelta \mathbf{b}_t$) is estimated by running several iterations until the error cannot be improved. We proceed as follows.

Starting from $\mathbf{b} = \hat{\mathbf{b}}_{t-1}$, we compute the error vector $(\mathbf{x}(\hat{\mathbf{b}}_{t-1}) - \mu_t)$ and the corresponding error measure $e(\mathbf{b})$, given by (14). We find a shift $\varDelta \mathbf{b}$ by multiplying the error vector with the negative pseudo-inverse of the gradient matrix using (15). $\varDelta \mathbf{b}$ gives a displacement in the search space for which the error, e, can be minimized. We compute a new parameter vector and a new error:

$$\mathbf{b}' = \mathbf{b} + \theta \, \varDelta \mathbf{b} \tag{16}$$

$$e' = e(\mathbf{b}') \tag{17}$$

where θ is a positive real.

If $e' < e$, $\mathbf{b}$ is updated according to (16) and the process is iterated until convergence. If $e' \geq e$, smaller update steps are tested, using the same direction (i.e., smaller θ is used). Convergence is declared when the error cannot be improved anymore.

Gradient matrix computation

The gradient matrix is given by:

$$\mathbf{G} = \frac{\partial \mathcal{W}(\mathbf{y}_t, \mathbf{b}_t)}{\partial \mathbf{b}} = \frac{\partial \mathbf{x}_t}{\partial \mathbf{b}}$$

It is approximated by numerical differences, as explained in [5]. Once the solution $\hat{\mathbf{b}}_t$ becomes available for a given frame, it is possible to compute the gradient matrix from the associated input image. The jth column of $\mathbf{G}$ $(j = 1, \ldots, \dim(\mathbf{b}))$ is given by:

$$\mathbf{G}_j = \frac{\partial \mathcal{W}(\mathbf{y}_t, \mathbf{b}_t)}{\partial b_j}$$

and is estimated using differences

$$\mathbf{G}_j \simeq \frac{\mathbf{x}(\mathbf{b}_t) - \mathbf{x}(\mathbf{b}_t + \delta \, \mathbf{q}_j)}{\delta}$$

where δ is a suitable step size and $\mathbf{q}_j$ is a vector with all elements zero except the jth element that equals one. To gain more accuracy, the jth column of $\mathbf{G}$ is estimated using several steps around the current component value b_j, and then averaging over all these, we get our final $\mathbf{G}_j$ as

$$\mathbf{G}_j = \frac{1}{K} \sum_{0 < |k| \leq K/2} \frac{\mathbf{x}(\mathbf{b}_t) - \mathbf{x}(\mathbf{b}_t + k \, \delta_j \, \mathbf{q}_j)}{k \, \delta_j}$$

where δ_j is the smallest perturbation associated with the parameter b_j and K is the number of steps (in our experiments, K is set to 8).

Note that the computation of the gradient matrix $\mathbf{G}_t$ at time t is carried out using the estimated geometric parameters $\hat{\mathbf{b}}_{t-1}$ and the associated input image $\mathbf{y}_{t-1}$ since the adaptation for the time t has not been computed. It is worthwhile noting that the gradient matrix is computed for each time step. The advantage is twofold. First, a varying gradient matrix is able to accommodate appearance changes. Second, it will be closer to the exact gradient matrix since it is computed for the current geometric configuration (3D head pose and facial animations) whereas a fixed gradient matrix can be a source of errors for some kinds of motions such as out-of-plane motions.

4.4 Handling Outliers and Occlusions

We assume that occlusion and large image differences can be treated as outliers. Outlier pixels cannot be explained by the underlying process (the current appearance model A_t) and their influences on the estimation process should be reduced. Robust statistics provide such mechanisms [9].

The mechanism will have impact on three items: (i) the likelihood measure, (ii) the gradient descent method, and (iii) the update of the online appearance model A_t.

Following the ideas developed in Zhou et al. [16], we use the Huber's cost function ρ defined as follows [9]:

$$\rho(x) = \begin{cases} \frac{1}{2} x^2 & \text{if } |x| \leq h \\ h \, |x| - \frac{1}{2} h^2 & \text{if } |x| > h \quad \text{(outlier detection)} \end{cases}$$

where x is the value of a pixel, i, in the patch $\mathbf{x}$, normalized by the mean and the variance of the appearance at the same pixel, i.e., μ_i and σ_i. This function is a hybrid between the L^1 and least-squares function. It is continuous, with continuous first derivative. The cutoff threshold h controls the outlier rate. In our application, we take $h = 3$ based on experimental experience.

Likelihood measure

To make the likelihood measure robust, we replace the one-dimensional normal density $\mathbf{N}(x; \mu_i, \sigma_i)$ by

$$\hat{\mathbf{N}}(x; \mu_i, \sigma_i) = \frac{1}{Z} \exp\left[-\rho\left(\frac{x - \mu_i}{\sigma_i}\right)\right]$$

where Z is a constant.

Gradient method

To downweight the influence of the outlier pixels in the registration technique, we introduce a $d \times d$ diagonal matrix L_t with its ith diagonal element being $L_t(i) = \eta(x_i)$ where x_i is the ith element of the difference image $(\mathbf{x}(\hat{\mathbf{b}}_{t-1}) - \mu_t)$ normalized by the corresponding variance σ_i and

$$\eta(x) = \frac{1}{x}\frac{d\rho(x)}{dx} = \begin{cases} 1 & \text{if } |x| \leq h \\ \frac{h}{|x|} & \text{if } |x| > h \quad \text{(outlier detection)} \end{cases}$$

$\eta(x)$ is used to attenuate the influence of the outliers. Therefore, the shift used in the gradient-descent registration becomes

$$\Delta\mathbf{b}_t = -\mathbf{G}_t^+ L_t \left(\mathbf{x}(\hat{\mathbf{b}}_{t-1}) - \mu_t\right) \tag{18}$$

Appearance update

Once the solution $\mathbf{b}_t$ is ready, the corresponding patch $\mathbf{x}$ will be used to update the appearance. For non-outlier pixels the update equations are given by (11) and (12); for outlier pixels the corresponding means and variances are not updated. This mechanism is very useful for preventing occlusions from deteriorating the online appearance model.

4.5 The Tracking Algorithm

Tracking the 3D head pose and the facial animations is performed as follows. Starting from the solution, $\hat{\mathbf{b}}_{t-1}$, associated with the previous frame, we predict the state using (13) in which the deterministic part of the prediction, i.e., $\hat{\mathbf{b}}_{t-1} + \Delta\mathbf{b}_t$, is computed by the registration technique and the noise variance was set as a monotonically increasing function of the registration error obtained at convergence. Once a set of particles is obtained, the MAP of (9) is again chosen to be the solution of the current frame.

   As can be seen, unlike the classical particle filtering, the propagation concerns the MAP solution only and not the whole particle set. It is worthwhile noting that although the solutions provided by the deterministic and stochastic parts of (13) have utilized the same observation model, there are some differences. The deterministic solution is obtained by a directed continuous search starting from the solution associated with the previous frame. The stochastic solution is obtained by diffusing the deterministic solution in order to obtain possible refinement.

4.6 Experiments

Figure 5 displays the head and facial animation tracking results associated with a 800 frame long (only four frames are shown). These results correspond to the real-time tracker based on appearance-adaptive model (described above).

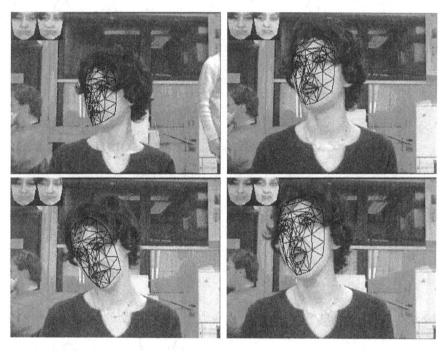

Fig. 5. Illustration of our framework for tracking the 3D head pose and the facial animations with an appearance-adaptive model. The sequence length is 800 frames. In the upper left corner, from left to right: the current adaptive appearance and the current shape-free texture

The sequence features quite large head pose variations as well as large facial animations. The sequence is of resolution 640×480 pixels. As can be seen with the very little prior information, the 3D motion of the face as well as the facial animations associated with the mouth and the eyebrows are accurately recovered. The upper left corner shows the current appearance μ_t and the current shape-free texture $\hat{\mathbf{x}}_t$.

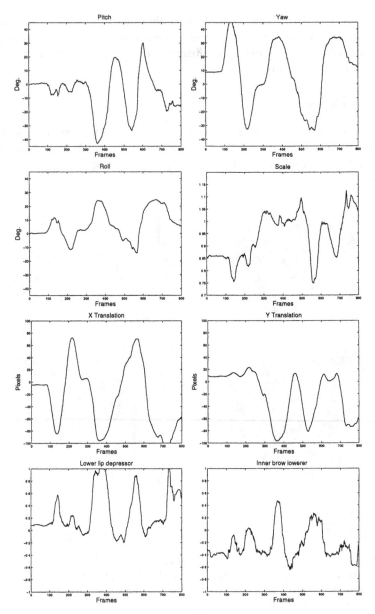

Fig. 6. The tracked parameters as a function of time associated with the 800 frame long sequence. The first six plots display the six degrees of freedom of the 3D head pose. The two bottom plots display the lower lip depressor and inner brow parameters, respectively

Figure 6 displays the estimated values of the 3D head pose parameters (the three rotations and the three translations) as well as the lower lip depressor, and the inner brow lowerer as a function of the frames of the same sequence. Figure 7 displays the face and facial animation results associated with a 602 frame long sequence. The left column displays the tracking results of the real-time tracker using the appearance-adaptive model with a fixed gradient matrix computed at the first video frame. The right column displays the tracking results when a time-varying gradient matrix has been used. We have noticed, for this sequence, that whenever the face performs an out-of-plane motion the tracker with a time-varying gradient is more accurate than the one using a fixed gradient. Moreover, in other experiments, the tracker using a fixed gradient matrix has totally lost the track.

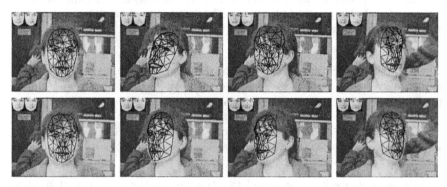

Fig. 7. From left to right: frames 94, 201, 376, and 569. The upper raw displays the head and facial animation tracking using the appearance-adaptive framework with a fixed gradient. The lower raw displays the tracking result when a time-varying gradient is used

Figure 8 displays the face and facial animation results associated with another 402 frame long sequence featuring two occlusions (only the second occlusion is displayed). The two occlusions are caused by putting the hand in front of the face. The frames 218 and 265 show the start and the end of the second occlusion, respectively. As can be seen on the the bottom row, pixels associated with the region of smiling and occlusions are considered as outliers.

On a 2 GHz PC, a non-optimized C code of the algorithm computes the adaptation parameters associated to one image in about 50 ms assuming that the patch resolution is 1310 pixels, K is eight. 80% of the CPU power is devoted to the gradient matrix computation.

In order to explore the behavior of the time-varying gradient based registration method in the presence of fast head movements and facial animations, we have conducted the following experiment. A video sequence was captured. This 708 frame long sequence features a bearded subject putting on his glasses. The sequence was tracked by the registration technique. Figure 9 displays the tracking results associated with four frames of the sequence. In order to simulate rapid movements, the sequence was subjected to a temporal

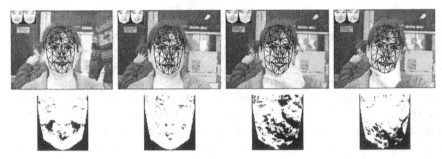

Fig. 8. Tracking another test sequence featuring two occlusions. Frames 36, 58, 218, and 265 are displayed. Frames 218 and 265 show respectively the start and the end of the second occlusion present in the video. The bottom row shows the corresponding shape-free map of the outlier pixels (shown in black)

downsampling factor of four. In other words, every fourth image of the original sequence was used. As can be seen, the tracking is still accurate and almost the same accurate tracking results were obtained in both cases.

5 Conclusion

In this chapter, we have proposed two tracking methods. The first method is fully stochastic and uses a particle filter with an observation likelihood based on statistical facial textures. This method has been utilized for 3D head tracking. The second method combines the merits of both stochastic and deterministic methods and is capable of tracking the head and facial animation. It employs an Online Appearance Model where both the observation and transition models are adaptive. The deterministic part exploits a directed continuous search aiming at minimizing the discrepancy between the upcoming observation and the current appearance model. Tracking long video sequences demonstrated the effectiveness of the developed methods. Accurate tracking was obtained even in the presence of perturbing factors such as illumination changes, significant head pose and facial expression variations as well as occlusions. Currently, we are investigating the recognition of facial expressions and gestures from the tracked parameters.

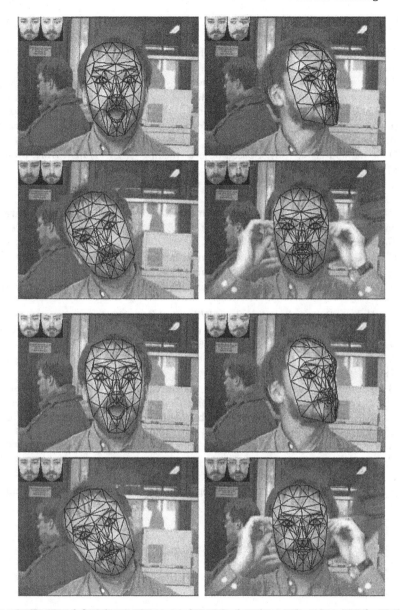

Fig. 9. Face and facial animation tracking results obtained with a 708 frame long sequence using the gradient-based registration method. At the end of the sequence the person is putting on his glasses. The two upper raws display tracking results obtained without any temporal downsampling. The two lower raws display tracking results obtained when every fourth image was used, i.e., the temporal downsampling factor is set to four

References

1. J Ahlberg. An active model for facial feature tracking. *J Applied Signal Proc*, pp 566–571, 2002.
2. S Baker and I Matthews. Lucas–Kanade 20 years on: A unifying framework. *Int J Computer Vision*, pp 221–255, 2004.
3. M Black and A Jepson. Eigen-tracking: Robust matching and tracking of articulated objects using a view-based representation. *Int J Computer Vision*, pp 101–130, 1998.
4. D Comaniciu et al. Kernel-based object tracking. *IEEE Trans PAMI*, pp 564–577, 2003.
5. T F Cootes et al. Active appearance models. *IEEE Trans PAMI*, pp 681–684, 2001.
6. F de la Torre et al. A probabilistic framework for rigid and non-rigid appearance based tracking and recognition. *Proc IEEE Int Conf on Automatic Face and Gesture Recognition*, 2000.
7. F Dornaika et al. 3D head tracking with particle filters. *Proc Int Workshop on Image Analysis for Multimedia Interactive Services*, 2004.
8. A Doucet et al. *Sequential Monte Carlo Methods in Practice*. Springer-Verlag, 2001.
9. P J Huber. *Robust Statistics*. John Wiley and Sons, 1981.
10. M Isard and A Blake. Condensation - conditional density propagation for visual tracking. *Int J Computer Vision*, pp 5–28, 1998.
11. A D Jepson et al. Robust online appearance models for visual tracking. *IEEE Trans PAMI*, pp 1296–1311, 2003.
12. B Lucas and T Kanade. An iterative image registration technique with an application to stereo vision. *Proc Int Joint Conf on Artificial Intelligence*, 1981.
13. B Moghaddam and A Pentland. Probabilistic visual learning for object representation. *IEEE Trans PAMI*, pp 696–710, 1997.
14. B North et al. Learning and classification of complex dynamics. *IEEE Trans PAMI*, pp 1016–1034, 2000.
15. P Pérez et al. Color-based probabilistic tracking. *Proc ECCV*, 2002.
16. S Zhou et al. Visual tracking and recognition using appearance-adaptive models in particle filters. *IEEE Trans Image Proc*, pp 1491–1506, 2004.

A Real-Time Vision Interface Based on Gaze Detection – EyeKeys

John J. Magee, Margrit Betke, Matthew R. Scott, and Benjamin N. Waber

Computer Science Department
Boston University
mageejo@cs.bu.edu
betke@cs.bu.edu
mrscott@cs.bu.edu
bwabes@cs.bu.edu

There are cases of paralysis so severe the ability to control movement is limited to the muscles around the eyes. In these cases, eye movements or blinks are the only way to communicate. Current computer interface systems are often intrusive, require special hardware, or use active infrared illumination. An interface system called EyeKeys is presented. EyeKeys runs on a consumer grade computer with video input from an inexpensive USB camera. The face is tracked using multi-scale template correlation. Symmetry between left and right eyes is exploited to detect if the computer user is looking at the camera, or to the left or right side. The detected eye direction can then be used to work with applications that can be controlled with only two inputs. The game "BlockEscape" was developed to gather quantitative results to evaluate EyeKeys with test subjects.

1 Introduction

Some people may be so severely paralyzed that their voluntary movements are limited to movements of the eyes. To communicate with family, friends, and care givers, they look in a certain direction or blink for "yes" and "no" responses. Innovative assistive technologies are needed to enable them to access the computer for communication, education, and entertainment. As progress toward that goal, we present an interface called EyeKeys that simulates computer keyboard input and is based on gaze detection that exploits the symmetry between left and right eyes.

There has been much previous work in computer assistive technologies, e.g., [2, 3, 6, 16, 17, 23, 29]. Most of these methods, though successful and useful, also have drawbacks. Many currently available or early systems are often intrusive, or use specialized hardware [29]. For example, the EagleEyes system [6] uses electrodes placed on the face to detect the movements of the eyes and has been used by disabled adults and children to navigate a computer mouse. Another approach [2] uses head mounted cameras to look at eye movements. It takes advantage of the fact that the face will always be in the same location in the video image if the head moves around. Large headgear is not suited for all users, especially small children. One of our goals is to design a non-intrusive system that does not need attachments.

Another successful system is the Camera Mouse [3]. People with disabilities can control a mouse pointer by moving their head, finger, or other limbs, while the system uses video to track the motion. This is successful for those who can move their heads or limbs; however, people who can only move their eyes are unable to use it. These are the people for whom we aim to provide a communication device. A goal of our system is therefore to use only information from the eyes.

Many systems that analyze eye information use specialized hardware. The use of active infrared illumination is one example [8, 12, 13, 14, 18, 28]. The infrared light reflects off the back of the eye to create a distinct "bright eye" effect in the image. If switching the infrared light on and off is synchronized with the camera, the pupils can be located by differencing the bright eye image obtained with infrared illumination from the subsequent image without infrared illumination. The illumination also creates a "glint," a reflection off the surface of the eye. One technique to find the gaze direction is to analyze the difference vector between pupil center and glint. There are concerns about the safety of prolonged exposure to infrared lighting. Another issue is that some of these systems require a complicated calibration procedure that is difficult for small children to follow.

Avoiding specialized hardware is another important goal of our system. This means that our system must run on a consumer grade computer. In addition to avoiding infrared light sources and cameras, we decided to build the system around an inexpensive USB camera. The system can therefore be run on any computer without the need for an expensive frame grabber or pan/tilt/zoom cameras as required in some previous work [5]. Our system must be able to work with images that have a lower resolution than the images used in previous approaches [15, 22, 25].

To be a useful human-computer interface, the system must run in real-time. This excludes existing approaches that do not run in real-time. In addition, the system can not use all of the processing power of the computer because the same computer will have to run both the vision based interface as well as user programs such as web browsers or games.

EyeKeys tracks the face using multi-scale template correlation. The left and right eyes are compared to determine if the user is looking center, or to the left or right side. This is accomplished by exploiting the symmetry between the left and the right eyes. If one eye image is mirrored and subtracted from the other, the large differences will be due to the difference in pupil location.

The output of our system can be used to control applications such as spelling programs or games.

We tested EyeKeys on the BlockEscape game. This game was developed specifically as an engaging way to test our interface system while reporting quantitative results. This is important because it motivates users and test subjects to try the system. We can use the game to gather statistics on how well the interface works for various situations that we create.

This chapter is organized in the following manner: Section 2 discusses the methods employed in the EyeKeys system itself, including a thorough description of the EyeKeys' modules and the BlockEscape game. Section 3 details our experiments and results, while Sect. 4 presents an in-depth discussion of our results, comparisons to other HCI systems, and plans for future extensions to our system.

2 Method

The EyeKeys system performs two main tasks: (1) face detection and tracking, and (2) eye analysis. Throughout the system, efficient processing techniques are used to enable real-time performance. Major components of the system are presented in Fig. 1.

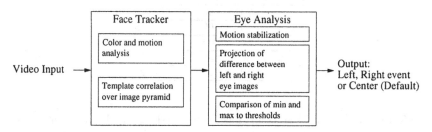

Fig. 1. System Diagram for EyeKeys

In order to facilitate working with the eyes, we developed a fast two-dimensional (2D) face tracker. From the scale and location of the face located by this tracker, regions of interest for the eye analysis are obtained. The eye analysis algorithm then determines if the eyes are looking toward the center, or have moved to the left, or to the right of the camera.

The output from the eye module can be the input to a computer control interface. Usually, looking center means "do nothing." The interface system can then map the left and right outputs to events such as mouse movements, left and right arrow keys, or other key combinations. This allows the system to be configured for a variety of applications such as playing games, entering text, or navigating a web site.

2.1 Face Detection and Tracking

The face detection and tracking method consists of various parts, some of which were used in previous face tracking approaches, e.g., [11, 27]. Color and motion information is combined to create a mask to exclude areas of the search space for the correlation-based matching of a 12×16-pixel face template. To enable detection of faces that differ in size (for example, a user may have a large head or sit close to the camera), the system uses image pyramids [1] along each step of the face detection. To avoid the large size difference between traditional pyramid levels, where the image at each successive level is half the size of the previous image, the pyramid structure has been modified to include images with intermediate resolutions. This allows the system to find face scales at smaller discrete steps. The resolutions of the images of the pyramids are listed in Table 1.

Table 1. Resolutions used by the image pyramids. Coordinates in any level can be transformed into coordinates in the 640×480 input frame by multiplying by the scale factor. Levels 2 through 7 are used to find the face

Level	Width	Height	Scale Factor
0	640	480	1
1	320	240	2
2	160	120	4
3	128	96	5
4	80	60	8
5	64	48	10
6	40	30	16
7	32	24	20

Color analysis. Skin color has been used to track faces previously, e.g., [19]. Here, it is used as a preprocessing mask. The color input image is converted into the YUV color space [24]. YUV was chosen because the camera can be configured to provide images in that format, and the color information is contained within two dimensions. A binary image is created with a 2D histogram lookup in UV space. If a pixel's lookup on the histogram for the specified UV value is over a threshold, then the pixel is marked as skin, otherwise not. The binary image is then decimated into the other levels using Gaussian blurring [1]. A box filter that smoothes an image by averaging with a support of 12×16 pixels is applied to each image in the pyramid so that each pyramid level represents the color information for the appropriate scale of the face to search for. Thresholding then produces a binary pyramid mask P_{color} (Fig. 2).

The color histogram was trained on 15 face images which were marked by hand with a rectangle covering most of the facial regions. In cases where the color segmentation fails to provide good results, the histogram can be

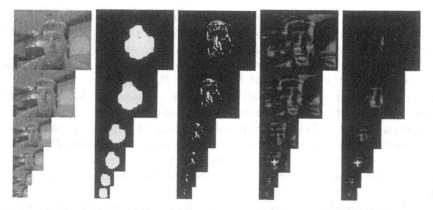

Fig. 2. Pyramids P_{input}, P_{color}, P_{motion} before application of box filter, $P_{\text{correlation}}$, and P_{masked} computed by the face detection and tracking algorithm. The cross indicates the maximum correlation peak in the pyramid and after applying the appropriate scale factor in Table 1, yields the location and scale of the face

retrained during system operation by clicking on areas of skin in the live video. The histogram can be saved and reloaded so that it can be used again for the same user or lighting conditions without retraining.

There are various situations when the UV-histogram might need to be retrained. Certain changes in lighting conditions can result in changes of the UV values of skin. A histogram trained on one person might not work well with a person with a different skin tone. Pixels corresponding to objects such as wooden doors or tan carpets can often have similar pixel values as skin. The default histogram will represent a wider range of skin tones, while a histogram trained on one person will represent that person's skin more exclusively. Since skin color segmentation may not yield accurate segmentation results due to the difficulties described above, UV-based segmentation is used only as a preprocessing mask for face localization.

Motion analysis. Frame differencing creates a motion image that is decimated into a pyramid (Fig. 2). Pixels in the face with large brightness gradients also have large values in the motion image if the face is moving. The box filter is applied again to each motion image in the pyramid to account for the appropriate scale of the face to search for. This yields, after thresholding, a binary pyramid mask P_{motion}. The pyramid P_{motion} computed from the scene shown in Fig. 2 looks similar to the color pyramid mask P_{color}.

In cases when there is little or no motion, the motion mask must be prevented from excluding the previously found face location from the correlation search. Locations near the previous face location are therefore set to one in the binary motion image. The other motion pyramid levels are also modified in this way to account for movements toward or away from the camera that are not caught by the motion segmentation. The area modified is proportional to the scale represented by the respective pyramid level.

Correlation matching. Template matching based on the normalized correlation coefficient [4] is used to find the location of the face. A small, 12×16 face template is correlated over all levels of the grayscale input pyramid P_{input} (Y channel from the YUV color image), which allows for fast processing. The resulting correlation values yield the pyramid $P_{correlation}$ (Fig. 2). The maximum correlation peak among all of the levels indicates the location of the face. The scale of the face is known by the level of the pyramid at which the maximum is found. To eliminate possible ambiguous correlation peaks in the background, the color and motion information masks are applied to $P_{correlation}$. An efficient implementation of the correlation function can also use the mask to save processing time by skipping background locations excluded by the mask.

The face template is created by averaging the brightness values of 8 face images. This ensures that the relevant information that it represents a face is preserved, while specific features of a particular person are smoothed, and thus allows the correlation method to find a "general" face in the image.

2.2 Eye Analysis

Given the estimate of face location provided by the face tracker, the approximate location and scale of the eyes can be inferred from simple anthropomorphic properties: The eyes must be located in a region above the center of the face, the left eye must be on the right side of this image region and the right eye on the left. Taking advantage of these properties, the eye analysis module crops out two subimages containing the eyes from the highest resolution image. The size of the subimages depends on the scale at which the face was found. To simplify the eye analysis, the system produces eye images of a fixed size of 60×80 pixels by linear interpolation.

Motion analysis and stabilization. Ideally, the two eyes would be centered in the respective eye images as the head moves. However, slight movements of the head by a few pixels may not be accurately tracked by the face tracker. A method must be used to "stabilize" the eye images for comparison. The method chosen here to locate the center of the eyes is frame differencing to create binary motion images (Fig. 3), followed by computing the first-order moments. These "centroid" points are used to adjust the estimates of the eye locations in the face image. Using this method, the eye images do not need to have as high a resolution as required by many feature-based eye localization methods, e.g., [25].

Left–right eye comparisons. The left and right eyes are compared to determine where the user is looking. The left eye image is mirrored and subtracted from the right eye image. If the user is looking straight at the camera, the difference is small. On the other hand, if the eyes are looking left, then the mirrored left eye image appears to be looking right as shown in Fig. 4.

The signed difference between the two images shows distinct pixel areas where the pupils are in different locations in each image. The unsigned dif-

Fig. 3. Motion detected by frame differencing is thresholded and used as a mask for the differencing of left-right eye images, and for finding the centroids for motion stabilization

ference can be seen in Fig. 5. To reduce extra information from the image areas outside of the eyes, the images are masked by their thresholded motion images (Fig. 3). To determine the direction of the eyes, the signed differences are projected onto the x–axis (Fig. 6). The signed difference creates peaks in the projection because eye sclera pixels are lighter than pupil pixels.

If the user is looking left, the signed difference operation creates large values in the projection because the dark-gray iris and pupil pixels in the left image are subtracted from the light-gray eye sclera pixels in the right image. This is followed by small values in the projection because light-gray eye sclera pixels in the left image are subtracted from dark-gray iris and pupil pixels in the right image. Vice versa, if the user is looking right, there will be a valley in the projection, followed by a peak (Fig. 6). If the peaks and valleys in the projection do not exceed a certain threshold, then the eye analysis method outputs the default value "looking center."

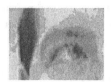

(a) Right eye looking left   (b) Mirrored left eye looking left

Fig. 4. Eye images automatically extracted from input video by face tracker

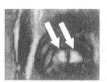

Fig. 5. Absolute difference between right and mirrored left eyes. Left: Eyes are looking to the left; arrows indicate large brightness differences due to pupil location. Right: Eyes are looking straight ahead

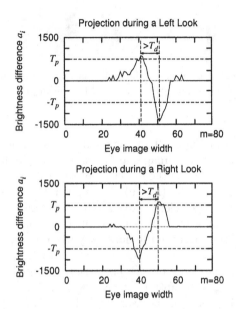

Fig. 6. Results of projecting the signed difference between right and mirrored left eyes onto the x−axis. The top graph is the result of left-looking eyes. The bottom graph is the result of right-looking eyes

Let I_ℓ and I_r be the $m \times n$ left and right eye images masked by motion information. The projection of the signed difference onto vector $\mathbf{a} = a_1, \ldots, a_m$ is computed by:

$$a_i = \sum_{j=1}^{n} (I_r(i,j) - I_\ell(m-i,j)) \tag{1}$$

Two thresholds T_p and T_d are used to evaluate whether a motion occurred to the right, left, or not at all. The thresholds can be adjusted to change the sensitivity of the system. First, the maximum and minimum components of the projection vector $\mathbf{a}$ and their respective indices are computed:

$$a_{\min} = \min_{i=\{1,\ldots,m\}} (a_i) \quad \text{and} \quad a_{\max} = \max_{i=\{1,\ldots,m\}} (a_i) \tag{2}$$

$$i_{\min} = \underset{i=\{1,\ldots,m\}}{\arg\min} (a_i) \quad \text{and} \quad i_{\max} = \underset{i=\{1,\ldots,m\}}{\arg\max} (a_i) \tag{3}$$

The minimum and maximum values are then compared to the projection threshold T_p:

$$a_{\min} < -T_p \quad \text{and} \quad a_{\max} > T_p \tag{4}$$

This threshold assures that there is a sufficient brightness difference to indicate a left or right motion. The second threshold T_d is used to guarantee a minimal spatial difference between the minimum and maximum projection values when motion is detected. The direction of motion is determined as follows:

$$i_{\max} - i_{\min} > T_d \qquad \Rightarrow \qquad \text{'right motion'} \qquad (5)$$

$$i_{\max} - i_{\min} < -T_d \qquad \Rightarrow \qquad \text{'left motion'} \qquad (6)$$

2.3 Classification

Information from both the motion and eye comparison analysis are combined to determine if there was an intentional look to the left or right. The system detects motion followed by eye direction to the left in order to trigger the "user has looked left" event. The corresponding right event is similarly triggered.

A limit was set on how frequently events can be triggered in order to avoid the system from becoming confused and triggering many events in quick succession. The limit was set experimentally at one event every 0.5 seconds. The user must move his or her eyes back to the center position before attempting to trigger another left or right event. In the future however, it may be preferable to let the user keep looking to one side in order to trigger many events in a row to simulate holding down a key. Audio feedback or multiple monitors would be needed to let the user know when events are triggered.

2.4 BlockEscape Game

The game BlockEscape was developed as a tool to test the performance of EyeKeys as an interface. It is a game that is easy to learn and provides an interactive and engaging user experience, which is particularly important for users with severe disabilities who have difficulty remaining physically active for long periods of time. Providing an enjoyable game as a statistics gathering device may encourage subjects to play for longer periods of time. Figure 7 shows a screenshot of BlockEscape.

The rules of the game are as follows. The walls, which are the black rectangles in Fig. 7, are fixed objects that move upward at a constant rate. The user, who controls a white block, must lead it into the holes between these walls, where it "falls through" to the next wall. The user is restricted to move the white block horizontally left and right. The block movement is *triggered* by issuing a 'left motion' or 'right motion' command. The command can be issued using the EyeKeys interface, the mouse, or the left/right keys on the keyboard. The block continues to move in that direction until it falls through a hole or the user issues a new direction command. If the block reaches the bottom of the screen, the user wins. If the block is pushed to the top of the screen by the walls, the user loses.

There are numerous ways to configure game play. The significant configuration variables are game speed and distance between walls. The game speed specifies how often the game state is updated: by increasing this setting, the game is made slower and therefore easier to play. The settings allow the game

Fig. 7. Screenshot of the BlockEscape game. The player navigates the block through the holes by moving the mouse left or right or pressing keys as the block falls toward the bottom of the screen

to be configured appropriately for the abilities of the user with a chosen interface method.

Methods for gathering statistics. During playing, usage statistics, in particular, the departure of the user-controlled block from an optimal path, were computed based on the positions of the block, walls, and holes and compiled into XML (Extensible Markup Language) documents. If the block is on the rightmost side of the screen, and there is one hole on the leftmost side of the screen, the user should obviously move the block left. In cases with multiple holes on a particular wall, the user should move the block in the direction to the closest hole. The following equations are used to determine the player deviations:

$$d_{ij} = |x_{ij} - h_i| \tag{7}$$

$$D_{ij} = \begin{cases} 0 & \text{if } d_{ij} < d_{i\,j-1} \text{ or } j = 0 \\ 1 & \text{otherwise} \end{cases} \tag{8}$$

where h_i is the hole's position on wall i and x_{ij} is the block's position on wall i at time j. Distance d_{ij} is defined as the distance from the block's current position to the hole and D_{ij} determines whether the block is closer or farther away from the nearest hole. We define the deviation for wall i as:

$$\sigma_i = \sum_{j=1}^{W_i} D_{ij} \tag{9}$$

where W_i is the number of game-update cycles during which the block is on wall i. The deviation σ_{avg}, averaged over all walls, was approximately zero in our tests with users employing a keyboard. Therefore, we can assume that all movement errors encountered during testing are not due to user error resulting from difficulty of the game itself, but are instead due to the interface system being employed.

The XML document includes a coordinate-pair listing denoting the configuration of each individual wall during a game play. This information may then be used to reconstruct the exact wall sequence that was seen in a previous game, allowing the user to play the same game multiple times. This is also useful for playing the same sequence with multiple users.

3 Experiments and Results

This section describes experiments to evaluate the performance of EyeKeys.

3.1 EyeKeys Performance Evaluation

Experimental setup. EyeKeys is designed to be used by a person sitting in front of a computer display. The camera is mounted on the end of an articulated arm, which allows the camera to be optimally positioned in front of a computer monitor. The USB camera we used is a Logitech Quickcam Pro 4000, with a retail price of $79.99. The tests were run on an Athlon 2100.

The EyeKeys system was tested by 8 able-bodied people. Tests were created to determine if the system can detect when a user intentionally looks to the left or to the right. The average face template used by the face detection and tracking method was first updated with a template representing the face of the test subject. Testers were told to look at the computer monitor. When asked to look left, the tester should quickly move their eyes to look at a target point to the left of the monitor. A similar target was to the right side of the monitor. After the "look" was completed, the user should move his or her eyes back at the monitor.

We created a random ordered sequence of twenty "looks:" ten to the left and ten to the right. The same sequence was used for all the test subjects. If the system did not recognize a look, the user was asked to repeat it. The number of tries required to recognize the look was recorded. We also recorded when the system misinterpreted a left or right look, and the test proceeded to the next look in the sequence.

Results. The faces of all test subjects were correctly tracked in both location and scale while they were moving between 2 and 5 feet from the camera. Our system correctly identified 140 out of 160 intentional looks to the left or right. This corresponds to an 87.5% success rate. For the system to detect and classify 160 looks, the users had to make 248 attempts. On average, 1.55 actual looks are made for each correctly identified look event. The results are summarized in Table 2.

Table 2. Number of actual and detected left and right looks in testing the EyeKeys system

		Actual		
		Left	Right	Correct
Observed	Left	72	12	90.0%
	Right	8	68	85.0%
	Missed	40	48	

EyeKeys was more successful with some of the test subjects than others. For example, one subject had all 20 looks correctly identified while only making 24 actual look attempts. Cases where an incorrect recognition occurred were likely due to a problem with alignment of the right and mirrored-left eyes. The number of extra look attempts is due to high thresholds that were chosen to avoid false detection of looks, since it was decided that it is better to miss a look than to misclassify a look. Other incorrect recognitions were due to the system missing a look in one direction, but detecting eye movement back to the center position as a move in the opposite direction.

3.2 BlockEscape Experiment

Experimental setup. Four test subjects participating in this experiment were read the rules of BlockEscape, followed by two demonstrations of the game using a mouse. We chose to test the Camera Mouse in this experiment in order to measure the effectiveness of EyeKeys against a previously developed HCI system for people with disabilities. The keyboard was chosen as a control against the HCI systems. All subjects were unfamiliar with Block-Escape, EyeKeys, and the Camera Mouse.

In the "practice" phase, the subjects were allowed to become familiar with the game and the interfaces. They played up to three trial games, or for up to three minutes, on the keyboard, Camera Mouse and EyeKeys. They were then asked to play at least one game for 30 seconds with each device.

For the "trial" phase, the test subjects played three games on each input device, the results are shown in Table 3.

Table 3. Results of four users employing three devices to play BlockEscape. Units are percentage of game playing area

	Device		
	EyeKeys	Camera Mouse	Keyboard
σ_{avg}	2.9	2.27	0
Median	2.54	0	0
Std. Dev.	4.01	2.68	0
Wins	$\frac{10}{12}$ (83%)	$\frac{10}{12}$ (83%)	$\frac{12}{12}$ (100%)

Results. The win percentage of EyeKeys compared to the Camera Mouse was the same, although EyeKeys had a higher σ_{avg}, median, and standard deviation. We also noted that a Camera Mouse failure requires manual intervention to correct, while an EyeKeys user could frequently make another look in the appropriate direction to correct a mistake. However, the median deviation for the Camera Mouse system indicates that errors were quickly corrected by the user in most instances. The median deviation for EyeKeys is due to the time restriction limit between detections. The keyboard control is obviously the most accurate way to play the game for those that are able, however, the results demonstrate that EyeKeys works well enough as an interface to play this game, and that it is comparable in performance to an existing assistive-technology interface that is in current use.

Users had different levels of success playing BlockEscape with EyeKeys. One user mastered EyeKeys quickly, winning all three games, but had trouble with the Camera Mouse. With EyeKeys, all the other users improved their performance on succeeding games. This did not hold true for the Camera Mouse experiments.

3.3 Initial Experience: A Test User with Severe Disabilities

We were able to hold a preliminary test of the EyeKeys system with a user with cerebral palsy. This user can control his eyes and has some control over head movements. However, he also has involuntary head movements.

We asked him to use the EyeKeys system to move a window left and right across the screen. We observed that he was frequently able to move the window in the direction that we asked him. Sometimes, involuntary head motion would cause the system to detect an unintentional eye event. Since he has used the Camera Mouse on numerous occasions, he would often move his head in a motion that would work with the Camera Mouse, but caused problems with EyeKeys. Adjusting the thresholds in future tests may allow the system to work better with these head motions. The system could also be configured to ignore eye movements when head movements are detected.

3.4 Real-Time Performance of System

Our system achieves real-time performance at 15 frames per second, which is the limit of the USB camera at 640×480 resolution. The BlockEscape game had no problem running concurrently with the real-time vision interface system. The performance of EyeKeys easily enables it to run concurrently with other applications such as spelling programs and web browsers.

4 Discussion and Future Work

Real-time performance. Correlation-based face tracking is the most computationally expensive procedure in our system. The face tracker employs multi-scale techniques in order to improve real-time performance. The template correlation over the image pyramid is more efficient than performing multiple correlations with a scaled template. In addition to improving accuracy, the color and motion information could be used to reduce the search space of the template correlation, further improving efficiency.

The eye analysis is relatively computationally inexpensive. The eye direction is computed in time proportional to the size of the eye image.

Design motivations. The approach of EyeKeys to exploit symmetry works well with eye images of low resolution. Other approaches to gaze detection that model eye features require higher resolution eye images, e.g., [25]. If such images cannot be obtained, and therefore eye features such as corners of the eyes or curve of the iris cannot be used, the difference mirroring approach allows eye direction classification to be successful.

The two thresholds that determine when the user looks right or left are adjustable. Increasing T_p makes the system more likely to miss an intentional look, but less likely to misclassify a look. Increasing T_d has the effect of requiring that the looks be faster and more deliberate. While this can decrease false detections, it also makes the system difficult and uncomfortable to use.

The template can be updated from the current video feed by clicking on the nose and then selecting the correct scale of the face from a slide bar. This is useful in cases when a person's face does not correlate well with the default template. Detection methods based on the normalized correlation coefficient can work well with uniform changes in brightness [4], however, problems may occur if the user becomes more brightly lit from one side. In addition, the template-based detection method works well if the template face and the user's face remain in the same orientation. If the default template is applied, the user should face the camera and hold his or her head straight. An updated template can work with specific head tilts and lighting conditions.

Testing experience and comparisons. Our test subjects had little difficulty learning the EyeKeys interface. After only a minute of practice, users were able to play BlockEscape. In addition, most subjects improved after each game, leading us to believe that EyeKeys users will become as proficient as Camera Mouse users over time.

EyeKeys performed well in comparison to the Camera Mouse. When the Camera Mouse loses track, the performance decreases dramatically. In our system, a false detection can be rectified by a correct detection. This, however, is specific to certain applications. For instance, if our system caused a web browser to follow a hyperlink in error, then it would be difficult to return to the original page without manual intervention. Since this system was designed as an HCI application, it was expected that the user would be cooperative and *try* to make it work. Future tests will determine the limitations for EyeKeys to detect head tilts or rotations.

Future work and improvements. EyeKeys has the potential to become an integral part of a complete HCI system, e.g., perceptual interface systems described in references [20, 26]. Combining EyeKeys with other HCI applications would give the user greater control over the computer, and if utilized with other facial processing techniques, could prove to be part of an all-purpose command interface. While the current research is focused on creating an interface system for people with severe disabilities, gaze detection systems such as EyeKeys can be useful in other areas such as linguistic and communication research, or monitoring a vehicle driver's attention.

EyeKeys can be adapted for specific applications such as text entering. Text can be entered in a variety of ways, for example, an on-screen keyboard can scan to the intended letter, or letters can be selected by following a binary search of the alphabet. Some of this type of software is already in use with current interfaces for people with disabilities [3, 6, 7, 9, 10, 21].

Another important application for EyeKeys is navigating a web browser. The two commands, left and right looks, could map to the *Tab* and *Enter* keys of the keyboard. This allows the user to tab through the links on a page, and then select a link to follow. If the user starts on a web page with a hierarchical structure of the web, such as Yahoo, then information can be retrieved by following a few links. This would allow access to news, weather, sports, entertainment, and educational material. A current issue is that following an incorrect link by mistake results in the user on the wrong page. A possible solution would be to detect other events, such as blinks [10], to serve as an undo command. Alternatively, a confirmation step could be built into the interface before a link was followed to add one level of protection against this kind of problem.

The EyeKeys system could be improved with an algorithm to more precisely locate the eyes. The current method relies on eye motion for position refinement. Our system should also work better with head motion. One solution could be to not allow eye movement detection when the head is moving. However, that may cause a problem for disabled users that have involuntary head movements. Another extension would be an analysis of the difference projection by fitting a polynomial function instead of thresholding. The current system assumes that the head is held vertically and faces toward the camera. When the user's head tilts, the eyes are no longer symmetrical across a vertical axis, which causes problems in detecting the gaze. Extending the system to find the amount of head tilt would improve the detection rate. This could be done by rotating the template, or by finding the rotated line of symmetry of the face or between the eyes.

Future possibilities for extending this system include the addition of a blink analysis module [10], which would give the interface three events to work with. Unfortunately, some subjects with severe cerebral palsy cannot control their eye blinks. Another way to extend the system is with further analysis of the duration that the user looks left or right to allow mapping of more events to additional commands. Eventually, it would be useful to increase the number of gaze directions that can be detected reliably, but this is a very challenging problem with the low-grade cameras and low-resolution eye images used here.

Acknowledgments

Funding was provided by the National Science Foundation (IIS-0308213, IIS-039009, IIS-0093367, P200A01031, and EIA-0202067).

References

1. E H Adelson et al. Pyramid methods in image processing. *RCA Engineer*, pp 33–41, 1984.
2. Applied Science Laboratories. http://www.a-s-l.com
3. M Betke et al. The Camera Mouse: Visual tracking of body features to provide computer access for people with severe disabilities. *IEEE Trans Neural Systems and Rehabilitation Engineering*, pp 1–10, 2002.
4. M Betke and N C Makris. Recognition, resolution, and complexity of objects subject to affine transformation. *Int J Computer Vision*, pp 5–40, 2001.
5. M Betke et al. Active detection of eye scleras in real time. *Proc IEEE Workshop on Human Modeling, Analysis, and Synthesis*, 2000.
6. P DiMattia et al. *An Eye Control Teaching Device for Students without Language Expressive Capacity – EagleEyes*. The Edwin Mellen Press, 2001.
7. L A Frey et al. Eye-gaze word processing. *IEEE Trans Systems, Man, and Cybernetics*, pp 944–950, 1990.
8. A Gee and R Cipolla. Determining the gaze of faces in images. *Image and Vision Computing*, pp 639–647, 1994.
9. J Gips and J Gips. A computer program based on Rick Hoyt's spelling method for people with profound special needs. *Proc Int Conf on Computers Helping People with Special Needs*, 2000.
10. K Grauman et al. Communication via eye blinks and eyebrow raises: Video-based human-computer interfaces. *Universal Access in the Information Society*, pp 359–373, 2003.
11. E Hjelmas and B K Low. Face detection: A survey. *Computer Vision and Image Understanding*, pp 236–274, 2001.
12. T Hutchinson et al. Human-computer interaction using eye-gaze input. *IEEE Trans Systems, Man, and Cybernetics*, pp 1527–1533, 1989.
13. Q Ji and Z Zhu. Eye and gaze tracking for interactive graphic display. *Proc Int Symp on Smart Graphics*, 2002.
14. A Kapoor and R W Picard. Real-time, fully automatic upper facial feature tracking. *Proc IEEE Int Conf on Automatic Face Gesture Recognition*, 2002.
15. K-N Kim and R S Ramakrishna. Vision-based eye-gaze tracking for human computer interface. *Proc IEEE Int Conf on Systems, Man, and Cybernetics*, 1999.
16. J J Magee. A real-time human-computer interface based on gaze detection from a low-grade video camera. MS Thesis, Boston University, 2004.
17. J J Magee et al. EyeKeys: A real-time vision interface based on gaze detection from a low-grade video camera. *Proc IEEE Workshop on Real-Time Vision for Human-Computer Interaction*, 2004.
18. C H Morimoto et al. Pupil detection and tracking using multiple light sources. Technical Report RJ-10177, IBM Almaden Research Center, 1998.
19. K Schwerdt and J L Crowley. Robust face tracking using color. *Proc IEEE Int Conf on Automatic Face and Gesture Recognition*, 2000.
20. R Sharma et al. Toward multimodal human-computer interfaces. *Proceedings of the IEEE*, pp 853–869, 1998.
21. R C Simpson and H H Koester. Adaptive one-switch row-column scanning. *IEEE Trans Rehabilitation Engineering*, pp 464–473, 1999.
22. S Sirohey et al. A method of detecting and tracking irises and eyelids in video. *Pattern Recognition*, pp 1389–1401, 2002.

23. O Takami et al. Computer interface to use head and eyeball movement for handicapped people. *Proc IEEE Int Conf on Systems, Man, and Cybernetics*, 1995.
24. J-C Terrillon and S Akamatsu. Comparative performance of different chrominance spaces for color segmentation and detection of human faces in complex scene images. *Proc IEEE Int Conf on Automatic Face and Gesture Recognition*, 2000.
25. Y Tian et al. Dual-state parametric eye tracking. *Proc IEEE Int Conf on Automatic Face and Gesture Recognition*, 2000.
26. M Turk and G Robertson. Perceptual user interfaces. *Comm ACM*, pp 32–34, 2000.
27. M Yang et al. Detecting faces in images: A survey. *IEEE Trans PAMI*, pp 34–58, 2002.
28. D H Yoo et al. Non-contact eye gaze tracking system by mapping of corneal reflections. *Proc IEEE Int Conf on Automatic Face and Gesture Recognition*, 2002.
29. L Young and D Sheena. Survey of eye movement recording methods. *Behavior Research Methods and Instrumentation*, pp 397–429, 1975.

Map Building from Human-Computer Interactions

Artur M. Arsenio

Computer Science and Artificial Intelligence Laboratory
Massachusetts Institute of Technology
arsenio@csail.mit.edu

Online help from a human actor has a lot of potential to facilitate computer perception. This chapter proposes an innovative real-time algorithm – running on an active vision head – to build 3D scene descriptions from human cues. The theory is supported by experimental results both for figure/ground segregation of typical heavy objects in a scene (such as furniture) and for object/scene recognition and 3D reconstruction.

1 Introduction

Embodied and situated perception [5] consists of boosting the vision capabilities of an artificial creature by fully exploiting the opportunities created by an embodied agent situated in the world [2].

Active vision proponents [1, 7], contrary to passive vision, argue for active control of the visual perception mechanism so that perception is facilitated. Percepts can indeed be acquired in a purposive way by the active control of a camera [1]. This approach has been successfully applied to several computer vision problems, such as stereo vision – by dynamically changing the baseline distance between the cameras or by active focus selection [19].

We argue for solving a visual problem by not only actively controlling the perceptual mechanism, but also and foremost actively changing the environment through experimental manipulation. The human body plays an essential role in such a framework, being applied not only to facilitate perception, but also to change the world context so that percepts are easily understood [5].

1.1 Motivation

Besides binocular cues, the human visual system also processes monocular data for depth inference, such as focus, perspective distortion, among others. Previous attempts have been made on exploring scene context for depth inference [34]. However, these passive techniques make use of contextual cues already present on the scene. They do not actively change the context of the scene through manipulation to improve the robot's perception. We propose an active, embodied approach that actively changes the context of a scene, extracting monocular depth measures (see Fig. 1).

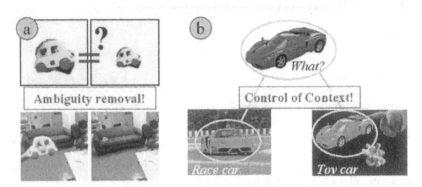

Fig. 1. Control of contextual information in a scene. (a) Top: Two images: same object at different depths? or distinct size objects? Bottom: Contextual information removes ambiguity. The background image provides enough information for a human to infer that there us a high probability for being the same object at different depths (b) Information from viewing a car without being in context may result in categorical ambiguity. If the car is viewed on a race track with trees, then it is probably a real race car. But for toy cars, a human can easily control context, introducing contextual references by manipulating the object

We propose an algorithm to infer depth and build 3-dimensional maps from a distinct monocular cue: the relative size of objects on a monocular image – special focus will be placed on using the human's arm as a reference measure. Another algorithm's novelty is the real-time transmission of world-structure to the perceptual system from the action of an embodied agent (the human tutor). This real-time algorithm builds scene descriptions as a function of objects, together with 3D coarse maps for the scene, through the analysis of cues provided by an interacting human. Scene representations are then the training inputs for a statistical real-time scene recognition algorithm, which exploits world contextual cues.

1.2 Human-Robot Interactive Communication

Previous approaches for transferring skills from human to computers rely heavily on human gesture recognition, or haptic interfaces for detecting human motion. Environments are often over-simplified to facilitate the perception of the task sequence [20]. Other approaches consist of visually identifying simple guiding actions (such as direction following, or collision), for which both the task's structure and goal are well known [24].

Teaching a visual system information concerning the surrounding world is a difficult task, which takes several years for a child, equipped with evolutionary mechanisms stored in its genes, to accomplish. Our approach exploits help from a human in a robot's learning loop to extract meaningful percepts from the world. However, it should be emphasized that such help does not aim at constraining the world structure (for instance by removing environment cluttering or careful luminosity setup). The focus will be placed on communicating information to a robot which boosts its perceptual skills, helping the visual system to filter out irrelevant information. Indeed, while teaching a toddler, parents do not remove the room's furniture or buy extra lights to just show the child a book. Help instead is given by facilitating the child's task of stimulus selection (for example, by pointing or tapping into a book's image [5]).

1.3 Map Building

Several techniques have been proposed for three-dimensional reconstruction of environments, ranging from passive sensing techniques to active sensing using laser range finders, or both [29]. Indeed, there is a wide selection of algorithms available in the literature to infer depth or shape [18, 11, 17]:

- Monocular techniques for depth inference include, among others, Depth from Motion or Shading [18], Depth from Disparity [11], Depth from Focus [19], and Shape from Texture [13].
- Stereo techniques most often extract depth from a binocular system of cameras [6] or by integrating multiple simultaneous views from a configuration of several cameras. [17, 12].

We will focus on learning topological map representations [9] from cues provided by interactive humans. It should be emphasized we will not argue for more accurate results than other Stereo or Monocular depth inference techniques. Indeed, the technique here proposed provides solely coarse depth information. Its power relies on providing an additional cue for depth inference, which could be augmented by using cues from other scene objects besides the human arm. In addition, the proposed algorithm has complementary properties to other depth inference algorithms, it does not require special hardware (low-cost cameras will suffice) and it also outputs object segmentations.

2 Object Processing from Human-Robot Interactive Cues

Real-time object segmentation on unstructured, non-static, noisy and low resolution (128×128) images is a hard problem subject to a large variety of disturbances:

- target object with similar color/texture as background
- multiple objects moving simultaneously in a scene
- object is the union of a large number of color regions

Robustness to luminosity and world structure variations is also of paramount importance. Mobility constraints (such as segmenting heavy objects) poses additional difficulties, since motion cannot be used to facilitate the problem.

We argue for a visual embodied strategy which is not limited to active robotic heads. Instead, embodiment of an agent is exploited by probing the world with a human arm. This strategy proves not only useful to segment object descriptions from books [4], but also to segment large, stationary objects (such as a table) from monocular images.

2.1 Figure-Ground Segregation

We propose a human aided object segmentation algorithm to tackle the figure-ground problem, formulated as follows:

> Given a monocular image which contains an object of interest, the problem consists in determining the clusters of features in the image which correspond to the correct representation of the apparent visual appearance of the object.

Objects might have multiple colors, as well as multiple textures. Furthermore, their shape might be composed of several groups of closed contours. In addition, this same richness in descriptive features usually applies for the object background as well (for non-trivial environments). Hence, to solve the aforementioned problem, one needs to:

- reject all clusters of features which belong to the object background
- group all clusters of features which make part of the object.

Embodiment of an agent is exploited through probing the world with a human arm, creating a salient stimuli in the robot's attentional system (which is described in Sect. 2.2). The retinal location of the salient stimuli is thus near the object. Hence the robot moves its head to gaze at it, and becomes stationary thereafter. After saving a stationary image (no motion detected), a batch sequence of images is acquired to extract the human arm oscillating trajectory. Color clusters of perceptual elements in the stationary image which intersect the human arm trajectory are grouped together to segment the visual appearance of the object from the background.

Our approach is therefore to have a human actor to tell the robot, by repetitive gestures, which are the set of feature clusters which make part of an object, by pointing repetitively at them. Indeed, a significant amount of contextual information may be extracted from a periodically moving actuator. This can be framed as the problem of estimating $p(o_n | v_{B_{\mathbf{p}, \epsilon}}, act^{per}_{\mathbf{p}, S})$, the probability of finding object n given a set of local, stationary features v on a neighborhood ball B of radius ϵ centered on location p, and a periodic actuator on such neighborhood with trajectory points in the set $S \subseteq B$. The following algorithm implements the estimation process to solve this figure-ground separation problem (see Fig. 2):

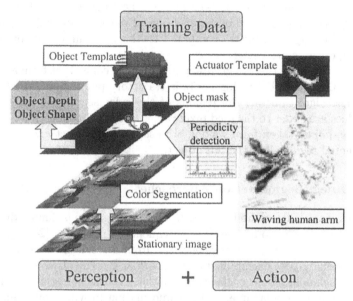

Fig. 2. Algorithm for segmentation of heavy, stationary objects. A standard color segmentation algorithm computes a compact cover of color clusters for the image. A human actor *shows* the sofa to the robot, by waving on the objects' surface. The human actuator's periodic trajectory is used to extract the object's compact cover – the collection of color cluster sets which composes the object

1. A standard color segmentation [10] algorithm is applied to a stationary image.
2. A human actor waves an arm on top of the target object.
3. The motion of skin-tone pixels is tracked over a time interval (by the Lucas-Kanade Pyramidal algorithm). The energy per frequency content – using Short-Time Fourier Transform (STFT) – is determined for each point's trajectory [21].
4. Periodic, skin-tone points are grouped together into the arm mask [5].
5. The trajectory of the arm's endpoint describes an algebraic variety [16] over N^2 (N stands for natural integers). The target object's template is then given by the union of all bounded subsets (the color regions of the stationary image) which intersect this variety.

Periodic detection is applied at multiple scales. Indeed, for an arm oscillating during a short period of time, the movement might not appear periodic at a coarser scale, but appear as such at a finer scale. If a strong periodicity is not found at a larger scale, the window size is halved and the procedure is repeated again. Periodicity is estimated from a periodogram built for all signals from the energy of the STFTs over the frequency spectrum. These periodograms are processed by a collection of narrow bandwidth band-pass filters. Periodicity is found if, compared to the maximum filter output, all remaining outputs are negligible.

The algorithm consists in grouping together the colors that form an object. This grouping works by having periodic trajectory points being used as seed pixels. The algorithm fills the regions of the color segmented image whose pixel values are closer to the seed pixel values, using a 8-connectivity strategy. Therefore, points taken from waving are used to both select and group a set of segmented regions into the full object.

Other Object Segmentation Approaches

Previous research literature for figure/ground segregation is mainly divided in object segmentation from video (i.e., a sequence of images) – [27] reports one such approach – and object segmentation from a single monocular image – which is perhaps best exemplified by the work at Berkeley University [30, 22]. Our approach does not fit exclusively in either of these: it segments an object from a single monocular image, using information provided by humans and extracted over a sequence of images.

Instead of using *offline* knowledge, our approach exploits *online* information introduced in real-time by the human helper, using such information as cues to agglomerate image regions into a coherent object. Hence, the robot is able to infer which collection of features groups form a particular object.

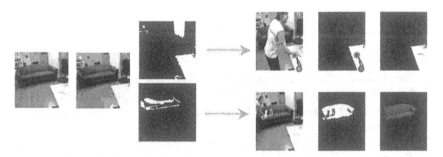

Fig. 3. Segmentation of heavy, stationary objects. The arm trajectory links the objects to the corresponding color regions

Experimental Results

Considering Fig. 3, both sofa and table segmentations are hard cases to solve. The clustering of regions by table-like color content produces two disjoint regions. One of them corresponds to the table, but it is not possible to infer which just from the color content. But a human teacher can *show* the table to the robot by waving on the table's surface. The arm trajectory then links the table to the correct region. For the sofa case, segmentation is hard because the sofa appearance consists of a collection of color regions. It is necessary additional information to group such regions without including the background. Once more, a human tutor *describes* the object, so that the arm trajectory groups several color regions into the same object – the sofa.

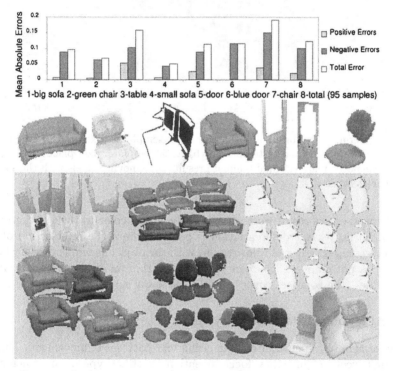

Fig. 4. Statistics for furniture items (random segmentation samples are also shown). Errors given by (template area – object's real area)/(real area). Positive/negative errors stand for templates with larger/smaller area than the real area. Total stands for both errors. The real area values were determined manually. A chair is grouped from two disconnect regions by merging temporally and spatially close segmentations

Figure 4 shows segmentations for a random sample of objects segmentations (furniture items), together with statistical results for such objects.

Clusters grouped by a single trajectory might either form (e.g., table) or not form (e.g., black chair – a union of two disconnected regions) the smallest compact cover which contains the object (depending on intersecting or not all the clusters that form the object). After the detection of two or more temporally and spatially closed trajectories this problem vanishes – the black chair is grouped from two disconnect regions by merging temporally and spatially close segmentations. This last step for building templates from merging several segmentations is more robust to errors than extracting templates from a single event (such process is illustrated in Fig. 5).

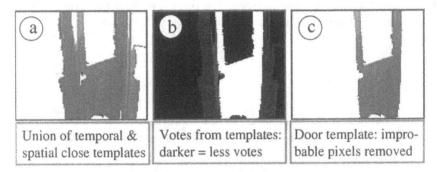

| Union of temporal & spatial close templates | Votes from templates: darker = less votes | Door template: improbable pixels removed |

Fig. 5. Merging temporally and spatially close templates. Example for segmenting a door (a) Superposition of templates; (b) Each template pixel places one vote in an accumulator map; (c) final template results by removing pixels with the smaller number of votes

Typical errors result from objects with similar color to their background, for which no perfect differentiation is possible, since the intersection of the object's compact cover of color regions with the object's complementary background is not empty. High color variability within an object create grouping difficulties (the compact cover contains too many sets – hard to group).

2.2 A Logpolar Attentional System

Newborns have a special interest in oscillatory patterns of movements. During the first weeks of life, they focus attention on these type of movements for long periods of time. As previously described, we developed a mechanism that filters image data over time intervals according to its frequency content. However, this strategy only works if the human actor is able to engage the visual system, by having the active head gazing towards the object to be segmented.

An attentional Visual System [35] was therefore implemented to facilitate human-computer communication. This system combines salient stimulus from different feature modalities into a saliency map. The human actor gets visual attention to a desired object by creating a salient stimulus on such a target.

The human waving behavior then primes the attentional system (such bias decreases with time) towards this stimulus (as shown in Fig. 6).

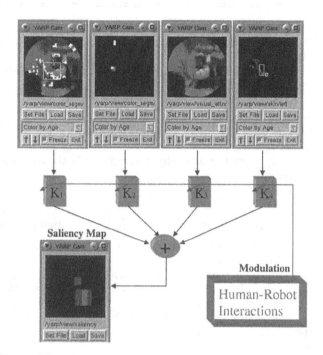

Fig. 6. The attentional system running on the humanoid robot

2.3 Object Recognition – Color Histograms

As just described, a human-computer interactive approach was implemented to introduce a humanoid robot to new percepts stored in its surrounding world. Such percepts are then converted into an useful format through an object recognition scheme, which enables the robot to recognize an object in several contexts and under different perspective views. This object recognition algorithm needs to cluster object templates by classes according to their identity. Such a task was implemented through color histograms – objects are classified based on the relative distribution of their color pixels. A multi-target tracking algorithm (which tracks *good features* [31] using a pyramidal implementation of the Lucas-Kanade algorithm), keeps track of object locations as the visual percepts change due to movement of the robot's active head.

New object templates are classified according to their similarity with other object templates in an object database [3], as follows:

Given:
- a batch of n query images (from tracking) of object templates (no background)
- training data: 20 averaged color histograms in memory for each of the m object categories learned

Recognize the set of objects:
- for $k = 1, \ldots, n$,
    1. Compute color histograms for query image k (denoted G^k)
    2. set best=(-1,-1,-1)
    3. for $l = 1, \ldots, m$ (for each object category l in the database of m categories)
        a) set $p_{max} = (-1, -1)$
        b) for $j = 1, \ldots, 20$,
            i. compute the probability $p = \sum_{i=1}^{8^3} minimum \left(n_{G_i}, n_{G_i''^{lj}} \right)$, where G''^{lj} is the j average color histogram in category l
            ii. if $p \geq 0.7$
                - $p_{max} = maximum_p(p_{max}, (j, p)))$
        c) if $p_{max} \neq (-1, -1)$ (a matching occurs for this category)
            - $best_k = maximum_p(best_k, (l, j, p))$, where j and p are the two elements of p_{max} (in that order)
- set category$(1, \ldots, m+1)=0$
- for $k = 1, \ldots, n$,
    1. if $best_k \neq (-1, -1, -1)$ (a match occurred)
        - category(l)=category(l)+1, where l is the category given by the first element of $best_k$
    2. else (no match occurred)
        - category(m+1)=category(m+1)+1
- find max_{cat}, the index of the maximum value in category
- if $equal(max_{cat}, m+1)$ (create new object category)
    1. Set $m = m + 1$, $minc = minimum(category(max_{cat}), 20)$
    2. initialize the average color histograms $G'^{m, \{1, \ldots, minc\}}_{1, \ldots, 8^3} = G^{1, \ldots, minc}_{1, \ldots, 8^3}$
    3. $histogramsavg_m(\{1, \ldots, minc\}) = 1$
    else (match – update object category max_{cat})
    - for $k = 1, \ldots, n$
        1. set j as the second element of $best_k$
        2. update (by weight average) the average histogram $G'^{max_{cat}, j}$ with G^k
        $$G'^{max_{cat}, j}_{1, \ldots, 8^3} = \frac{histogramsavg_m(j) \times G'^{max_{cat}, j}_{1, \ldots, 8^3} + G^k_{1, \ldots, 8^3}}{histogramsavg_m(j) + 1}$$
        3. $histogramsavg_{max_{cat}}(j) = histogramsavg_{max_{cat}}(j) + 1$
- output identifier max_{cat}

Experimental Results

Figure 7 presents quantitative performance statistics for this algorithm (which was extensively applied for building maps of scenes, a topic described in the next section). The quantitative evaluation was performed from data extracted while running online experiments on the humanoid robot Cog. The batch number was reduced to $n = 1$ (object templates were classified one at a time), and the training data consisted of stored object template images annotated by the tracking algorithm. This table also shows the system running on the humanoid robot Cog, while recognizing previously learned objects. Incorrect matches occurred due to color similarity among different objects (such as a big and a small sofa). Errors arising from labeling an object in the database as a new object result are chiefly due to drastic variations in light sources.

Recog. objects	Errors %	Recog. objects	Errors %
Big sofa	4.35 (23)	Green chair	0.0 (4)
Small sofa	18.2 (11)	Door	3.57 (28)
Table	5.56 (18)	Blue door	14.29 (7)
Black chair	0.0 (18)	Total	5.5 (109)

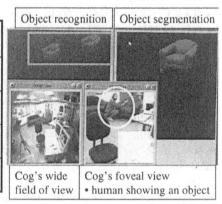

Object recognition	Object segmentation
Cog's wide field of view	Cog's foveal view • human showing an object

Fig. 7. (left) Recognition errors. It shows the number of matches evaluated from a total of 11 scenes (objects may be segmented and recognized more than once per scene) and $m = 7$ object categories. A scene is composed by several objects extracted from an unbounded number of images. The number in parenthesis shows the total number of times a given object was recognized (correctly or incorrectly). Incorrect matches occurred due to color similarity among big/small sofas or between different objects. Missed matches result from drastic variations in light sources (right) sofa is segmented and recognized. Out of around 100 samples from online experiments, recognition accuracy averaged 95%

3 Three-Dimensional Environment Map Building

The world structure is a rich source of information for a visual system – even without visual feedback, people expect to find books on shelves. We argue that world structural information should be exploited in an active manner. For instance, there is a high probability of finding objects along the pointing direction of a human arm [26]. In addition, a human can be helpful for ambiguity removal: a human hand grabbing a Ferrari car implies that the latter is a toy car model, instead of a real car. Hence, humans can control the image context to facilitate the acquisition of percepts from a visual system.

We propose a real-time strategy to acquire depth information from monocular cues by having a human actor actively controlling the image context. It consists in automatically extracting the size of objects and their depth as a function of the human arm diameter. This diameter measure solves the image ambiguity between the depth and size of an object situated in the world.

3.1 Coarse Depth Measures from Human Cues

Given the image of an object, its meaning is often a function of the surrounding context. The human arm diameter (which is assumed to remain approximately constant for the same depth, except for degenerate cases) is used as a reference for extracting relative depth information – without camera calibration. This measure is extracted from periodic signals of a human hand as follows:

1. Detection of skin-tone pixels over a image sequence.
2. A blob detector labels these pixels into regions.
3. These regions are tracked over the image sequence, and all non-periodic blobs are filtered out.
4. A region filling algorithm (8-connectivity) extracts a mask for the arm.
5. A color histogram is built for the background image. Points in the arm's mask having a large frequency on such histogram are labeled as background.
6. The smallest eigenvalue of the arm's mask gives an approximate measure of a fraction of the arm radius (templates shown in Fig. 8).

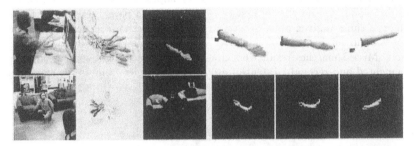

Fig. 8. Human waving the arm to facilitate object segmentation. Upper row shows a sequence for which the skin-tone detector performs reasonably well under light saturation. Lower row shows background sofas with skin-like colors. The arm's reference size was manually measured as 5.83 pixels, while the estimated value was 5.70 pixels with standard deviation of 0.95 pixels

Fig. 9. (left) An image of the lab. (right) Depth map (lighter=closer) for a table and a chair. Perpendicularity is preserved for the chair's disconnected regions (3D plot)

Once a reference measure is available, it provides a coarse depth estimation in retinal coordinates for each arm's trajectory point. The following factors affect the depth estimation process (see Fig. 9 for object reconstruction results, and Table 1 for an error analysis):

Light sensitivity: This is mainly a limitation of the skin-color algorithm. We noticed a variation in between 10–25% on size diameter for variations in light intensity (no a-priori environment setup – the only requirement concerns object visibility). High levels of light exposure increase average errors.

Human arm diameter variability: Variations along people diversity are negligible if the same person describes objects in a scene to the visual system, while depth is extracted relative to that person's arm diameter.

Background texture interference: The algorithm that we propose minimizes this disturbance by background removal. But in a worst case scenario of saturated, skin-color backgrounds, the largest variability detected for the arm's diameter was 35% larger than its real size.

Hence, we argue that this technique provides coarse depth estimates, instead of precise, accurate ones (a statistical scheme which augments the power of this algorithm by using cues from other scene objects besides the human arm is described in [3]). The average depth of an object can be estimated by averaging measures using a least squares minimization criterion – errors are even further reduced if large trajectories are available. The algorithm has complementary properties to other depth inference algorithms, it does not

Table 1. Depth estimation errors for objects from 5 scenes (as percentage of real size). T stands for number of templates, N for average number of trajectory points per template, S for light source, H and L for High/Low luminosity levels, respectively. (left) Overall results (right) Depth errors for different luminosity conditions are shown for the two sofas – top – and from all objects– bottom

Errors in avg. depth	T	N	Mean error	Error Std	Mean abs error
big sofa	46	305	6.02	19.41	17.76
small sofa	28	326	-7.79	19.02	18.16
black chair	31	655	8.63	3.95	8.63
table	17	326	15.75	5.80	15.75
door	11	126	8.00	34.94	27.05
green chair	24	703	17.9	3.87	17.93

	S	T	N	Mean error
big sofa	H	7	146	27.96
	L	39	384	1.84
small sofa	H	25	369	-12.2
	L	3	158	33.4

S	Mean error	Error Std	Mean abs error
H	0.74	25.3	16.35
L	-0.98	10.6	7.44

require special hardware (low-cost cameras will suffice) and it also outputs object segmentations. And there are cases in which it can provide more accurate results than standard depth inference techniques. Examples of such cases include textureless images, or low resolution representations (e.g., a foveated camera looking at a completely white table or a white wall, with no visible boundaries). Stereo, Depth from Motion and most algorithms will fail for these cases, but not our approach.

The availability of a collection of 3D trajectories (2-dimensional positions and depth) from temporally and spatially closed segmentations makes possible to determine a coarse estimate for the shape of an object from such data. A plane is fitted (in the least square sense) to the 3D data, for each connected region in the object's template – although hyperplanes of higher dimensions or even splines could be used. Outliers are removed by imposing upper bounds on the distance from each point to the plane (normalized by the data standard deviation). Such fitting depends significantly on the area covered by the arm's trajectory and the amount of available data. The estimation problem is ill-conditioned if not enough trajectory points are extracted along one object's eigendirection. Therefore, the fitting estimation depends on the human description of the object – accuracy increases with the area span by the human trajectories and the number of extracted trajectory points.

3.2 Map Building from Human Contextual Cues

The object location $p = (\theta, \psi)$ in the active vision head's gazing angles (egocentric coordinates), together with the estimated depth and the object's size

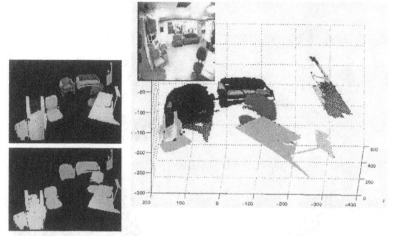

Fig. 10. (left) Furniture image segmentations – on top – and depth map – bottom – for the scene shown; (right) Coarse 3D map of the same scene. Depth is represented on the axis pointing inside, while the two other axis correspond to egocentric gazing angles (and hence the spherical deformation)

and orientation, are saved for further processing. Each point in the object's template is converted to egocentric coordinates using a motor-retinal map (obtained by locally weighted regression).

A scene was defined as a collection of objects with an uncertain geometric configuration, each object being within a minimum distance from at least one other object in the scene. Figure 10 presents both coarse depth images and 3D reconstruction data for a typical scene in the robot's lab. The geometry of a scene was reconstructed from the egocentric coordinates of all points lying on the most recent object's template. Figure 11 presents further scene reconstruction results without deformation for a typical scene on Cog's room, while Fig. 12 shows 3D plots for the same scene.

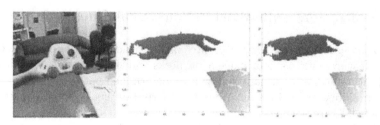

Fig. 11. (left) Scene on Cog's room, showing stationary objects such as a sofa and a table. A toy car waved by a human is also shown. (center) Coarse depth information (lighter corresponds to closer). Depth information on which object is modeled by planes. (right) Coarse depth information for the stationary scene (toy car removed)

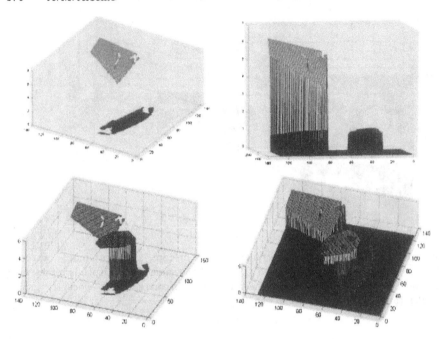

Fig. 12. (top) Two different views of coarse 3D information (with color values rendered) for a stationary scene. (bottom) Two different views of coarse 3D information for the same stationary scene plus a movable toy car

Scene reconstruction was evaluated from a set of 11 scenes built from human cues, with an average of 4.8 objects per scene (from a set of ten different furniture items). Seven of such scenes were reconstructed with no object recognition error, and hence for such cases the scene organization was recovered without structural errors. An average of 0.45 object recognition errors occurred per scene.

4 Localization from World Contextual Cues

Although environmental textures are also dependent on human selection, global features such as door placement, desks and shelf location, wall division or furniture geometry usually follow a predetermined pattern which presents low variability. Therefore, in order to incorporate such global constraints, wavelets [32] are selected as contextual features.

Wavelet components are obtained by transforming input monochrome images using a Daubechies-4 wavelet tree [32]. Processing is applied iteratively through the low frequency branch of the transform over $T = 5$ scales, while higher frequencies along the vertical, horizontal and diagonal orientations are stored (because of signal polarity, this corresponds to a compact represen-

Fig. 13. Reconstruction of the original image (by the inverse Wavelet transform). As suggested by [33], this corresponds to an holistic representation of the scene. Instead of building the holistic representation using STFTs [25] or Gabor filters (as in [33]), our approach applies Wavelets decomposition. Original and reconstruction images are shown in pairs, with the original placed at the left side

tation of six orientations in three images). The input is thus represented by $v(x, y) = v(\mathbf{p}) = \{v_k(x, y), \ k = 1, \ldots, N\}$, with $N = 3T$ ($N = 15$). Each wavelet component at the ith level has dimensions $256/2^i \times 256/2^i$, and is downsampled to a 8×8 image:

$$\bar{v}(x, y) = \sum_{i,j} v(i, j) h(i - x, j - y) \tag{1}$$

where h(x,y) is a Gaussian window. Thus, $\bar{v}(x, y)$ has dimension 960. Figure 13 shows image reconstructions from sets of features **p**, which are also called image sketches or holistic representation [25] of a scene. This representation bypasses object identities, since the scene is represented as a single identity [25], holistically. [25] and [33] apply Windowed Fourier Transforms (similar to STFTs) and Gabor filters, respectively, as contextual features. This chapter proposes instead wavelets coefficients as contextual information.

Other contextual features can be found in the research literature. The approach presented by [14] assumes prior knowledge about regularities of a reduced world where the system is situated. [23] assumes as well a prior model, that of a particular fixed scene. In yet another approach presented by [8], visual routines are selected from contextual information. Unlike these approaches, our system does not assumes any offline information or constraint about the real-world scene. Such information is transmitted online by a human to the robot in real-time.

Similarly to the approach in [33], the dimensionality problem is reduced to become tractable by applying Principal Component Analysis (PCA). The image features $\bar{v}(\mathbf{p})$ are decomposed into basis functions provided by the PCA, encoding the main spectral characteristics of a scene with a coarse description of its spatial arrangement:

$$\bar{v}(\mathbf{p}) = \sum_{i=1}^{D} c_i \varphi_k^i(\mathbf{p}) \quad \text{with} \quad c_i = \sum_{\mathbf{p},k} \bar{v}_k(\mathbf{p}) \varphi_k^i(\mathbf{p}) \tag{2}$$

where the functions $\varphi_k^i(\mathbf{p})$ are the eigenfunctions of the covariance operator given by $\bar{v}_k(\mathbf{p})$. These functions incorporate both spatial and spectral information. The decomposition coefficients are obtained by projecting the image features $\bar{v}_k(\mathbf{p})$ into the principal components c_i. This is computed using a database of images automatically annotated by the robot. The vector $\mathbf{c} = \{c_i, \ i = 1, \ldots, D\}$ denotes the resulting D-dimensional input vector, with $D = E_m$, $2 \leq D \leq Th_o$, where m denotes a class, Th_o an upper threshold and E_m denotes the number of eigenvalues within 5% of the maximum eigenvalue. The coefficients c_i are thereafter used as input context features. They can be viewed as a scene's holistic representation since all the regions of the image contribute to all the coefficients, as objects are not encoded individually.

Mixture models are applied to find interesting places to put a bounded number of local kernels that can model large neighborhoods. In D-dimensions a mixture model is denoted by density factorization over multivariate Gaussians (spherical Gaussians for faster processing times), for each object class n. The estimation of the parameters will follow the EM algorithm [15], denoting G_m as the mth Gaussian with mean μ_m and covariance matrix C_m, M as the number of Gaussian clusters, and $b_m = p(g_m)$ as the weights of the local models.

E-step for k-iteration: From the observed data $\mathbf{c}$, this step computes the a-posteriori probabilities $e_{m,n}^k(l)$ of the clusters:

$$e_{m,n}^k(l) = p(c_{m,n}|\mathbf{c}) = \frac{b_{m,n}^k G(\mathbf{c}, \mu_{m,n}^k, C_{m,n}^k)}{\sum_{m=1}^{M} b_{m,n}^k G(\mathbf{c}, \mu_{m,n}^k, C_{m,n}^k)} \tag{3}$$

M-step for k-iteration: Cluster parameters are estimated according to the maximization of the joint likelihood of the L training data samples:

$$b_{m,n}^{k+1} = \frac{\sum_{l=1}^{L} e_{m,n}^k(l)}{L} \tag{4}$$

$$\mu_{m,n}^{k+1} = <\mathbf{c}>_m = \frac{\sum_{l=1}^{L} e_{m,n}^k(l)\mathbf{c}_l}{\sum_{l=1}^{L} e_{m,n}^k(l)} \tag{5}$$

$$C_{m,n}^{k+1} = \frac{\sum_{l=1}^{L} e_{m,n}^k(l)(\mathbf{c}_l - \mu_{m,n}^{k+1})(\mathbf{c}_l - \mu_{m,n}^{k+1})^T}{\sum_{l=1}^{L} e_{m,n}^k(l)} \tag{6}$$

All vectors are column vectors and $<>_m$ in (5) represents the weighted average with respect to the posterior probabilities of cluster m. The EM algorithm converges as soon as the cost gradient is small enough or a maximum number of iterations is reached. The probability density function (PDF) for an object n is then given by Bayes' rule:

$$p(o_n|\mathbf{c}) = p(\mathbf{c}|o_n)p(o_n)/p(\mathbf{c}) \tag{7}$$

where $p(\mathbf{c}) = p(\mathbf{c}|o_n)p(o_n) + p(\mathbf{c}|\neg o_n)p(\neg o_n)$. The same method applies for the out-of-class PDF $p(\mathbf{c}|\neg o_n)$ which represents the statistical feature distribution for the input data in which o_n is not present.

Finally, it is necessary to select the number M of gaussian clusters. This number can be selected as the one that maximizes the joint likelihood of the data. An agglomerative clustering approach based on the Rissanen Minimum Description Length (MDL) order identification criterion [28] was implemented to automatically estimate M. In summary:

Given:
- for all m scene categories learned, it has in memory for each scene l
  - a maximum of $h_l = 800$ wavelet coefficient images [3], and h vectors with the components of the PCA applied to this set of images $(\mathbf{c}^{\{1,...,h_l\},l})$
  - the parameters of the K mixture of gaussians: $e_{\{1,...,K\},l}(\{1,...,h_l\})$, $b_{\{1,...,K\},l}$, $\mu_{\{1,...,K\},l}$ and $C_{\{1,...,K\},l}$.
- *Training Data:*
  - a batch of n wide-field of view scene images annotated to a scene l_q by the algorithm described in the previous section.
- *Classification Data:*
  - a query wide-field of view scene image
- TRAINING – Update scene category l with new images of the scene:
  - set $h_{l_q} = minimum(800, h_{l_q} + n)$ and store the additional n wavelet decomposition of scene images
  - apply PCA to all images in the category, and extract the new h_{l_q} coefficient vectors $(\mathbf{c}^{\{1,...,h_{l_q}\},l_q})$ obtained from the PCA
  - apply EM to train the new mixture of gaussians, initializing the number of mixtures to a large value
  - after convergence, a new K is estimated (Rissanen method) for the number of gaussians, together with a new set of parameters for the mixture of gaussians
- CLASSIFICATION – Recognize query scene image:
  - for $l = 1, ..., m$ (for each scene category l in the database of m categories)
    · compute the probability $p(\mathbf{c}|o_l)$ of the query scene in the mixture of gaussians
  - $best = (-1, MAX_{FLOAT})$
  - for $l = 1, ..., m$
    1. compute $p(o_l|\mathbf{c})$
    2. $best = minimum_{p(o_l|\mathbf{c})}(best, (l, p(o_l|\mathbf{c})))$
  - set max_{cat} as the first element of $best$
  - output scene identifier max_{cat}

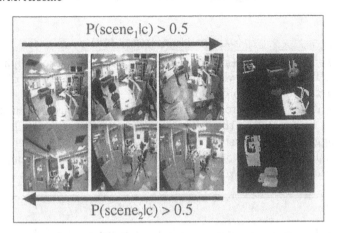

Fig. 14. Test images (wide field of view) organized with respect to $p(o_n|\mathbf{c})$. Top row: $o_n = scene_1$, $p(scene_1|\mathbf{c}) > 0.5$; Bottom row: $o_n = scene_2$, $p(scene_2|\mathbf{c}) > 0.5$

Figure 14 shows results for classifying two different scenes, which were built using the method described in the previous section. Each time a human presents a scene object to the robot, both foveal and wide field of view images are saved and automatically annotated to the corresponding scene.

5 Conclusions

This chapter presented an alternative strategy to extract depth information. The method proposed relies on a human actor to modify image context so that percepts are easily perceived – a waving human arm in front of an object provides an important cue concerning the size of such object.

Throughout this discussion percepts were acquired by an active vision head on a stationary platform (the humanoid robot). This work can be extended to a mobile platform, for performing simultaneously map building and robot localization in real-time. Whenever a scene object is recognized, the corresponding scene 3D model where it appears and the scene's spatial distribution of objects are updated. Images of that scene are hence annotated automatically. The system is then able to future recognize a scene from its image.

This human-centered framework was also applied extensively to solve other research problems, such as teaching robots from books [4]; generating training data for contextual priming of the attentional focus from holistic cues [3]; or learning cross-modal properties of objects, by correlating periodic visual events with periodic acoustic signals [3]. And there is still a high number of potential applications for which this approach might bring benefits.

Acknowledgments

Project funded by DARPA's project "Natural Tasking of Robots Based on Human Interaction Cues" under contract number DABT 63-00-C-10102, and by the Nippon Telegraph and Telephone Corporation as part of the NTT/MIT Collaboration Agreement. Author is supported by Portuguese grant PRAXIS XXI BD/15851/98.

References

1. J Y Aloimonos et al. Active vision. *Int J Computer Vision*, pp 333–356, 1987.
2. M Anderson. Embodied cognition: A field guide. *Artificial Intelligence*, pp 91–130, 2003.
3. A M Arsenio. Cognitive-developmental learning for a humanoid robot: A caregiver's gift. PhD Thesis, MIT, 2004.
4. A M Arsenio. Teaching a humanoid robot from books. *Proc Int Symp on Robotics*, 2004.
5. A M Arsenio. Towards an embodied and situated AI. *Proc Int FLAIRS Conf*, 2004.
6. A M Arsenio and J S Marques. Performance analysis and characterization of matching algorithms. *Proc Int Symp on Intelligent Robotic Systems*, 1997.
7. R K Bajcsy. Active perception. *Proceedings of the IEEE*, pp 996–1005, 1988.
8. A Bobick and C Pinhanez. Using approximate models as source of contextual information for vision processing. *Proc Workshop on Context-Based Vision*, 1995.
9. R Chatila and J Laumond. Position referencing and consistent world modelling for mobile robots. *Proc IEEE Int Conf on Robotics and Automation*, 1985.
10. D Comaniciu and P Meer. Robust analysis of feature spaces: Color image segmentation. *Proc CVPR*, 1997.
11. O Faugeras. *Three-Dimensional Computer Vision: A Geometric Viewpoint*. MIT Press, 1993.
12. O Faugeras et al. *The Geometry of Multiple Images: The Laws that Govern the Formation of Multiple Images of a Scene and some of their Applications*. MIT Press, 2001.
13. D Forsyth. Shape from texture and integrability. *Proc ICCV*, 2001.
14. D D Fu et al. Vision and navigation in man-made environments: Looking for syrup in all the right places. *Proc Workshop on Visual Behaviors*, 1994.
15. N Gershenfeld. *The Nature of Mathematical Modeling*. Cambridge University Press, 1999.
16. J Harris. *Algebraic Geometry: A First Course*. Springer-Verlag, 1994.
17. R Hartley and A Zisserman. *Multiple View Geometry in Computer Vision*. Cambridge University Press, 2000.
18. B K P Horn. *Robot Vision*. MIT Press, 1986.
19. E Krotkov et al. Stereo ranging from verging cameras. *IEEE Trans PAMI*, pp 1200–1205, 1990.
20. Y Kuniyoshi et al. Learning by watching: Extracting reusable task knowledge from visual observation of human performance. *IEEE Trans Robotics and Automation*, pp 799–822, 1994.
21. J S Lim. *Two-Dimensional Signal and Image Processing*. Prentice Hall, 1990.

22. J Malik et al. Textons, contours, and regions: Cue integration in image segmentation. *Proc ICCV*, 1999.
23. D J Moore et al. Exploiting human actions and object context for recognition tasks. *Proc IEEE Int Conf on Image Processing*, 1999.
24. M Nicolescu and M J Mataric. Experience-based learning of task representations from human-robot interaction. *Proc IEEE Int Symp on Computational Intelligence in Robotics and Automation*, 2001.
25. A Oliva and A Torralba. Modeling the shape of the scene: A holistic representation of the spatial envelope. *Int J Computer Vision*, pp 145–175, 2001.
26. D I Perrett et al. Understanding the visual appearance and consequence of hand action. In: M A Goodale. *Vision and Action: The Control of Grasping*, Cromland, 1990.
27. F M Porikli. Object segmentation of color video sequences. *Proc Int Conf on Computer Analysis of Images and Pattern*, 2001.
28. J Rissanen. A universal prior for integers and estimation by minimum description length. *Annals of Statistics*, pp 417–431, 1983.
29. V Sequeira. Active range sensing for three-dimensional environment reconstruction. PhD Thesis, IST/UTL, 1996.
30. J Shi and J Malik. Normalized cuts and image segmentation. *IEEE Trans PAMI*, pp 888–905, 2000.
31. J Shi and C Tomasi. Good features to track. *Proc CVPR*, 1994.
32. G Strang and T Nguyen. *Wavelets and Filter Banks*. Wellesley-Cambridge Press, 1996.
33. A Torralba. Contextual priming for object detection. *Int J Computer Vision*, pp 153–167, 2003.
34. A Torralba and A Oliva. Global depth perception from familiar scene structure. MIT AI-Memo 2001-036, CBCL Memo 213, 2001.
35. J M Wolfe. Guided search 2.0: A revised model of visual search. *Psychonomic Bulletin and Review*, pp 202–238, 1994.

Real-Time Inference of Complex Mental States from Facial Expressions and Head Gestures

Rana el Kaliouby and Peter Robinson

Computer Laboratory
University of Cambridge
rana.el-kaliouby@cl.cam.ac.uk
peter.robinson@cl.cam.ac.uk

In this chapter, we describe a system for inferring complex mental states from a video stream of facial expressions and head gestures in real-time. The system abstracts video input into three levels, each representing head and facial events at different granularities of spatial and temporal abstraction. We use Dynamic Bayesian Networks to model the unfolding of head and facial displays, and corresponding mental states over time. We evaluate the system's recognition accuracy and real-time performance for 6 classes of complex mental states – *agreeing, concentrating, disagreeing, interested, thinking* and *unsure*. Real-time performance, unobtrusiveness and lack of preprocessing make our system suitable for user-independent human-computer interaction.

1 Introduction

People exhibit and communicate a wide range of affective and cognitive mental states. This process of mind-reading, or attributing a mental state to a person from the observed behaviour of that person is fundamental to social interaction. Mind-reading allows people to make sense of other's actions within an intentional framework [1]. The majority of people read the minds of others all the time, and those who lack the ability to do so, such as people diagnosed along the autism spectrum, are at a disadvantage [2]. Beyond social interaction, there is growing evidence to show that emotions regulate and bias processes such as perception, decision-making and empathic understanding, in a way that contributes positively to intelligent functioning [8, 13, 23].

The human face provides an important, spontaneous channel for the communication of mental states. Facial expressions function as conversation enhancers, communicate feelings and cognitive mental states, show empathy and acknowledge the actions of other people [6, 15]. Over the past decade there has been significant progress on automated facial expression analysis (see Pantic and Rothkrantz [35] for a survey). The application of automated

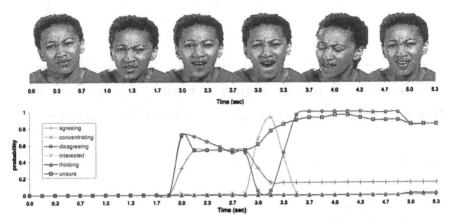

Fig. 1. Mental state inference in a video labelled as *discouraging* from the Mind Reading DVD [5]: (top) Selected frames sampled every 1 s. (bottom) Results of mental state inference. The overall probability of *disagreeing* is 0.75, a correct classification

facial expression analysis to human-computer interaction (HCI) however, is limited to basic, inconsequential scenarios. This is because the majority of existing systems either attempt to identify basic units of muscular activity in the human face (action units or AUs) based on the Facial Action Coding System (FACS) [16], or only go as far as recognizing the set of basic emotions [11, 12, 14, 29, 36, 39]. The basic emotions comprise only a small subset of the mental states that people can experience, and are arguably not the most frequently occurring in day-to-day interactions [38].

In this chapter, we describe a system for inferring complex mental states from a video stream of facial expressions and head gestures in real-time. The term complex mental states collectively refers to those mental states – both affective and cognitive – that are not part of the classic basic emotions, and which, as a result have not been addressed by the computer science research community. The system makes two principal contributions. First, it classifies different shades of complex mental state classes, and second, it does so from a video stream of facial events in real-time. Figure 1 shows the output of the system for a video labelled as *discouraging* from the Mind Reading DVD [5]. It is our belief that by building systems that recognize a wide range of mental states, we widen the scope of HCI scenarios in which this technology can be integrated.

2 Related Work

We begin our review of related work with Garg et al.'s approach to multimodal speaker detection [19] as this provides the inspiration for our present work. In their work, asynchronous audio and visual cues are fused along with contextual information and expert knowledge within a Dynamic Bayesian Network (DBN) framework. DBNs are a class of graphical probabilistic models which encode dependencies among sets of random variables evolving in time, with efficient algorithms for inference and learning. DBNs have also been used in activity recognition and facial event analysis. Park and Aggarwal [37] present a DBN framework for analyzing human actions and interactions in video. Hoey and Little [22] use DBNs in the unsupervised learning and clustering of facial displays. Zhang and Ji [42] apply DBNs to recognize facial expressions of basic emotions. Gu and Ji [20] use DBNs to classify facial events for monitoring driver vigilance. Other classifiers that have been applied to facial expression analysis include static ones such as Bayesian Networks and Support Vector Machines that classify single frames into an emotion class [11, 32].

The input to the classifiers are features extracted from still or video sequences. While numerous approaches to feature extraction exist, those meeting the real-time constraints required for man-machine contexts are of particular interest. Methods such as principal component analysis and linear discriminant analysis of 2D face models (e.g., [34]), can potentially run in real-time but require initial pre-processing to put images in correspondence. Gabor wavelets as in Littlewort et al. [30] are feature independent but are less robust to rigid head motion and require extensive (sometimes manual) alignment of frames in a video sequence. The approach that we adopt for feature extraction is based on the movement of points belonging to facial features [12, 36, 32]. Facial analysis based on feature-point tracking compares favourably to manual FACS coding [12].

3 The Mind Reading DVD

Existing corpora of nonverbal expressions, such as the Cohn-Kanade facial expression database [26], are of limited use to our research since they only cover enactments of the classic basic emotions. Instead, we use the Mind Reading DVD [5], a computer-based guide to emotions, developed by a team of psychologists led by Professor Simon Baron-Cohen at the Autism Research Centre, University of Cambridge. The DVD was designed to help individuals diagnosed along the autism spectrum recognize facial expressions of emotions.

The DVD is based on a taxonomy of emotion by Baron-Cohen et al. [4] that covers a wide range of affective and cognitive mental states. The taxonomy lists 412 mental state concepts, each assigned to one (and only one) of 24 mental state classes. The 24 classes were chosen such that the semantic distinctiveness of the emotion concepts within one class is preserved. The number of concepts within a mental state class that one is able to identify reflect one's empathizing ability [3].

Out of the 24 classes, we focus on the automated recognition of 6 classes that are particularly relevant in a human-computer interaction context, and that are not in the basic emotion set. The 6 classes are: *agreeing, concentrating, disagreeing, interested, thinking* and *unsure*. The classes include affective states such as *interested*, and cognitive ones such as *thinking*, and encompass 29 mental state concepts, or fine shades, of the 6 mental states. For instance, *brooding, calculating*, and *fantasizing* are different shades of the *thinking* class; likewise, *baffled, confused* and *puzzled* are concepts within the *unsure* class.

Each of the 29 mental states is captured through six video clips. The resulting 174 videos were recorded at 30 frames per second, and last between 5 to 8 seconds, compared to a mean duration of .67 seconds per sequence in the Cohn-Kanade database [26]. The resolution is 320×240. The videos were acted by 30 actors of varying age ranges and ethnic origins. All the videos were frontal with a uniform white background. The process of labelling the videos involved a panel of 10 judges who were asked 'could this be *the emotion name?*' When 8 out of 10 judges agreed, a statistically significant majority, the video was included. To the best of our knowledge, the Mind Reading DVD is the only available, labelled resource with such a rich collection of mental states, even if they are posed.

4 The Automated Mind-Reading System

A person's mental state is not directly available to an observer (the machine in this case) and as a result has to be inferred from observable behaviour such as facial signals. The process of reading a person's mental state in the face is inherently uncertain. Different people with the same mental state may exhibit very different facial expressions, with varying intensities and durations. In addition, the recognition of head and facial displays is a noisy process.

To account for this uncertainty, we pursued a multi-level representation of the video input, combined in a Bayesian inference framework. Our system abstracts raw video input into three levels, each conveying face-based events at different granularities of spatial and temporal abstraction. Each level captures a different degree of temporal detail depicted by the physical property of the events at that level. As shown in Fig. 2, the observation (input) at any one level is a temporal sequence of the output of lower layers.

Our approach has a number of advantages. First, higher-level classifiers are less sensitive to variations in the environment because their observations are the outputs of the middle classifiers. Second, with each of the layers being trained independently, the system is easier to interpret and improve at different levels. Third, the Bayesian framework provides a principled approach to combine multiple sources of information. Finally, by combining dynamic modelling with multi-level temporal abstraction, the model fully accounts for the dynamics inherent in facial behaviour. In terms of implementation, the system is user-independent, unobtrusive, and accounts for rigid head motion while recognizing meaningful head gestures.

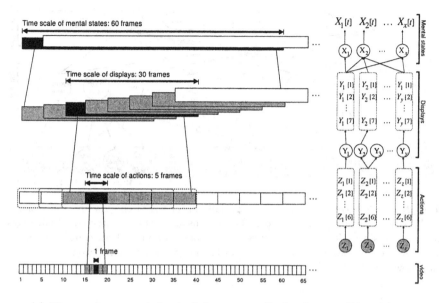

(a) Time scales at each level of the system. On level L a single event is shown in black. The input to this event is a sequence of events from level $L-1$ (shown in gray). A single action spans 5 frames (166 ms), a display spans 30 frames (1 s), and a mental state spans 60 frames (2 s)

(b)   Matrix representation of the output at each level of the system

Fig. 2. Multi-level temporal abstraction in the system

4.1 Extraction of Head and Facial Actions

The first level of the system models the basic spatial and motion characteristics of the face including the head pose. These are described by z facial actions $\mathbf{Z} = \{Z_1, \ldots, Z_z\}$ based on the FACS. Each action describes the underlying motion of an abstraction across multiple frames. Figure 3 summarizes the spatial abstractions currently supported by the model: head rotation along each of the three rotation axes (pitch, yaw and roll) and facial components (lips, mouth and eyebrows). For example, $Z_1[t]$ may represent the head pose along the pitch axis at time t; the possible values of Z_1 are {AU53, AU54, *null*} or the head-up AU, head-down, or neither respectively. To determine the time scale of head and facial actions, we timed the duration of 80 head-up and 97 head-down motions in head nod gestures, sampled from 20 videos by 15 people representing a range of complex mental states such as *convinced, encouraging* and *willing*. The movements lasted at least 170 ms, a result similar to that in the kinematics of gestures [9]. The system produces facial or head actions every 5 frames at 30 fps, or approximately every 166 ms.

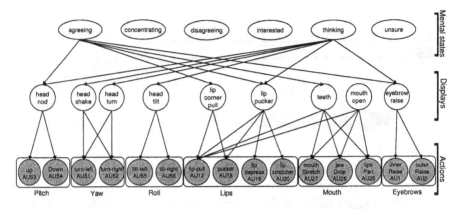

Fig. 3. A video stream is abstracted spatially into head pitch, yaw and roll actions, and lips, mouth and eyebrow actions. The actions are in turn abstracted into displays and mental states. The displays present in a model of a mental state are determined by a feature selection mechanism. For clarity, the displays for only two mental states are shown

For head and facial action extraction, feature points are first located on the face and tracked across consecutive frames using FaceTracker [18], part of Nevenvision's facial feature tracking SDK. Figure 4 describes the 2D model of the face used by the system, and how the head and facial AUs are measured. The motion of expression-invariant feature points over successive frames such as the nose tip, nose root, and inner and outer eye corners are used to extract head rotation parameters. This approach has been successfully used in a number of existing systems [33, 28, 39, 27]. A more accurate, but computationally intensive approach involves tracking the entire head region using a 3D head model [10, 17, 41]. Since our objective was to identify head actions automatically and in real-time, rather than come up with a precise 3D estimate of the head pose, a feature-point based approach was deemed more suitable than a model-based one. Facial actions are identified from motion, shape and colour descriptors derived from the feature points. The shape descriptors capture the deformation of the lips and eyebrows, while the colour-based analysis is used to extract the mouth actions (aperture and teeth).

4.2 Recognition of Head and Facial Displays

Head and facial actions are in turn abstracted into $y = 9$ head and facial displays $\mathbf{Y} = \{Y_1, \ldots, Y_y\}$. Displays are communicative facial events such as a head nod, smile or eyebrow flash. Each display is described by an event that is associated with a particular spatial abstraction as in the action level. Like actions, display events can occur simultaneously. $P(Y_j[t])$ describes the probability that display event j has occurred at time t. For example, Y_1 may

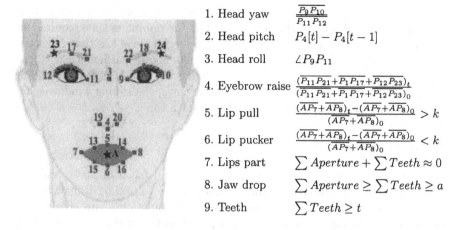

	1. Head yaw	$\frac{P_9 P_{10}}{P_{11} P_{12}}$
	2. Head pitch	$P_4[t] - P_4[t-1]$
	3. Head roll	$\angle P_9 P_{11}$
	4. Eyebrow raise	$\frac{(P_{11}P_{21}+P_1 P_{17}+P_{12}P_{23})_t}{(P_{11}P_{21}+P_1 P_{17}+P_{12}P_{23})_0}$
	5. Lip pull	$\frac{(\overline{AP_7}+\overline{AP_8})_t-(\overline{AP_7}+\overline{AP_8})_0}{(\overline{AP_7}+\overline{AP_8})_0} > k$
	6. Lip pucker	$\frac{(\overline{AP_7}+\overline{AP_8})_t-(\overline{AP_7}+\overline{AP_8})_0}{(\overline{AP_7}+\overline{AP_8})_0} < k$
	7. Lips part	$\sum Aperture + \sum Teeth \approx 0$
	8. Jaw drop	$\sum Aperture \geq \sum Teeth \geq a$
	9. Teeth	$\sum Teeth \geq t$

Fig. 4. Extraction of head and facial actions: (left) the 25 fiducial landmarks tracker per frame; (right) action descriptors. P_i represents point i in the face model

represent the head nod event; $P(Y_1[t]|Z_1[1:t])$ is the probability that a head nod has occurred at time t given a sequence of head pitch actions. We timed the temporal intervals of 50 head-nod (AU53) and 50 head-shake gestures; a single display lasted 1 second on average. Accordingly, the time scale of a single display is 30 frames at 30 fps, or 6 actions. The output progresses one action at a time, i.e., every 166 ms.

To exploit the dynamics of displays, we use Hidden Markov Models (HMMs) for the classification of temporal sequences of actions into a corresponding head or facial display. Although defining the topology of an HMM is essentially a trial-and-error process, the number of states in each HMM were picked such that it is proportional to the complexity of the patterns that each HMM will need to distinguish; the number of symbols were determined by the number of identifiable actions per HMM. Accordingly, the head nod and head shake were implemented as a 2-state, 3-symbol ergodic HMM; episodic head turn and tilt displays as 2-state, 7-symbol HMMs to encode intensity, lip displays such as a smile, or pucker and mouth displays as in a jaw drop or mouth stretch, are represented by a 2-state 3-symbol HMM; the eye-brow raise as a 2-state, 2-symbol HMM. We decided to model the HMM level separately rather than part of the DBN to make the system more modular. For our purposes the two approaches have the same computational complexity.

4.3 Mental State Inference

Finally, at the topmost level, the system represents $x = 6$ mental state events $\{X_1, \ldots, X_x\}$. For example, X_1 may represent the mental state *agreeing*; $P(X_1[t])$ is the probability that *agreeing* was detected at time t. The probability $P(X_i[t])$ of a mental state event is conditioned on the most recently observed displays $\mathbf{Y}[1:t]$, and previous inferences of that mental state $P(X_i[1:t-1])$. We found that two seconds is the minimum time required for a human to reliably infer a mental state; video segments of less than 2 seconds result in inaccurate recognition results [25]. As shown earlier in Fig. 2, we chose to sample these 2 seconds using a sliding window of 30 frames, sliding it 6 times, 5 frames at a time. In terms of displays, the sliding window spans 1 display and progresses 6 times one display at a time.

Representation

We use DBNs to model the unfolding of head and facial displays, and corresponding mental states over time. DBNs are an appealing framework for complex vision-based inference problems. DBNs function as an ensemble of classifiers, where the combined classifier performs better than any individual one in the set [19]. They also incorporate multiple asynchronous cues within a coherent framework, and can model data at multiple temporal scales making them well suited to modelling hierarchically structured human behaviour.

To represent the x mental state classes, we decided to model each mental state as a separate DBN, where the hidden mental state of each DBN represents a mental state event. The event has two possible outcomes: it is true whenever the user is experiencing that mental state, and false otherwise. Having a DBN per class means that the hidden state of more than one DBN can be true; mental states that are not mutually exclusive or may co-occur can be represented by the system.

Like all probabilistic graphical models, a DBN is depicted by its structure and a set of parameters. The structure of the model consists of the specification of a set of conditional independence relations for the probability model, or a set of (missing) edges in the graph. The parameter set θ_i for mental state i is described in terms of an observation function, a state-transition function, and a prior. The observation function B_ϕ is parameterized by conditional probability distributions that model the dependencies between the two nodes. The transition function A encodes temporal dependency between the variable in two slices of the network. The prior π the initial state distributions. The model is given by its joint probability distribution:

$$P(X_i, \mathbf{Y}, \theta) = P(\mathbf{Y}|X_i, B_\phi)P(X_i|A, \pi)$$

4.4 Parameter Learning

When the data is fully observed and the network structure is known, Maximum Likelihood Estimation (MLE) can be used to estimate the parameters of a DBN. When all the nodes are observed, the parameters B_ϕ can be determined by counting how often particular combinations of hidden state and observation values occur. The transition matrix A can be viewed as a second

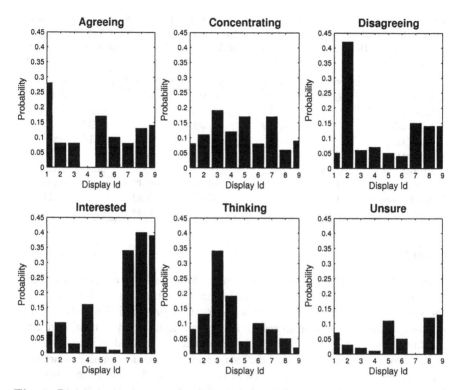

Fig. 5. Discriminative power of head and facial displays in complex mental states. Display Ids: 1:nod, 2:shake, 3:tilt, 4:turn, 5:lip-pull, 6:pucker, 7:mouth open, 8:teeth present, 9:eyebrow raise

histogram which counts the number of transitions between the hidden state values over time.

In addition to the above parameters, we define a heuristic H that quantifies the discriminative power of a display for a mental state: $H = P(Y_j|X_i) - P(Y_j|\overline{X}_i)$. The magnitude of H is an indication of which displays contribute the most (or least) to recognizing specific mental states. The sign depicts whether it increases or decreases the probability of the mental state. Figure 5 summarizes the discriminative power of head and facial displays for 6 different complex mental states.

A post-hoc analysis of the results of parameter estimation yields an insight into the facial expressions of complex mental states. The exercise is an important one given the little literature there is on the facial expressions of these states. The strongest discriminator was the head shake for *disagreeing* (0.42), followed by an eyebrow raise for *interested* (0.40). The analysis shows that single displays are weak classifiers that do not capture complex mental states, verifying the suitability of DBNs.

Table 1. Summary of model selection results. Column i summarizes how the probability of mental state i is affected by observing evidence on each of the displays. Row j depicts the effect of observing display j on the probability of each of the mental states

	agreeing	concentrating	disagreeing	interested	thinking	unsure
head nod	+0.28	-0.08	-0.05	-0.07	-0.08	-0.07
head shake		-0.11	+0.42		-0.13	+0.04
head tilt		-.019	-0.06		+0.34	
head turn					+0.18	
lip corner pull	+0.17	-0.17				-0.1
lip pucker	-0.10				+0.1	+0.06
mouth open	-0.13	+0.07	-0.14	+0.40		-0.05
teeth present	-0.14		-0.14	+0.39		-0.17
eyebrow raise	-0.08	-0.17	-0.15	+0.34	-0.08	

Model Selection

The results of parameter estimation show that the head and facial displays that are most relevant in discriminating mental states are not by necessity the same across mental states. This observation provided the motivation to implement model selection in search for the optimal subset of head and facial displays most relevant in identifying each of the mental states. Using only the most relevant features for the DBN structure reduces the model dimensions without impeding the performance of the learning algorithm, and improves the generalization power of each class by filtering irrelevant features.

Assuming the inter-slice topology is fixed, the problem of feature selection is an optimization one defined as follows: given the set of y displays **Y**, select a subset that leads to the smallest classification error for videos in a test set of size S. Each video in the set yields T instances of mental state inference. The classification error per video per instance is $1 - P(X_i[t])$. Accordingly, the classification error of mental state i is given by the sum of the error over the T instances for all S videos:

$$e_i = \frac{1}{ST} \sum_{s=1}^{S} \sum_{t=1}^{T} (1 - P(X_i[t])) \qquad (1)$$

We implemented sequential backward elimination [31] to find the optimal subset of observation nodes for each mental state. Features are removed recursively such that the classification error, e_i, of the DBN model is minimized. Note that the algorithm does not guarantee a global optima since that depends on the training and test sets used.

The results of sequential backward elimination are summarized in Table 1. A non-blank entry at cell (j, i) implies that display j is present in the DBN model of mental state i; the number is the value of the discriminative-power heuristic H of display j for mental state i. A positive value means that observing display j increases $P(X_i)$; a negative one means that observing display j

decreases that probability. The magnitude depicts the extent with which the probability will change. The columns summarize how each mental state is affected by observing evidence on each of the displays. For instance, the table predicts that an open mouth, teeth or eyebrow raise would increase the probability of *interested*, but a head nod would decrease it (assuming it was non-zero). The row depict the effect of observing a display on the probability of each of the mental states. For instance, observing a head shake would increase the probability of *disagreeing* and *unsure* but would decrease that of *concentrating* and *thinking*. Note that the table only provides a prediction; the actual behaviour of the DBNs will depend on the combination of displays recognized, their dynamics, and the probability of the previous mental states.

5 Recognition Accuracy

The accuracy is a measure of the classification performance of the system on a pre-defined set of classes. Those classes are *agreeing, concentrating, disagreeing, interested, thinking* and *unsure*. The objective of this experiment was to test how well the system performs when the 29 mental state concepts in each of the 6 classes are included. Each concept is represented by 6 videos from the Mind Reading DVD for a total of 174 videos. The challenge that the test posed is that while the concepts share the semantic meaning of the class they belong to, they differ in intensity, in the underlying head and facial displays, and in the dynamics of these displays. To the best of our knowledge, this is the first time different shades of a mental state are included in the evaluation of an automated facial expression analysis system.

5.1 Classification Rule

A classification rule is needed to determine whether or not the result of classifying each video in the test set is a correct one. The classification rule that we have used is a combination of the least-error rule with a threshold rule. The threshold rule was necessary because the least-error rule alone ignores the system's explicit representation of co-occurring mental states. The classification result for a video that is truth-labelled as i is a correct one if $e_i = e_{min}$ or $e_i \leq 0.4$, that is, if the class with the least-error matches the label of the video, or if on the whole the inferences result in the label of the video at least 60% of the time. Figure 6 shows an example display recognition and mental state inference in a 6-second long video labelled as *undecided* from the Mind Reading DVD. Throughout the video, a number of asynchronous displays that vary in duration are recognized: a head shake, a head tilt, a head turn, a lip pucker, and an eye-brow raise. The displays affect the inferred mental states over time as shown in the figure. The error value e is shown for each of the classes over the entire video as in (1). Since *undecided* belongs to the *unsure* class, and *unsure* scored the least error (and also meets the threshold), this is an example of a correct classification.

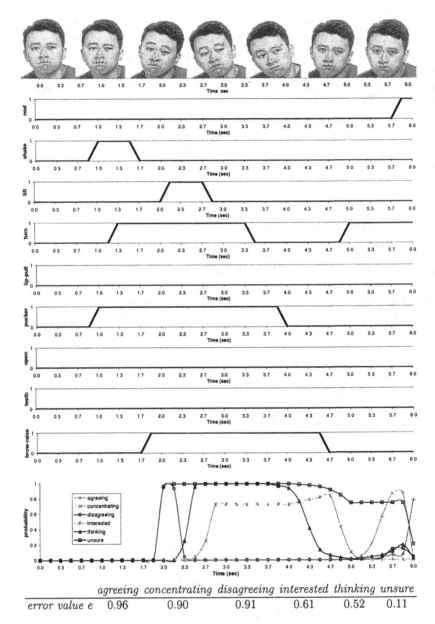

	agreeing	concentrating	disagreeing	interested	thinking	unsure
error value e	0.96	0.90	0.91	0.61	0.52	0.11

Fig. 6. Trace of display recognition and mental state inference in a video labelled as *undecided* from the DVD [5]: (top) selected frames from the video sampled every 1 second; (middle) head and facial displays; (bottom) mental state inferences for each of the six mental state classes and corresponding table of errors. Since the least error is *unsure* and *undecided* belongs to the *unsure* class, this is a correct classification

5.2 Results

Out of the 174 videos, 10 were discarded because `FaceTracker` failed to locate the non-frontal face on the initial frames of the videos. We tested the system on the remaining 164 videos, which spanned 25645 frames or approximately 855 seconds. Using a leave-one-out methodology, 164 runs were carried out, where for each run the system was trained on all but one video, and then tested with that video. Note that chance responding is at 16.7% since this is effectively a 6-way forced choice procedure. Chance responding describes a classifier that picks a class at random, i.e., does not encode any useful information.

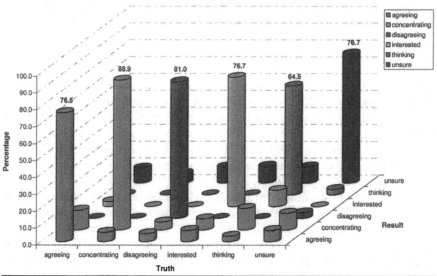

mental state	agreeing	concentrating	disagreeing	interested	thinking	unsure	TP %
agreeing	**26**	4	0	1	0	3	76.5
concentrating	1	**16**	0	0	0	1	88.9
disagreeing	1	1	**17**	0	0	2	81.0
interested	2	2	0	**23**	0	3	76.7
thinking	1	4	0	3	**20**	3	64.5
unsure	2	3	1	0	1	**23**	76.7
FP %	5.4	9.6	0.7	3.0	0.8	9.0	**77.4**

Fig. 7. Recognition accuracy: (top) 3D bar chart of results (bottom) confusion matrix. The last column of the matrix is the true positive (TP) or classification rate for each class; the last row yields the false positive (FP) rate. For a false positive rate of 4.7%, the overall recognition accuracy of the system is 77.4%

The results are summarized in the confusion matrix and 3D bar chart in Fig. 7. Row i of the matrix describes the classification results for mental state i. Column i states the number of times mental state i was recognized. The last column states the true positive (TP) or classification rate for class i. It is given by the ratio of videos correctly classified as mental state i to the total number of videos truth-labelled as i. The bottom row yields the false positive (FP) rate for class i, computed as the ratio of videos falsely classified as i to the total number of videos truth-labelled as anything but i. In the 3D bar chart, the horizontal axis describes the classification results of each mental state class. The percentage that a certain mental state was recognized is given along the z−axis. The classification rate is highest for *concentrating* (88.9%) and lowest for *thinking* (64.5%). The false positive rate is highest for *concentrating* (9.6%) and lowest for *disagreeing* (0.7%). For a mean false positive rate of 5.1%, the overall accuracy of the system is 77.4%.

5.3 Discussion

The overall accuracy of the system (77.4%) and the classification rates of each of the 6 classes are all substantially higher than chance responding (16.7%). Unfortunately, it is not possible to compare the results to those of other systems since there are no prior results on the automated recognition of complex mental states. Instead we compare the results to those reported in the literature of automated recognition of basic emotions, and to human recognition of complex mental states.

The accuracy of automated classifiers of basic emotions typically range between 85–95% [35]. Although this is higher than the results reported here, it is somewhat expected since the basic emotions are by definition easier to identify than complex ones, especially in stimuli that is stripped out of context. From an engineering point of view, the automated recognition of complex mental states is a challenging endeavour compared to basic emotions. This is because basic emotions have distinct facial expressions that are exploited by automated classifiers, while the facial expressions of complex mental states remains an open research problem. In addition, the DVD was not developed with automation in mind, so the videos are technically challenging compared to existing facial expression databases in a number of ways:

- Within-class variation
- Uncontrolled rigid head motion
- Multiple, asynchronous displays
- noisy evidence

Videos within a class vary along several dimensions including the specific mental states they communicate, the underlying configuration and dynamics of head and facial displays, and the physiognomies of the actors. In contrast, the stimuli used in training and evaluating existing automated facial analysis systems are typically more homogeneous, confined to a single prototypic expression of an emotion class. Hence, a video that varies substantially compared to other videos in the class along any of these dimension may end up being misclassified. For instance, only 60% of the videos labelled as *assertive* were correctly classified as *agreeing*. The rest were misclassified as *concentrating* or *unsure* since the underlying displays did not contain a head nod or a lip-corner pull (a smile) the most frequently observed displays in the *agreeing* class. The accuracy results then, will largely depend on the specific concepts that are picked for training and testing in each class and how different are their underlying displays. When the mental state concepts that share the underlying head/facial displays are only the ones picked for training and testing the system, the results reported are much higher. For example, in an earlier version of the system we reported an overall accuracy of 89.5% for 106 videos that cover 24 mental state concepts [24].

In terms of the underlying head and facial displays, there were no restrictions on the head or body movements of the actors, and there were no instructions given on how to act a mental state. Hence, the resulting head gestures and facial expressions are natural, even if the mental state is posed. In addition, while each video is given a single mental state label, it comprises of several asynchronous head and facial displays. Processing displays in context of each other by considering the transitions between displays, boosts the recognition results of humans for complex mental states [25]. Existing automated facial analysis systems of basic emotions, on the other hand, rely solely on facial expressions for classification and do not support the recognition of head gestures. Accordingly, the stimuli used in evaluating these systems is often restricted in terms of rigid head motion: the actors of these images or videos are either asked not to move their head, or are asked to exhibit very controlled head motion, and typically consists of a small number of frames limited to a single facial expression.

Finally, the head and facial display HMM classifiers are imperfect: displays may be misclassified or may pass undetected by the system altogether. Both cases will result in incorrect evidence being presented to the mental state DBNs. Depending on the persistence of the erroneous evidence, its location within the video, and its discriminative power, the resulting mental state inferences may be incorrect. Figure 8 shows an example of misclassification due to noisy evidence. The 5.7 second long video is labelled as *vigilant*, and is in the *concentrating* class. The output starts with a high probability of *concentrating*, which drops to 0 when a head shake is observed at 3.0 seconds. The head shake however, is a falsely detected display that persists for 1 second. At 5.0 seconds the head shake is no longer observed, and the probability of *concentrating* shoots up again. Unfortunately though, the effect of the head shake was such that *concentrating* did not score the least error and did not meet the 0.4 threshold and the video ended up being misclassified.

In a preliminary study [25] we show that human recognition of complex mental states from the Mind Reading DVD [5] is lower than that of the classic basic emotions, and reaches an upper bound of 71% for videos from the DVD.

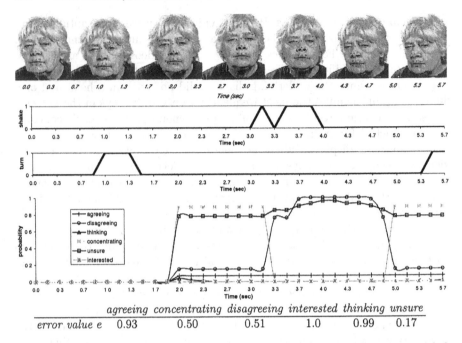

	agreeing	concentrating	disagreeing	interested	thinking	unsure
error value e	0.93	0.50	0.51	1.0	0.99	0.17

Fig. 8. Incorrect classification due to noisy evidence: (top) selected frames – sampled every 1 second – from a video labelled as *vigilant* from the DVD [5]; (middle) head and facial displays; (bottom) mental state inferences for each of the six mental state classes and corresponding table of errors. Note the effect of the false head shake on decreasing the probability of *concentrating*. The rest of the displays are not shown since there was nothing detected by the HMMs

At 77.4%, the results of the automated mind-reading system are comparable to that of humans.

6 Real-Time Performance

Real-time performance pertains to a system's ability to respond to an event without a noticeable delay. Executing in real-time is crucial since the idea is that applications adapt their responses depending on the inferred mental state of the user; it is pointless for an application to respond to a confused user long after she is no longer experiencing this mental state.

6.1 Objectives

The objective of this analysis is to quantify the real-time performance of the automated mind-reading system. The throughput and the latency are typically used to quantify the real-time performance of a vision-based system [40].

The **throughput** is the number of events that are processed per unit time. For the automated mind-reading system, the throughput translates to the number of mental state inferences made per second. The **latency** is defined as the time elapsed, or delay, between the onset of an event and when the system recognizes it. For the automated mind-reading system, the latency translates to the time it takes the system to infer the mental state, from the time a frame is captured.

6.2 Results

The processing time at each level of the system was measured on a 3.4 GHz Pentium IV processor with 2 GB of memory. The results are summarized in Table 2. For feature point tracking, `Facetracker` runs at an average of 3.0 ms per frame of video at a resolution of 320×240 captured at 30 fps. The time taken to extract a single action was sampled over 180 function calls. On average, head-action function calls took 0.02 ms per frame depending on the amount of head motion in the frame; facial-action function calls lasted 0.01 ms per frame. In total, this level of the system executes at 0.09 ms per frame. The time taken to compute the probability of a head/facial display was also sampled over 180 invocations of the HMM inference algorithm. On average, a call to the HMM inference lasts 0.016 ms. Since there are nine displays implemented so far, this level of the system executes at 0.14 ms every five frames. Finally, the implementation of fixed lag smoothing of the six previous inferences using unrolled junction tree inference for a DBN with an average of seven nodes (one hidden mental state and six observation nodes) takes 6.85 ms per slice. Hence, this level executes at 41.10 ms for the six complex mental states.

Table 2. The processing time at each level of the automated mind-reading system (measured on a 3.4 GHz Pentium IV processor with 2 GB of memory)

level	tracking	action-level	display-level	mental state-level	total
time (ms)	3.00	0.09	0.14	41.10	**44.33**

6.3 Discussion

To be deemed as real-time, the throughput of the system has to be at least six instances of mental states inferences per second to keep up with the input. This is because the DBNs are invoked every 5 frames at a capture rate of 30 frames per second. Also, the latency of the system has to be comparable to the latency of high-level facial expression recognition in humans, which ranges between 140–160 ms [7]. In our current implementation, the DBNs are the bottleneck of the system. Nonetheless, since 41.1 ms is less than 166 ms, the system runs in real-time. The total processing time for a frame is 44.34 ms. In terms of scalability, feature-point tracking, the extraction of head and facial actions and displays all run in linear time. At the mental state level, inference runs in polynomial time in the number of nodes [21].

7 Conclusion

The two principal contributions of this chapter are: 1) an automated system for inferring complex mental states, 2) a system that classifies the video input in real-time. The results also yield an insight into the optimal subset of facial and head displays most relevant in identifying different mental states. We reported promising results for the recognition accuracy and speed performance of 6 classes of complex mental states. Further research is needed to test the generalization power of the system by evaluating the system on a completely different previously unseen corpus of videos. The system we have presented serves as an important step towards integrating real-time facial affect inference in man-machine interfaces.

Acknowledgments

The authors would like to thank Professor Simon Baron-Cohen and Ofer Golan at the Autism Research Centre, University of Cambridge for making the Mind Reading DVD available to our research. This research was funded by the Computer Laboratory's Wiseman Fund, the Overseas Research Student Award, the Cambridge Overseas Trust, and Newnham College Studentship Research Award.

References

1. S Baron-Cohen. How to build a baby that can read minds: Cognitive mechanisms in mindreading. *Current Psychology of Cognition*, pp 513–552, 1994.
2. S Baron-Cohen. *Mindblindness: An Essay on Autism and Theory of Mind*. MIT Press, 1995.
3. S Baron-Cohen. *The Essential Difference: The Truth about the Male and Female Brain*. Perseus Publishing, 2003.
4. S Baron-Cohen et al. *A New Taxonomy of Human Emotions*. 2004.
5. S Baron-Cohen et al. *Mind Reading: The Interactive Guide to Emotions*. Jessica Kingsley Publishers, 2004.
6. S Baron-Cohen et al. Reading the mind in the face: A cross-cultural and developmental Study. *Visual Cognition*, pp 39–59, 1996.
7. M Batty and M J Taylor. Early processing of the six basic facial emotional expressions. *Cognitive Brain Research*, pp 613–620, 2003.

8. A Bechara et al. Emotion, decision making, and the orbitofrontal cortex. *Cereb Cortex*, pp 295–307, 2000.
9. R Birdwhistell. *Kinesics and Context*. University of Pennsylvania Press, 1970.
10. M La Cascia et al. Fast, reliable head tracking under varying illumination: An approach based on registration of texture-mapped 3D models. *IEEE Trans PAMI*, pp 322–336, 2000.
11. I Cohen et al. Learning Bayesian network classifiers for facial expression recognition with both labeled and unlabeled data. *Proc CVPR*, 2003.
12. J F Cohn et al. Automated face analysis by feature point tracking has high concurrent validity with manual FACS coding. *Psychophysiology*, pp 35–43, 1999.
13. A R Damasio. *Descartes Error: Emotion, Reason, and the Human Brain*. Putnam Sons, 1994.
14. G Donato et al. Classifying facial actions. *IEEE Trans PAMI*, pp 974–989, 1999.
15. P Ekman. About brows: Emotional and conversational signals. In: M von Cranach (Editor). *Human Ethology*. Cambridge University Press, 1979.
16. P Ekman and W V Friesen. *Facial Action Coding System: A Technique for the Measurement of Facial Movement*. Consulting Psychologists Press, 1978.
17. M Erdem and S Sclaroff. Automatic detection of relevant head gestures in American Sign Language communication. *Proc ICPR*, 2002.
18. FaceTracker. *Facial Feature Tracking SDK*. Neven Vision, 2002.
19. A Garg et al. Bayesian networks as ensemble of classifiers. *Proc ICPR*, 2002.
20. H Gu and Q Ji. Facial event classification with task oriented Dynamic Bayesian Network. *Proc CVPR*, 2004.
21. H Guo and W H Hsu. A Survey of algorithms for real-time Bayesian network inference. *Proc Joint Workshop on Real-Time Decision Support and Diagnosis Systems*, 2002.
22. J Hoey and J J Little. Bayesian clustering of optical flow fields. *Proc ICCV*, 2003.
23. A M Isen. Positive affect and decision making. In: M Lewis and J M Haviland–Jones (Editors). *Handbook of Emotions*. Guilford Press, 2000.
24. R el Kaliouby and P Robinson. Real-time inference of complex mental states from facial expressions and head gestures. *Proc IEEE Workshop on Real-Time Vision for Human-Computer Interaction*, 2004.
25. R el Kaliouby et al. Temporal context and the recognition of emotion from facial expression. *Proc of HCI Int Conf*, 2003.
26. T Kanade et al. Comprehensive database for facial expression analysis. *Proc Int Conf on Automatic Face and Gesture Recognition*, 2000.
27. A Kapoor and R W Picard. A real-time head nod and shake detector. *Proc Workshop on Perceptive User Interfaces*, 2001.
28. S Kawato and J Ohya. Real-time detection of nodding and head-shaking by directly detecting and tracking the "Between-Eyes." *Proc Int Conf on Automatic Face and Gesture Recognition*, 2000.
29. J J Lien et al. Automated facial expression recognition. *Proc Int Conf on Automatic Face and Gesture Recognition*, 1998.
30. G Littlewort et al. Towards social robots: Automatic evaluation of human-robot interaction by face detection and expression classification. In: S Thrun and B Schoelkopf (Editors). *Advances in Neural Information Processing Systems*. MIT Press, 2004.
31. T Marill and D M Green. On the effectiveness of receptors recognition systems. *IEEE Trans IT-9*, pp 11–27, 1963.

32. P Michel and R el Kaliouby. Real-time facial expression recognition in video using Support Vector Machines. *Proc IEEE Int Conf on Multimodal Interfaces*, 2003.
33. C Morimoto et al. Recognition of head gestures using Hidden Markov Models. *Proc ICPR*, 1996.
34. C Padgett and G Cottrell. Identifying emotion in static images. *Proc Joint Symp of Neural Computation*, 1995.
35. M Pantic and L J M Rothkrantz. Automatic analysis of facial expressions: The state of the art. *IEEE Trans PAMI*, pp 1424–1445, 2000.
36. M Pantic and L J M Rothkrantz. Expert system for automatic analysis of facial expressions. *Image and Vision Computing*, pp 881–905, 2000.
37. S Park and J K Aggarwal. Semantic-level understanding of human actions and interactions using event hierarchy. *Proc IEEE Workshop on Articulated and Non-Rigid Motion*, 2004.
38. P Rozin and A B Cohen. High frequency of facial expressions corresponding to confusion, concentration, and worry in an analysis of naturally occurring facial expressions of Americans. *Emotion*, pp 68–75, 2003.
39. Y-L Tian et al. Recognizing action units for facial expression analysis. *IEEE Trans PAMI*, pp 97–115, 2001.
40. M Turk and M Kölsch. Perceptual interfaces. In: G Medioni and S B Kang (Editors). *Emerging Topics in Computer Vision*. Prentice Hall, 2004.
41. J Xiao et al. Robust full motion recovery of head by dynamic templates and re-registration techniques. *Proc Int Conf on Automatic Face and Gesture Recognition*, 2002.
42. Y Zhang and Q Ji. Facial expression understanding in image sequences using dynamic and active visual information fusion. *Proc ICCV*, 2003.

Epipolar Constrained User Pushbutton Selection in Projected Interfaces

Amit Kale, Kenneth Kwan, and Christopher Jaynes

Department of Computer Science and
Center for Visualization and Virtual Environments
University of Kentucky, Lexington
amit@cs.uky.edu
khkwan0@cs.uky.edu
jaynes@cs.uky.edu

An almost ubiquitous user interaction in most HCI applications is the task of selecting one out of a given list of options. For example, in common desktop environments, the user moves the mouse pointer to the desired option and clicks it. The analog of this action in projector-camera HCI environments involves the user raising her finger to touch one of the different virtual buttons projected on a display surface. In this chapter, we discuss some of the challenges involved in tracking and recognizing this task in a projected immersive environment and present a hierarchical vision based approach to detect intuitive gesture-based "mouse clicks" in a front-projected virtual interface.

Given the difficulty of tracking user gestures directly in a projected environment, our approach first tracks shadows cast on the display by the user and exploits the multi-view geometry of the camera-projector pair to constrain a subsequent search for the user's hand position in the scene. The method only requires a simple setup step in which the projector's epipole in the camera's frame is estimated. We demonstrate how this approach is capable of detecting a contact event as a user interacts with a virtual pushbutton display. Results demonstrate that camera-based monitoring of user gesture is feasible even under difficult conditions in which the user is illuminated by changing and saturated colors.

1 Introduction

In the recent past there has been a significant body of research focused on camera projector systems. This is partly due to the observation that camera-based calibration of projected displays allows very-large, cost-effective immersive displays with very little setup or maintenance burden placed on the user [7, 14, 2].

This research has spawned many smart projector applications such as scalable alignment of large multi-projector displays [14, 9], smarter interfaces for controlling computer based presentations [22, 11], and dynamic shadow elimination [8, 1]. Perhaps most importantly, camera-projector research has begun to explore the development of very flexible visually immersive environments, e.g., "Office of the Future" [15] that offer completely new applications.

Given the scientific and commercial interest in these emerging technologies, a natural next step is to exploit the the camera-projector system to support human-computer interaction (HCI) [20, 21]. The system must be able to detect human gesture, interpret the context of the action, and respond appropriately. Understanding human actions is an active area of research in computer vision. However, when this task is transferred from the domain of an ambient (or controlled) environment to a situation in which the user may be illuminated by the projected imagery, the problem takes on a new dimension. For instance, traditional approaches to tracking may fail when the user is illuminated by varying (and saturated) colors. Surprisingly, this situation is likely to occur in many of the new display environments that are emerging from the multi-projector display community.

Although the work presented here assumes the presence of a front-projected display (and cast shadow of the gesture), the assumption is not overly restrictive. In addition, some of the principles used to track and recognize gesture in a front-projection environment can be used to alleviate some of the same problems with tracking user gestures against a changing back-projected display. Front-projected displays are recently used in favor of back-projected and controlled display walls due to lower cost, space savings, and ease of maintenance. Immersive environments that emphasize reconfigurability, and rapid deployment [8], almost certainly cannot assume the presence of backprojection screens. Finally, new applications that emphasize display on everyday surfaces, anywhere [20, 23], by definition cannot support controlled backprojection display. Given these new applications, it is important that camera-based HCI methods are developed that do not degrade when users are illuminated by a projector.

One approach to camera-based HCI in a projected display is to opportunistically capture and process imagery while the projectors are synchronously turned off. This is the approach taken by the the blue-c project [6] that acquires a volumetric model of the user within a projected display. Given the 3D reconstruction of the subject in an immersive environment, event detection can be achieved by directly analyzing the three-dimensional configuration of the user and determining if it corresponds to a particular event. This and similar approaches address the problem of projected illumination by shuttering the projected light to remove its effects from the user [6], detecting and eliminating light projected on the user altogether [1], or simply by disallowing HCI to occur in the frustum of a projector. Although these approaches have met various levels of success, they require specialized hardware (gen-lock and expensive high shutter rate projectors), or make assumptions about the environment (i.e., that the projected image is known or fixed).

A common user input in many HCI applications is the task of selecting one out of a given list of options. Users of common desktop environments achieve this by moving the mouse pointer to the desired option and clicking it. The analog of this action in an immersive environment involves the user raising her finger to touch one of several virtual buttons projected on the display surface. In this chapter, we discuss some of the challenges involved in performing this task in an immersive projected environment and present a hierarchical vision based approach to detect this "mouse click" or contact event. This work is motivated by the following observation: shadows cast by users interacting within an immersive environment are often simpler to detect than the occluder. Detected shadows can constrain the location of the occluder and are often sufficient to recognize simple gestures. Rather than viewing shadows as an obstacle, we can exploit information given by the shadow to expedite the detection of a contact event. Segen and Kumar [16] have used joint shadow and hand information for gesture recognition. However their approach relies on using hue values of skin for detection of the hand region. In projected interfaces or immersive environments detection of skin region (as we shall see in Sect. 2) can be quite difficult.

Initially, the epipole of the projector in the camera's frame is estimated using a novel approach that requires very little user input. The shadow of the hand is detected and tracked using a mean-shift tracker. Using appropriate histogram metrics, the onset of the contact event is detected. The tracked shadow and the projector epipole define a constrained region that could contain the occluding object (hand). Background subtraction is used to extract the hand from the restricted epipolar swath region. The Euclidean distance between the hand centroid and the tracked hand-shadow is computed to detect the contact event. Because we employ geometric constraints, the computational burden normally associated with tracking and monitoring can be reduced and real-time rates can be achieved. Experimental results are presented for the case where a user interacts with three virtual buttons on the screen. Initial results demonstrate that contact approach, and the contact event itself can be measured robustly using our method.

This chapter is organized as follows: in Sect. 2 we discuss challenges in gesture recognition in immersive environments. In Sect. 3 the details of the algorithm are covered. Section 4 presents the experimental results and Sect. 5 concludes the chapter with speculation about how constrained tracking of user gesture via detected shadows may be applied to a wider range of gestures common to user interfaces.

2 Challenges for HCI in Immersive Environments

Most current automated approaches for recognizing hand gestures [12] rely on detection and tracking of skin regions. In order to detect skin regions the raw RGB color values are usually transformed to a color-space where hue is measured against known target values. A comparison of different color-space transformations for skin detection is discussed in [17]. As an example, consider the transformation to the HSV space. Independent of ethnicity, skin regions are restricted to either very low or very high values of hue under ambient lighting and a simple algorithm for skin detection can be obtained by setting appropriate thresholds on hue values in the scene. These settings are fairly robust for a particular (non-changing) lighting scenario.

An immersive environment or even projected interface is fundamentally a constantly changing, interactive display. The changing radiometric characteristics may be approximated and taken into account [8], by underlying image processing algorithms, but these approximations are often insufficient to support straightforward skin detection or are far too complex to estimate and then use at real-time rates. As a user is illuminated with projected information the hue of the skin is transformed based on the color being projected.

One of the ways to deal with this problem is to perform automatic white balancing [4] under a given colored lighting. Assuming that a certain region viewed by the camera is white, we can compensate its color values to remove the bias introduced by non-white illumination. However, white balancing may not correctly restore the hue of the skin regions to their ambient values. Furthermore if more than one color is projected white balancing may become complicated and expensive. This is an issue when real-time performance is desired. Another approach is to model skin appearance under different illuminations by building histograms of skin pixels under different illuminations [18]. Figure 1 shows the RGB and hue images of the hand for ambient and color illuminations. As can be seen, under color illumination some backgrounds can attain hue characteristics of skin. Detection and tracking of skin regions under varying illumination is thus a hard problem. To circumvent this difficulty, it would then be necessary to simply shutter off the projected information [6, 1], or require that the user does not enter the frustum of any projector. Fast shuttering of projected energy requires additional expensive hardware and may not be feasible for large scale multi-projector environments. Turning off projected information has been explored for situations in which users may be "blinded" by projected energy, but requires an accurate model of what is projected at each frame. This information is simply unavailable to an interactive display.

3 Proposed Methodology

The work presented here is motivated by the observation that shadow regions are relatively easy to detect and track even under widely varying illumination.

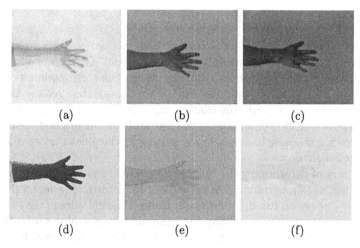

(a)   (b)   (c)

(d)   (e)   (f)

Fig. 1. Images of the hand taken under different illuminations. RGB images for (a) Ambient lighting. (b) Saturated Blue Color. (c) Saturated Magenta Color. Hue images for (d) Ambient lighting. (e) Saturated Blue Color. (f) Saturated Magenta Color

Detection and tracking of the hand regions is a rather formidable problem as we saw in Sect. 2. Ultimately, interface gestures are performed by the user and his/her hands and not the shadows on the display surface. However, by tracking the shadow we can infer the appropriate search region for the hand in the scene. Moreover, the position of *both* the shadow and the casting object can yield information to a gesture recognition system. Here we detail how we track both regions (when appropriate) and how the measured distance between the hand and its shadow is a robust image-based measure of detecting the contact event.

Considering the non-rigid nature of the hand, a mean-shift tracker is used to track the centroid of this hand-shadow region. It is necessary to track the hand centroid only when the hand is close to the screen containing the virtual buttons. This proximity of the hand to the screen can be detected by the occlusion of the shadow of the hand by the hand itself. After detecting the onset of contact, the estimated epipolar geometry between the camera and projector can be used to restrict the search region for the hand. Additional information about the approximate color-mapping between the camera and projector as well as the contents of the projector frame buffer at any given instant is then used to detect the presence of the user's hand within this small search region. The Euclidean image distance between the centroid of the tracked hand shadow and the centroid of the hand region is measured and when this distance drops below a threshold, the color in the neighborhood of the hand shadow centroid is declared to be the corresponding virtual button "pressed" by the user.

3.1 Projector Epipole Estimation

A data projector is a dual of a camera and the projection process can be modeled using the standard pinhole camera model. Given a shadow on the display surface and detected in a camera image, the corresponding occluding object must lie along an epipolar line in the image that relates the multi-view geometry of the projector-camera pair. Our approach is to estimate the position of this projector epipole in the frame of the camera and the constrain the search for the user hand via the implied epipolar lines that emanate from the detected shadow.

One way of determining the epipole for a camera-projector pair is to compute a pair of homographies between them by determining matchpoints between the devices on two different world planes. The epipoles in the two images can then be computed by solving the generalized eigenvalue problem for the two homographies [10]. This idea was used by Raskar and Beardsley [13] as an intermediate step in the camera-projector calibration problem. In order to obtain the homographies it is necessary to vary the configuration of the system with respect to the plane which can prove to be cumbersome. For our problem all we need to restrict the search space for the hand is the location of the projector epipole. A much simpler approach can be used in order to do this. Presence of an occluder in the frustum of the projector will cast a shadow on the screen. In an image of the object and its shadow, the line joining a point on the object and its shadow will pass through the projector epipole. Thus, given two pairs of corresponding object-shadow points, the join of their lines determines the epipole. More formally, let (o_1, s_1) and (o_2, s_2) be the image plane coordinates (expressed in homogeneous coordinates) of two distinct world points. Then the epipole e can be determined as

$$e = l_1 \times l_2 \tag{1}$$

where $l_1 = o_1 \times s_1$ and $l_2 = o_2 \times s_2$ where $\times$ represents the cross product. In practice, it is necessary to consider more points when estimating the epipole. A simple way to do this is to simply move a suitable object in the field of view of the camera. Pairs of points on the object and their corresponding shadows can be used to generate the lines passing through the projector epipole. Using these lines and (1) estimates of the epipoles can be obtained. During this bootstrapping process, the projector is instructed to project white to alleviate the tracking problems that this chapter addresses.

3.2 Mean-Shift Tracking

In order to track the shadow it is necessary to compute the location of the hand shadow in the first image. Prior shape information about the hand shadow regions and the location of the shadow can constrain the initial tracking system. One way to compute the location of the hand shadow is to use the chamfer

system [5]. Alternatively, if the approximate areas where shadows are likely
to emerge on the display are known, simpler search techniques can be used.

The intensity histogram of the image patch around the detected centroid of
the hand-shadow region as it emerges from the edge of the monitoring camera
defines the target histogram. Taking into account the non-rigid nature of
the hand, we use the mean-shift tracking algorithm of Comaniciu et al. [3] to
robustly update the estimated position of the cast shadow. Mean-shift tracking
is based on maximizing the likelihood of the model (hand shadow) intensity
distribution and the candidate intensity distribution using the Bhattacharyya
coefficient.

$$\rho(\mathbf{m}) = \sum_{u=1}^{n} \sqrt{q_u p_u(\mathbf{m})} \tag{2}$$

where $\mathbf{m}$ is the center of the hand region, n is the number of bins in the
distribution, and q_u and p_u are the weighted histograms of the model and
candidate respectively. The weights for the histograms are obtained using the
Epanechnikov kernel. The center of the hand region in the next frame is found
using

$$\mathbf{m}_{\mathrm{new}} = \frac{\sum_{i=1}^{n_h} \mathbf{x}_i w_i g(\|\mathbf{m}_{\mathrm{old}} - \mathbf{x}_i\|)}{\sum_{i=1}^{n_h} w_i g(\|\mathbf{m}_{\mathrm{old}} - \mathbf{x}_i\|)} \tag{3}$$

where $\mathbf{x}_i$ are the pixels in the image patch, g is the derivative of the Epanechnikov kernel and n_h denotes the number of pixels. The weights w_is are computed as

$$w_i = \sum_{u=1}^{n} \delta[b(\mathbf{x}_i) - u] \sqrt{\frac{q_u}{p_u(\mathbf{m})}} \tag{4}$$

where $\delta(.)$ is the Kronecker delta function and $b(.)$ is a function that associates
to a pixel the index of the histogram bin corresponding to the intensity value
associated with the pixel. As the hand starts making contact with the virtual
buttons the shadow of the hand starts getting occluded by the hand. This
occlusion of the hand-shadow indicates the onset of contact. In order to detect
this, it is necessary to compare the tracked shadow region in the neighborhood
of its centroid in the present frame to the target histogram. One measure could
simply be the number of shadow pixels. This measure is not scale invariant
however. It is more appropriate to consider scale invariant metrics, e.g., the
Bhattacharyya distance which is also used for the mean-shift tracker

$$d_{\mathrm{Bhattacharyya}}(p, q) = \sqrt{1 - \sum_{u=1}^{n} \sqrt{q_u p_u(\mathbf{m})}} \tag{5}$$

Another scale-invariant histogram distance metric is the chi-squared distance
defined by (6) which has been used in [19] for scene change detection in digital
video sequences

$$d_{\chi^2} = \sum_{u=1}^{n} \frac{(q_u - p_u(\mathbf{m}))^2}{(q_u + p_u(\mathbf{m}))} \tag{6}$$

Fig. 2. A few images taken from our experimental setup. The white lines connect the corners of the window enclosing the hand shadow region to the epipole

3.3 Detection of the Contact Event

A simple way of detecting contact is to consider the value of this metric as a function of time. When the metric is sufficiently large, contact can be assumed to have occurred. However this simple scheme has the disadvantage that the extent to which the hand occludes the shadow varies based on the location of the user with respect to the display. Hence it is more appropriate to use this temporal metric information only to signal the onset of contact. Once the onset of the contact has been detected it is necessary to detect the true hand position in the image plane. Knowing the projector epipole, a simple way to limit the search region is to construct a swath region starting at the corners of the window enclosing the hand shadow centroid. Furthermore, since the hand is assumed to be close to the shadow when the shadow begins to be occluded it is possible to limit the depth of this epipolar swath.

Given this implied search area on the image plane, there are several options to determining the location of the users hand. One way is to compute an edge-map within the swath region and compute its centroid. On nearing contact the centroid of this edge-map would be expected to merge with the centroid of the hand shadow. Alternatively if the image displayed by the projector does not change too rapidly and the color transfer function between the camera and projector is known, a simple background differencing between the swath region in the current image and the reference image can be used to detect the presence of the hand.

4 Experimental Results

The approach was tested using a single- ceiling mounted projector p while a camera, mounted approximately 20 degrees off-axis also on the ceiling monitors the scene. Three different colored buttons were projected and the subject was instructed to touch each button sequentially. Figure 2 shows a few images from the dataset. This section discusses the implementation details of our approach and explores the robustness of the virtual touchbutton detection system.

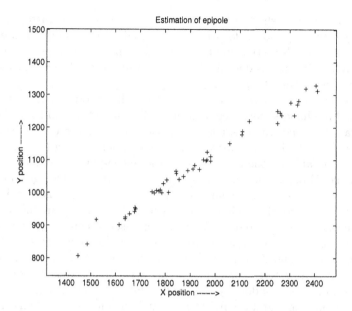

Fig. 3. Estimates of epipoles obtained by considering pairs of object-shadow points from several images of a rectangular board

In order to use this method it is necessary to compute the epipole. As discussed in Sect. 3, this requires several object-shadow point correspondences. In order to simplify the task of establishing correspondence, a rectangular board was moved around in the field of view of the camera. About 40 images were captured and the estimates of epipole locations were obtained using (1). Figure 3 shows the estimated epipoles. Since the camera and projector axes are almost parallel to each other there is considerable variance in the estimated epipoles. The epipole used in our experiments is the mean of this cloud of points. Clearly, the approach is unable to provide accurate information about the epipole position for traditional multi-view calibration tasks. However, only a rough estimate is required to constrain the subsequent search of the user's hand position.

Assuming that the person has an outstretched finger for the touchbutton gesture, the initial shadow region in the image is detected by thresholding the intensity values and analyzing the shape characteristics of the cast shadow. Of course the shadow changes shape according to a perspective projection of the hand to the display surface so these shape constraints must be quite weak. A rectangular binary mask is translated horizontally and its correlation with the shadow regions is computed. Since we assume an outstretched finger, the correlation in the finger (shadow) region will be smaller than that in the hand (shadow) region. The first instance of a large change in the correlation value can be used to approximately detect the hand shadow region. Given the estimated hand shadow location in the first frame, the histogram of the intensity values around the location is computed. This histogram is used as the target histogram. Note that unlike [3] the target histogram is one-dimensional. Mean shift iterations as described in [3] are used to track the centroid of the hand shadow in each frame.

In order to detect the onset of contact, the distance between the histogram of the hand-shadow region around the tracked centroid and the target histogram for each frame is computed. Note that at the end of each mean shift iteration the Bhattacharyya distance, computed using (5), between the target histogram and the histogram for the image-patch around the centroid is available. However we wanted to explore if a different histogram distance, e.g., chi-squared distance, computed using (6) would be more suitable for this task. Both the Bhattacharyya distance and the chi-square histogram distance measures were tested for detection of onset of contact. Figure 4 shows a comparison of the distance measures for a video sequence of the person touching the virtual buttons and then withdrawing. The peaks in the plot correspond to the person making contact with the virtual buttons (caused by occlusion of the shadow by the hand) while the valleys correspond to the persons hand being far away from the virtual buttons(no occlusion). The solid curve shows the chi-squared distance while the dash-dotted curve shows the Bhattacharyya distance as a function of time. As can be seen from this figure, for a fixed threshold, the chi-squared distance exceeds the threshold less frequently than the Bhattacharyya distance. This is because the chi-square distance, since it uses the square of the difference in the histogram values, penalizes differences more when they are large, whereas small differences are penalized less. For the case shown in Fig. 4 and for a threshold chosen to be 0.2, the chi-squared distance exceeds the threshold for 30% of the frames while the Bhattacharyya distance does so for 60% of the frames. Furthermore none of the true contact onsets were missed by the chi-squared distance for the chosen threshold. Since crossing the threshold implies that the hand centroid must be computed, using the chi-squared distance leads to a reduction in the amount of computation as compared to the Bhattacharyya distance. When the chi-squared distance exceeds the specified threshold, it is necessary to look for the hand. Given the approximate location of the epipole (obtained as discussed earlier) the search region is restricted appropriately. In particular we consider a window around the tracked position of the hand shadow. The epipolar swath region is determined by the lines joining the opposite corners of the window with the epipole. Figure 2 shows the epipolar swath region constructed for a few images in our dataset. Furthermore, since the onset of contact has been detected by the histogram distance, it is not necessary to consider the entire epipolar swath. It is sufficient to traverse a limited distance along the epipolar swath direction. Figure 5a shows the intensity image within the delimited swath region. Since the camera and projector axes are almost parallel the lines connecting the corners of the window to the epipole are almost parallel to each other. Given this delimited epipolar swath region

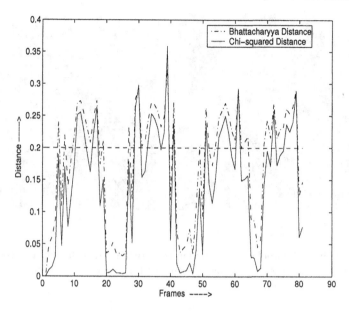

Fig. 4. Comparison between Bhattacharyya and chi-squared distances for detection of onset of contact. Observe that for a given threshold the chi-squared distance has fewer crossovers

it is necessary to compute the hand centroid in this region. One approach to this problem is to consider the edge-map within this region. This edge map would consist of edges from the hand as well as the shadow regions. As the hand starts making contact with the screen the centroid of the combined edge region would be expected to merge with the centroid of the hand shadow. However the drawback of this approach is that as the person makes contact with the middle and top buttons, his/her hand passes through at least one other button. This results in detection of spurious edges which causes the centroid computation to be unstable and resulting in false positives. Hence a more robust approach must be sought. Assuming that the display does not change very rapidly and that the color calibration between the camera and projector is known, one simple solution to this problem is to consider a simple pixel-wise background subtraction within the delimited swath region. As the number of pixels in this region is significantly smaller than that of the entire region (less than 4% of the total number of pixels in most cases)the added computational burden is not as significant as compared to an approach that uses background subtraction for the entire image. In particular the hand region is computed as

$$
I_{\text{hand}}(i,j) = \begin{cases} 1 & \text{if } (i,j) \in E_S \text{ and } |I_{\text{hand}}(i,j) - I_{\text{ref}}(i,j)| > T_1 \text{ and} \\ & \text{and } I_{\text{hand}}(i,j) > T_2 \\ 0 & \text{otherwise} \end{cases}
$$

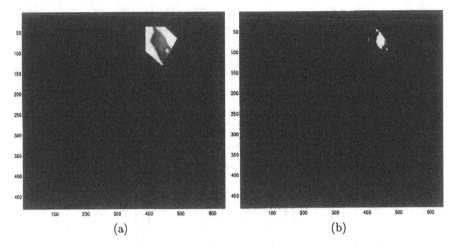

Fig. 5. Delimited epipolar swath region constructed after the onset of contact has been detected. (a) Intensity Image. (b) Binary Image showing the hand region after background subtraction

where E_S denotes the epipolar swath, T_1 denotes a threshold to determine if the pixel is a foreground pixel, and T_2 is a threshold to determine if the pixel is a shadow pixel. The estimated hand region corresponding to the intensity image in Fig. 5a is shown computed from the above equation is shown in Fig. 5b. The Euclidean distance between the tracked shadow centroid and the hand region is then computed. When the distance falls below a certain threshold, contact is declared. The color of region in the neighborhood of the contact region can be inspected to take the appropriate course of action.

Figure 6 shows the Receiver Operating Characteristics (ROC) plots for the contact event (hypothesis H_1) versus no contact (hypothesis H_0). The ROC plots the probability of detection of the contact event (P_D) against the probability of a false alarm (P_F). The video was analyzed manually to detect which frames had the contact event happen in them. The threshold for the histogram distance was set at a value so that no contact event was missed. The plot was generated by varying the threshold on the Euclidean distance between the hand and shadow regions and counting the number of times the contact event gets detected when no contact has occurred (for P_F) and when contact has occurred (for P_D), for a given threshold. The total number of frames was 243 out of which 31 frames had the contact event happen.

The ROC can be used to choose a threshold to get a good tradeoff between P_D and P_F.

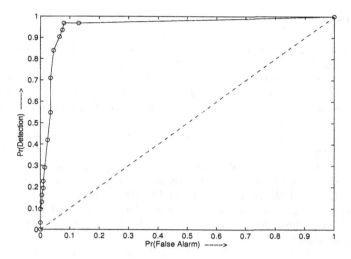

Fig. 6. Receiver Operating Characteristics for the contact event (hypothesis H_1) versus no contact (hypothesis H_0)

5 Conclusions and Future Work

In this chapter we presented a method for detecting contact events which can work under the arbitrary lighting conditions typically encountered in an interactive, projected display. Instead of using skin tone detection (which can be unreliable under varying lighting conditions), the approach focuses on the shadow cast by the hand. The location of the hand shadow is detected and tracked using a mean shift tracker. Since the hand occludes the shadow before contact happens, the deformation of the hand-shadow region is then used to detect the onset of contact. A novel method which required very little user input was introduced to estimate the projector epipole. After detecting the onset of contact, the epipole was used to define a restricted search region for the hand. Background subtraction was then used to extract the hand from the restricted epipolar swath region. The Euclidean distance between the hand centroid and the tracked hand-shadow was computed to detect the contact event. The experimental results showed that the contact approach and the contact event itself can be measured robustly using our method.

Our approach used a single-camera projector pair. Future work would focus on achieving greater view invariance. For instance, in the experimental setup we have considered, there are certain positions in the camera's field of view in which the person completely occluded the hand-shadow.One possible approach to remedy this situation would be to use multiple cameras. It would also be interesting to use 3D information about the hand by using the shadow and a full calibration between the camera-projector pair similar to Segen and Kumar [16].

References

1. T Cham et al. Shadow elimination and occluder light suppression for multi-projector displays. *Proc CVPR*, 2003.
2. H Chen et al. Scalable alignment of large-format multi-projector displays using camera homography trees. *Proc IEEE Visualization*, 2002.
3. D Comaniciu et al. Real time tracking of non-rigid objects using mean shift. *Proc CVPR*, 2000.
4. D A Forsyth. A novel algorithm for color constancy. *Int J Computer Vision*, pp 5–36, 1990.
5. D M Gavrila. Pedestrian detection from a moving vehicle. *Proc ECCV*, 2000.
6. M Gross et al. Blue-c: A spatially immersive display and 3D video portal for telepresence. *ACM Trans Graphics*, pp 819–827, 2003.
7. C Jaynes et al. The metaverse – A networked collection of inexpensive, self-configuring immersive environments. *Proc Int Workshop on Immersive Projection Technology*, 2003.
8. C Jaynes et al. Dynamic shadow removal from front projection displays. *Proc ACM SIGGRAPH*, 1998.
9. C Jaynes et al. A scalable framework for high-resolution immersive displays. *Int J Electrical and Technical Engineering Research*, pp 278–285, 2002.
10. B Johansson. View synthesis and 3D reconstruction of piecewise planar scenes using intersection lines between the planes. *Proc ICCV*, 1999.
11. C Pinhanez. Creating ubiquitous interactive games using everywhere displays projectors. *Proc Int Workshop on Entertainment Computing*, 2002.
12. C Rao et al. View-invariant representation and recognition of actions. *Int J Computer Vision*, pp 203-226, 2002.
13. R Raskar and P A Beardsley. A self-correcting projector. *Proc CVPR*, 2001.
14. R Raskar et al. Multi-projector displays using camera-based registration. *Proc IEEE Visualization*, 1999.
15. R Raskar et al. The office of the future: A unified approach to image-based modeling and spatially immersive displays. *Proc ACM SIGGRAPH*, 1998.
16. J Segen and S Kumar. Shadow gestures: 3D hand pose estimation using a single camera. *Proc CVPR*, 1999.
17. M C Shin et al. Does colorspace transformation make any difference on skin detection? *Proc Workshop on Applications of Computer Vision*, 2002.
18. M Soriano et al. Skin detection in video under changing illumination conditions. *Proc ICPR*, 2000.
19. R M Soriano et al. Metrics for scene change detection in digital video sequences. *Proc IEEE Int Conf on Multimedia Computing and Systems*, 1997.
20. N Sukaviriya et al. Augmenting a retail environment using steerable interactive displays. *Proc Conf on Human Factors in Computing Systems*, 2003.
21. R Sukthankar et al. Self-calibrating camera-assisted presentation interface. *Proc Int Conf on Control, Automation, Robotics, and Computer Vision*, 2000.
22. R Sukthankar et al. Smarter presentations: Exploiting homography in camera-projector systems. *Proc ICCV*, 2001.
23. R Yang and G Welch. Automatic projector display surface estimation using every-day imagery. *Proc Int Conf on Computer Graphics, Visualization, and Computer*, 2001.

## Part III

Looking Ahead

## Book III

Vision-Based HCI Applications

Eric Petajan

face2face animation, inc.
eric@f2f-inc.com

Vision-based HCI promises to simultaneously provide much more efficient communication from human to computer, and increased security using biometric identity verification. This chapter describes mature and currently deployed applications while offering reasons for slow deployment. System architecture and social issues are also explored resulting in the recommendation of a client-server architecture with standards like MPEG-4 Face and Body Animation (FBA) for optimal resource utilization; especially given the rapid adoption of powerful mobile devices as the primary HCI device.

1 Introduction

A growing number of people are spending more and more time interacting with electronic machines that are increasingly mobile, wireless, and compact. The world is in love with mobile devices as evidenced by the one billion phones in use today. While personal computer users will continue to spend time with larger fixed displays or medium sized portable displays, many times more people will own mobile phones with small displays. Eventually, the choice of display size will be independent of the choice of content. This independence is well on its way to realization as we watch video on our phones and drive our flat screen HDTV displays with computers. The cost of mobile web access is dropping rapidly while handsets are offered with a range of display sizes from tiny to a handful. The drop in cost of HD displays has caused a proliferation of flat panel displays in public spaces, the workplace, vehicles, and, of course, the home. In general, the flow of information from machine to human has progressed steadily with improvements in display technology, graphics chips, bandwidth, and battery life. However, the flow of information from human to machine is still mostly limited by the keyboard and mouse for the input of symbolic and spatial information. This one-way bottleneck in communication is especially constricted with mobile devices where keyboards are not very practical and require much more effort to use. If one's hands or eyes are busy while driving, walking, or handling something, the use of all but the simplest tactile interfaces is impractical or even hazardous for most people. Fortunately, the audio-visual computer input modalities can be used when the hands, eyes and ears are busy. Furthermore, the physical size of cameras, microphones, and processors will eventually be smaller than the smallest mobile display.

Each HCI modality has distinct advantages and limitations. An optimal HCI system should provide the user with the right combination of tactile, audio and visual modes given the amount of mobility and information exchange required at the time. The visual input modality is the least developed due to hardware cost and system complexity. The audio/speech input modality is still not reliable enough for widespread use, but integration with visual speech and gesture [1] recognition should significantly increase tolerance for audio mode recognition errors. Speech and gesture recognition are both the most widely used and natural human communication modes, and the least supported in current HCI systems. Most people can speak much faster than they can type and if Automatic Speech Recognition (ASR) was faster and more reliable it would be widely used for HCI. The incorporation of visual speech recognition into ASR promises [2, 3, 4] to provide sufficient robustness for general use. Simultaneously, face and voice recognition could also be deployed to identify the user. Finally, as vision-based HCI becomes a personal appliance that is always on and networked, audio and visual privacy will need to be secured and reliably controlled by the user. As the other electronic components continue miniaturization, the size and power consumption of the display will eventually be the first consideration when the user chooses an information appliance. Power consumption can be minimized at any time by placing as many applications on servers as possible while treating the personal appliance as a thin client.

While this book deals with vision-based interfaces, the audio modality is a necessary component of the ultimate HCI. Since the human face is the center of human communication, a primary requirement of vision-based HCI systems must be the capture and understanding of speech and emotional state using both audio and visual modalities. These two modes are uniquely suited for the acquisition of human behavior in that no physical contact is required, freeing the hands to perform other tasks. However, the lack of physical contact between human and device increases the possibility that audio or visual information about or associated with the user will be inadvertently transmitted to unintended recipients. Given the fallible nature of human beings and the lack of security inherent in legacy networks and computers, a secure privacy solution will necessarily be implemented as part of the local audio/visual acquisition system. It should also provide the user with continuous feedback and training for optimal positioning, voice level, and use of gestures, while maintaining awareness of the user's presence and identity. Limitations, some temporary and some fundamental, have impeded the realization of this utopian HCI system. This chapter explores how the receding of limitations should result in significant progress toward vision-based HCI for the masses, while certain applications are enabled in the short term.

2 System Architecture Considerations

The simultaneous demand for mobility, access to resources and information, and visual privacy points to the use of a client-server architecture where the HCI is part of a thin client with reliable data communication to the server. Given that state-of-the-art video codecs can't compress video enough for low latency transmission over consumer networks, the vision processing must be performed locally. The human features that result from vision processing can be easily compressed for further processing, either locally, or on a server depending on the remaining local resources. The avoidance of video transmission across the network is also required to protect visual privacy.

2.1 The Mobile Energy Crisis

The consumer electronics industry has succeeded in packing large amounts of processing power into small devices. If necessary, custom VLSI can be used to realize virtually any computer vision system on a single chip. Unfortunately, power requirements limit the clock speed and performance of VLSI in mobile applications. Fuel cells may eventually become practical but for now small, wireless devices are fundamentally limited in processing power by battery life and size, and storage capacity and retrieval speed are also limited by energy supply. The impact of energy storage limitations on mobile device performance is reduced by the availability of wireless communication networks that can provide distributed processing and data storage. However, wireless communication (and especially transmission from the wireless device) also consumes power in proportion to bandwidth. Fortunately, a variety of audio, video, graphics, and data compression standards are available to optimize the tradeoff between bandwidth and codec processing requirements.

Wireless vision-based HCI devices must process video from one or more cameras in real-time and deliver the resulting human behavior data stream to an application which performs a desired function. While video compression algorithms have progressed steadily over the years, the delivery of high quality video over wireless networks requires either too much power or too much bandwidth to be practical today. These limitations and the negative effects on vision algorithm performance from video coding artifacts will force the placement of vision processing onto the wireless device. Fortunately, the human behavior data stream is highly compressible and can be transmitted over any wireless network using standards such as MPEG-4 [5, 6].

2.2 User Imaging and Cooperation

An inherent challenge facing vision-based HCI is imaging of the user. The video camera solutions for a particular application environment must address both resolution requirements and camera position and orientation. The continued improvements and reduced cost of CCD and CMOS image sensors has recently made HD video capture available at SD video prices. In particular, the availability of 60 frame per second, HD progressive scan, color video cameras provides new levels of detail and increased field of view. The use of camera pan/tilt controllers further expands the user's freedom of movement.

If performance is more important than cost, size or power consumption, then multiple cameras should be used to provide depth from stereo, reduce occlusions, and reduce feature extraction errors by averaging or outlier removal. Stereo imaging certainly provides better face detection and tracking performance than single camera imaging and face tracking must be reliable enough to perform subsequent individual feature tracking (e.g., eyes and mouth). However, detailed stereo imaging of the face is fundamentally difficult due to a combination of smooth patches (cheeks), holes (nostrils, mouth), and hair; all of which can cause these algorithms to fail. Alternatively, features extracted from each camera can be combined by either averaging or removing outliers. Also note that stereo imaging performance is strongly affected by camera separation which should be optimized for the expected range of the subject. If stereo correspondence is not used, cameras can be placed to accommodate any range of subject motion, or placed in a cluster to increase resolution and/or field of view. Ultimately, a combination of stereo and feature integration can be deployed subject to camera placement constraints.

When automatic user imaging fails, the user can be engaged to either move the HCI device or move her self into view. At this point in the HCI session, the system must present an audio and/or visual display to the user assuming that she intends to interact with the system. In many application scenarios, the content of this display must be understandable to new users with neither experience nor prior intention to use the system. Since people are especially attentive to the human face and voice, the display of a talking human, humanoid, or character is the best way to engage the user in a dialog and optimize her position relative to the camera(s) and microphone(s). The implementation of a talking virtual agent is partitioned into the animation system and the language system. The language system sends animation instructions to the animation system with associated synchronized voice. The stream of animation instructions is inherently low in bit-rate after compression and the animation system is only moderately complex. However, the language system can be very complex and require access to large speech databases and sufficient processing power for real-time response. The best solution for this combination of conditions is, again, a client-server architecture.

2.3 Lighting

The type and position of light sources in the environment obviously directly determine the image signal to noise ratio and variations in appearance of objects in the scene. The degree to which lighting can be controlled or predicted depends on a variety of conditions including user comfort, level of mobility of the HCI device, exposure to sunlight, and the physical/economic practicality of light fixture placement. Non-visible light sources (near infrared) can provide some relief from user comfort issues but must be used cautiously to avoid injury to the retina. Infrared imaging can also be used for some applications.

One's face, body, clothing and accessories are rich with stable color information; at least for some period of time in the case of skin. The ideal camera would be sensitive from infrared to ultraviolet with each pixel expressed as a spectral array of intensities. Image sensors today have non-uniform sensitivity and rely on optical filters to quantize the spectrum. Therefore additional technology with significant additional cost is needed to produce broad-spectrum cameras. The camera is still the cost driver in many applications so the added cost of non-visible imaging may be difficult to justify in consumer applications.

People are quite sensitive to lighting; especially if they are trying to read a screen in a well-lit environment. Diffuse lighting is more comfortable than point sources, and minimizing lighting contrast is also important. Another advantage of diffuse lighting is that shadows are minimized and surface appearance is more stable. A disadvantage of diffuse lighting is that "shape from shading" algorithms are less useful.

2.4 Dialog Systems

The need for a dialog system [7] depends on the predictability of the user's behavior and objectives and also on the degree of user cooperation. For example, at one extreme, no dialog system is needed for vision-based surveillance because the user is not cooperative at all. An example at the other extreme would be an immersive virtual environment with interactive virtual humans or characters. The modes of a given dialog system are chosen based on each modes attributes and weaknesses. The dispersion of the human voice is both useful for broadcast communication and problematic when privacy is desired or noise pollution is a concern. The tactile input mode (keyboard, mouse, touch screen) is tedious for most people but privacy is easier to maintain. The visual capture of human behavior (emotional state, speech, body position) can be accomplished without disturbing others, at a distance, or covertly. However, the reliable capture of arbitrary human behavior in a surveillance environment is still a research frontier. In general, the presentation of audio and visual information to users can be accomplished with the desired degree of privacy; while the user's voice is the most difficult machine input mode to keep private. In addition, the acquisition and recognition of the user's voice is strongly affected by both voice volume and distance to the microphone, compelling users of current systems to speak loudly even if the microphone is close to the mouth. The acoustic input mode suffers from pollution, reliability, and privacy issues. The visual input mode also suffers from reliability issues but should enhance the performance of the acoustic input mode and reduce and possibly eliminate the need for higher voice volume.

The reliable capture of audio/visual user behavior is more easily accomplished when the user is guided and trained and the system can predict when additional guidance and training dialog are needed. While machine understanding of free speech has yet to be fully realized, user speech and emotional state recognition can be used to improve machine understanding of user intent, especially when the user is trained to limit the dialog domain. The achievement of unrestricted dialog between human and machine would be the most convincing demonstration of artificial intelligence. Only a client-server architecture can provide the heavy resources needed to achieve the most advanced dialog systems.

2.5 Privacy and Security

The need for security and user identity verification in all computing and network systems could be satisfied using audio/visual HCI. The rigorous engineering and careful deployment required for any secure system is especially needed with a vision-based system because security is needed for both the visual privacy control and access control subsystems. Fortunately, the real-time acquisition of human behavior data on a local device could provide protection of visual privacy while allowing accurate identity verification over a wireless network by avoiding the transmission of video over the network. The user must be able to reliably control the flow of camera-generated video that is output from the local device. Automatic camera control and video communication systems must be carefully designed to ensure that user cooperation and understanding are maintained. While consumer software companies are not accustomed to lawsuits for malfunction and the typical End User License Agreement (EULA) is notoriously one sided, violations of privacy and security that result from poor design could cause consumer revolt or impede adoption.

2.6 Multi-Model Biometrics

The post 9/11 focus on biometrics-based security has resulted in accelerated deployment of available systems and a government drive to collect biometrics information from as many citizens as possible. The need for identity verification is clear but commercial systems available today suffer from low accuracy, vulnerability to spoofing, or civil rights and privacy issues. For example, a static biometric such as fingerprints can be copied in order to spoof the system. Fingerprints can also be left behind and used to track the past location of people enrolled in the system without their knowledge. Face recognition is not very reliable and is also spoofable. It has the advantage of not requiring physical contact with the user and being socially acceptable. Voice recognition accuracy degrades badly in noisy environments but is difficult to spoof (in quiet conditions) if a challenge response protocol is used (prompting the user for particular utterances). The combination of face and voice recognition and visual speech recognition promises to provide identity verification with much greater accuracy than either mode alone without vulnerability to spoofing. Iris scan is also an option that can be incorporated into access control system applications where lighting and close-view cameras can be used. When the motivation to spoof the system is high and only static biometrics (hand, finger, face, and iris) are collected for unattended access there is a danger of dismemberment by violent criminals. The use of audio/visual biometrics promises to provide accurate identity verification at a distance without endangering the user or violating his privacy. A client-server architecture provides the best protection of user images and voice by secure containment in the HCI device while enabling access control over low bit-rate networks by transmission of compressed audio/visual biometric features (e.g., MPEG-4).

3 Common Application Environments

People need access to information and other people on a moment by moment basis using constantly varying modes that are optimized dynamically. The mobile phone/PDA is currently a handheld voice (and limited video) communicator with less than 50 kilobits per second of reliable bandwidth and adequate audio/visual display. Vision-based user input to mobile phones is currently processor limited but could be implemented in VLSI in the relative near term. Vision-based HCI in vehicles, home, office and public terminals is not constrained by stringent power and size requirements and will be deployed much sooner using commodity components. This section examines how each major application environment presents challenges and opportunities to developers of HCI.

3.1 Mobile

While mobile HCI devices are necessarily handled by the user, fixed HCI devices should interact with the user without requiring physical contact. Busy multitasking people need information and communication systems that work with whatever input modes are practical at the moment. We would all benefit from the option to interact with machines using human-to-human interaction modes (vision and voice) in addition to the traditional modes (tactile). All environments suffer from acoustic noise. This has required the use of close-talking microphones for reliable communication and machine recognition. The integration of visual speech processing into the HCI will bring speech recognition performance up to practical levels for a much greater number of applications without requiring close-talking microphones or elevated voice level. Visual communication with alternate appearance and face/voice recognition for identity verification can also be added as server applications.

3.2 Vehicles

The need for vision-based HCI is greatest for drivers of vehicles given that they are visually occupied while struggling to use tactile interfaces for phone, navigation, and entertainment control. This situation is hazardous enough to compel state lawmakers in a growing number of states to outlaw holding and talking on a cellphone while driving. While voice recognition in vehicles performs poorly due to acoustic noise, audio/visual speech recognition promises to perform reliably enough to be practical. In addition, the recognition of the user's mental state, e.g., fatigue level, using machine vision of head pose and eyelid opening will save lives. Multimodal biometrics applications could also be deployed using face and voice recognition to verify the identity of the driver. Trucks and other large vehicles should be equipped with reliable and convenient driver identification systems.

3.3 Public Terminals

Automatic teller machines (ATMs), vending machines, and grocery store checkout machines are located in public places and currently use simple tactile HCI and a magnetic strip. Public terminals must have robust and minimal tactile interfaces in order to survive dirt, weather, and hostile users. As the use of cash declines and is replaced with electronic payment systems that verify identity the incidence of theft and fraud has increased dramatically. Current credit card security measures do little to foil the determined criminal and electronic identity theft is increasing from already significant levels. Fingerprint readers are highly accurate but could endanger the user or violate his privacy. A major advantage of vision-based HCI for public terminal applications is the ability to complete transactions and verify identity while the user's hands are busy or gloved (no contact required). An advantage of public terminals for vision-based HCI (as opposed to mobile or desk-based locations) is the ability to control the camera placement and possibly the lighting, and model the variations in lighting and view of the users. The use of an animated talking face to engage the user in a dialog should help to reduce the variation in possible user responses. The user can be quickly trained to position herself within view of the camera(s) even if the user was not originally intending to interact with the system. For better or worse, vending machines with talking face dialog systems that beckon to passersby will eventually be deployed.

3.4 Vision-Based HCI for PCs and Game Consoles

The keyboard and mouse continue as the HCI of choice for personal computers in spite of the availability of speech recognition systems that require close-talking microphones for sufficient accuracy. Low typing speed and repetitive strain injuries are still preferred over state-of-the-art speech recognition systems. While CPU speeds have increased on schedule, the processing needs of vision algorithms still consume most or all of the latest PCs power. Just as graphics acceleration hardware became standard equipment on PCs to free the CPU for other applications, vision acceleration hardware will eventually become a standard for user identity verification, visual speech recognition, user state and gesture recognition. No head-mounted microphone will be required to interact with the PC using speech recognition. Gaze tracking will be used for spatial selection and mental state recognition, and gesture recognition will eventually become practical.

The deployment of vision-based HCI in the home requires that visual privacy be controlled in close cooperation with the user. Once the images from a camera are stored in a computer memory or disk, they are vulnerable to malicious or inadvertent transmission over the Internet by viruses or novice users. The vision-based HCI peripheral should be able to extract human behavior data from the video and transmit it to the PC without transmitting the video itself. This visually private operating state should be clear to the user and not changeable remotely. Consumers will need to learn to trust such systems before they are widely adopted.

4 Current and Emerging System Examples

So far, this chapter has analyzed the architectural requirements and environmental constraints that should inform the design and deployment of practical vision-based HCI systems. Given the small number of these systems in the field today, this analysis has been largely theoretical and somewhat speculative. This section describes commercial systems that are either available to consumers or employees now, or could be available now if the market were ready. Systems that involve direct contact with a sensor (e.g., fingerprint readers) or very close viewing and restricted user movement (e.g., iris scan) are not covered here.

4.1 EyeToy

Recently, a vision-based game controller called EyeToy [8] was successfully introduced to the consumer market by Sony for the PlayStation2 with games specifically designed to incorporate real-time imaging of the user. PS2 inputs video from the EyeToy camera via USB and performs all vision functions using the standard PS2 computing resources. A typical EyeToy game tracks gross body and arm movements in real-time and provides the user with visual feedback using overlay graphics on video of the user. As the first mass deployment of vision-based HCI to consumers, the evolution of EyeToy will be interesting to watch. Figure 1 shows the EyeToy in action from the gamers point of view as he attempts to bounce the virtual soccer ball off of his head. Special colored props can also be tracked by the system.

Fig. 1. Sony PlayStation EyeToy screen shot (courtesy R. Marks, Sony Computer Entertainment US)

4.2 Driver Eye Tracking

Vehicle driver face and eye tracking has not yet been commercially deployed but the technology has reached a level of maturity that makes it practical for prevention of falling asleep while driving. Cost and user resistance are the main barriers to deployment in the future. An example of a single camera system has been developed by the Delphi Corporation [9], and a stereo vision system has been developed by Seeing Machines [10].

4.3 Access Control Systems

The average consumer has to deal with several key or code based access control systems for use of vehicles, ATMs, credit cards, cellphones, computers, web sites, and buildings. These systems are not very secure as evidenced by the high rates of auto theft, credit card fraud, cellphone fraud, computer viruses, lock picking, key theft and duplication, etc. Biometrics access control technology [11] is available for much better security but cost and social issues are still holding back widespread deployment except for their mandated use at international border crossings since 9/11. Cost will continue to decline but the social and political issues could intensify as the need for security increases and personal privacy is challenged. Consumer adoption of biometric security for public terminals (ATMs, gambling and vending machines) will be limited by resistance to the enrollment process where the user provides proof of claimed identity and submits to the collection of biometrics. While everyone is affected by the cost of theft and fraud, the financial institutions, casinos, and vending machine companies have the greatest incentive to improve security using biometrics. Consumers will probably need additional incentives to cooperate; especially if fingerprints or other problematic biometrics are collected.

Biometric access control systems are currently being deployed in the workplace and in airports for both international passengers and workers. The US Visit program requires face and fingerprint biometrics to be used to verify the identity of Visa holders wishing to enter the US with the program expanding to all passport holders but the system is attended by customs and immigration agents. Schiphol Airport in Amsterdam has deployed iris recognition systems for automatic access control for volunteer passengers and airport employees [12]. Face recognition by itself has not been significantly deployed for access control [13] in the workplace or transportation systems.

The use of face recognition to access PCs, game consoles, and secure Internet locations can be deployed as a local application by the user as a replacement for passwords. A variety of systems are commercially available [14] but not widely used. Perhaps vision-based access control would be adopted more widely on PCs if other vision-based HCI applications were also deployed.

4.4 Immersive Simulation

The military is the leading developer of reality simulation systems with the "human in the loop." Head and eye tracking systems are currently deployed in many of these systems [15] as part of the HCI and for measurement of human performance. As real-time facial capture from video and audio/visual speech recognition systems mature, the emotional state, speech, and gestures of the user will also be available for simulation applications. The successful use of a complete vision-based HCI system in simulation should be rapidly followed by cost reduction, miniaturization, and ruggedization for deployment in vehicles, command and control centers, and finally mobile devices.

5 Conclusions

The adoption of technology by consumers is the ultimate validation of its maturity and utility. Vision-based HCI related applications have barely started to penetrate the consumer market and industrial deployment is mostly limited to access control systems where the period of use is inherently very brief. The potential for wide deployment of vision-based HCI is great; especially in applications where speech recognition is also needed. In particular, the rapid consumer adoption of advanced mobile phones [16] with video cameras promises to provide a platform for vision-based HCI using a client-server architecture and standards like MPEG-4 FBA. Rapid adoption is also possible on PCs, game consoles, and vehicles when enough vision-based HCI applications are available to justify the cost.

Acknowledgments

Thanks to the editors of this book for giving me the opportunity to express my views on the present state of vision-based HCI applications and the future paths to widespread adoption.

References

1. J Segen and S Kumar. Gesture VR: Vision-based 3D hand interface for spatial interaction. *Proc ACM Int Conf on Multimedia*, 1998.
2. E D Petajan. Automatic lipreading to enhance speech recognition. *Proc CVPR*, 1985.
3. A Goldschen et al. Continuous optical automatic speech recognition. *Proc Asilomar Conf on Signals, Systems, and Computers*, 1994.
4. G Potamianos et al. Large-vocabulary audio-visual speech recognition by machines and humans. *Proc Eurospeech*, 2001.
5. ISO/IEC 14496-1 IS (MPEG-4). Information Technology – Coding of audio-visual objects, Part 1: Systems. www.iso.org
6. ISO/IEC 14496-2 IS (MPEG-4). Information Technology – Coding of audio-visual objects, Part 2: Visual. www.iso.org
7. R Cole et al. Perceptive animated interfaces: First steps toward a new paradigm for human-computer interaction. *Proceedings of the IEEE.* pp 1391–1405, 2003.
8. R Marks. Natural interfaces via real-time video. *SIGGRAPH 2000 Sketch.* research.scea.com/research/pdfs/siggraph2000RICKnat_interfaces.pdf
9. B Kisačanin et al. Driver Drowsiness Monitor from DELPHI. *Proc CVPR Demonstrations (CD-ROM)*, 2004.
10. www.seeingmachines.com
11. www.biometrics.org/html/examples/examples.html
12. www.biometritech.com/features/deploywp1.htm
13. www.cisco.com/en/US/about/ac123/ac147/archived_issues/ipj_7-1/lures_of_biometrics.html
14. www.biomet.org/faceproducts.html
15. www.hf.faa.gov/docs/508/docs/VF-SNIPVFRDarken.pdf
16. www.mobilepipeline.com/59200081

The Office of the Past

Jiwon Kim[1], Steven M. Seitz[1], and Maneesh Agrawala[2]

[1] University of Washington
jwkim@cs.washington.edu
seitz@cs.washington.edu
[2] Microsoft Research
maneesh@microsoft.com

We propose a vision for the future office environment where the physical space is seamlessly integrated into the digital space by tracking and recognizing all physical artifacts in the office over time using overhead video cameras. In particular, we focus on the physical desktop and paper documents. The desktop system we envision is inspired by the search and organization capabilities of electronic desktops and provides similar affordances. In particular, we propose to automatically index the physical documents on the desk by tracking their locations in the stacks and linking them with their electronic versions. As a step towards this goal, we have implemented a prototype system that we demonstrate in the context of two sample scenarios, *paper tracking* and *photo sorting*. In both scenarios, the system tracks changes in the stacks of printed documents on the desk and builds a complete representation of the spatial structure of the desktop. Then the system is used for locating a paper document of interest in the stacks, and organizing digital photographs by sorting their printed versions into physical stacks on the desk.

1 Introduction

Most of our daily tasks in the office environment are carried out electronically on computers. However, our offices are still filled with physical artifacts such as books, papers, mail, pens, and telephones. Although we are accustomed to a separation of the office into the physical and digital space, new emerging technologies promise to close the gap between the two worlds by automatically recognizing individual physical artifacts and tracking their physical locations around the office.

The integration of the electronic and physical worlds will allow users to work in the office environment more efficiently, as well as enable novel and interesting interactions. For example, users will be able to quickly find lost objects (e.g., where is my key?), or locate objects of interest (e.g., all CVPR proceedings I have). Users may also organize the office more easily by grouping objects in various ways (e.g., all bills from the same credit card company, or all papers that I have not used for the past 30 days). Reminders may be attached to objects to alert the user about events related to the object (e.g., the due date of a book borrowed from the library).

Although research efforts are under way to develop technologies that link the physical and electronic worlds by attaching special tags to physical objects, such as RFID, these approaches require replacing or augmenting the current physical infrastructure, presenting a fundamental bottleneck for the adoption of the technology. Instead, we propose a computer vision based system that can be seamlessly integrated into the current office environment. In this approach, video cameras are installed on the ceiling to record the office over time, and the video is analyzed to track and recognize the physical objects. We call our approach *The Office of the Past*, in contrast to *The Office of the Future* [20] which also proposed a vision for future offices that leveraged display technologies to project onto walls or surfaces in the room. The name Office of the Past emphasizes the fact that the physical environment is allowed to remain the way it has been in the past, and that we store the entire history of the office into an indexable video archive.

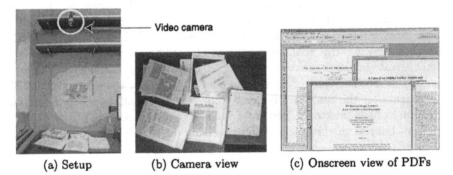

(a) Setup   (b) Camera view   (c) Onscreen view of PDFs

Fig. 1. Using a video camera mounted above a desktop (a), (b), our system tracks and recognizes all documents and links them to the electronic versions on the computer (c)

In this chapter, we focus on one particular surface in the office, the desktop, where most user interactions with physical artifacts take place, and among the physical artifacts, we concentrate on paper documents. An overhead video camera records the movements of physical documents stacked on the desk to link them with their electronic versions on disk and to track their physical locations in the stacks (Fig. 1). The ultimate goal of our desktop system is to extend the computer desktop metaphor back to the physical desktop. For example, we want the system to electronically index the paper documents on the physical desktop, as file systems do on the computer. The system should also allow users to search for papers both locally and remotely, analogous to tools for electronic desktops such as Google Desktop [1], Remote Desktop on Microsoft Windows [2] and VNC [4].

(a) Paper tracking sequence

(b) Photo sorting sequence

Fig. 2. (a) Sample input frames from the paper tracking sequence. Paper documents and books enter, exit the scene and change location in the stacks as the user shifts them around. (b) Sample input frames from the photo sorting sequence. The user sorts photographs in two source stacks (one on the desk in the lower right corner, the other outside the scene) into three target stacks

As a step towards this goal, we implemented a prototype system that tracks and recognizes stacks of physical documents on the desk using a feature-based technique, with certain constraints on the user interactions with documents [13]. The system also provides a user interface that allows users to issue queries about the documents in a few different ways: by appearance, keyword, access time and using a remote desktop interface. We demonstrate our system in two scenarios: *paper tracking* and *photo sorting*. In the first scenario, the system records a video of the desk as the user moves around printed documents and books, as shown in Fig. 2a. The captured video is subsequently analyzed to recognize each document by automatically matching it with the corresponding electronic document (e.g., PDF), and track its location in the stacks. The user can then query the system in a variety of ways to find particular documents of interest. The second scenario demonstrates the potential use of our system as a way to provide a tangible interface for organizing digital photographs. The system observes the user as he sorts printed photographs into stacks (Fig. 2b), and analyzes the video to recognize the photographs and infer the stack structure. The user then assigns each stack to a folder on disk to automatically organize the corresponding image files into the designated folder.

The remainder of the chapter is organized as follows. We first discuss related work in the following section. Section 3 describes our system in detail, explaining the tracking and recognition algorithm, and illustrating the user interface in the context of two sample scenarios. After presenting results in Sect. 4, we conclude the chapter with a discussion of future work and summary.

2 Related Work

There exists a significant body of previous work on camera and projector based augmented desktop systems [28, 25, 14, 5, 16]. However, their primary focus lies in supporting interaction with individual desktop objects or projected images using hand tracking, rather than building a representation of the structure on the desk. Although these systems are capable of simple object tracking, they do not support tracking stacks of papers, and they require either manual registration of objects or the use of specially designed visual tags and backdrops.

Tracking and ID technologies such as barcodes, IR/RFID tags and visual tags are already commonplace and becoming more prevalent in the context of finding lost objects [21, 27, 9, 19]. Although these techniques can be applied to paper documents, they all necessitate the use of physical tags and a specialized reader. Furthermore, they are not suitable for accurate tracking of object locations. Some vision-based tracking systems [17, 18] avoid the need for special tags and readers, but do not support tracking papers in stacks. More recently, Fujii et al. [8] demonstrated an experimental system for tracking stacked objects using stereo vision. However, as they used the physical height of the stacked objects to detect changes, their technique is not applicable to stacks of relatively thin paper documents.

In the computer vision and AI communities, a large body of work exists for object tracking and recognition. In particular, layer extraction ([26] and subsequent papers) is an area relevant to our work, as the document stack is by nature a layered structure. As we focus on documents, we are able to use specialized feature-based tracking techniques. Also, in our problem, the layered structure not only represents multiple objects with different motions, but also the complex spatial hierarchy of the documents on the desk.

Sanders et al. [23] proposed Object Discovery, a method to discover objects over time as they enter and leave the scene, by analyzing the temporal history of each pixel of the image sequence. They attempt to explain the temporal evolution of a scene with relatively infrequent object motions, and provided an initial inspiration for our work. However, our work differs from theirs in a few important aspects. First, in Object Discovery, the scene must satisfy the clean world assumption, i.e., each object must both enter and leave the scene. We remove this constraint in our work. We also combine temporal and spatial information instead of doing a pure temporal analysis, and are able to recognize a group of pixels as an object, as well as track its location over time. And while they focus on theory with limited experimental results, our objective is to build a practical system that can reconstruct the state of the desk, and we present two applications built on top of this system.

Perhaps most closely related to our work is the Self-Organizing Desk [22] which is also a camera-based system for tracking paper documents in stacks. However, it constrains the input in a few important ways, e.g., the papers must be of known size and are only allowed to translate. We overcome these limitations, and present a new framework that incorporates recognition at its core, a key capability that is not supported by either of the systems in [23, 22]. The incorporation of recognition techniques allows us to reliably track visually similar paper documents (i.e., text on white paper) and to link physical documents with their electronic versions on the computer.

3 Document Tracking and Recognition

In this section, we present a detailed description of how our system tracks and recognizes documents in the input video. We first provide a problem definition along with a list of the assumptions that we make, then explain the algorithm used to solve the problem.

3.1 Problem Definition

Given an input video of a desktop, our objective is to reconstruct the configuration of documents on the desk at each instant in time. We use the term *event* to refer to a change in the state of the document stacks. The state of the desk is represented by a directed acyclic graph called a *scene graph*, where each node corresponds to a document and edges exist between pairs of documents where one document is directly on top of the other (Fig. 3). The system produces as output a sequence of scene graphs representing the history of the desktop.

3.2 Assumptions

We make several simplifying assumptions to make the tracking problem more tractable.

- There are three types of events: entry, exit and move (Fig. 4).
- Only one document can move at a time.
- Only the document on the top of the stack can move, i.e., users cannot place documents in, or remove them from, the middle of a stack.
- Each document is unique, i.e., there is no duplicate copy of the same document on the desk.
- Each document on the desk has a corresponding electronic version on the computer that is used by the system to match and recognize the document. In the case of papers, an image of each page is extracted from the PDF file; for books, the image of the book cover is used; for digital photographs, the image file itself is used.

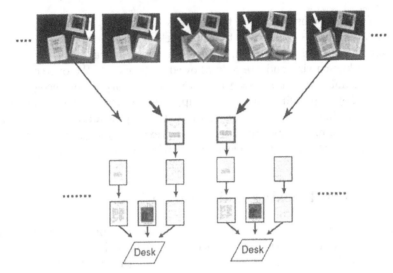

Fig. 3. A sequence of scene graphs represent the evolution of the desktop over time. The nodes correspond to documents and edges encode the occlusion relationship between them. The document pointed by a white arrow (top) moves from the top of one stack to another. The scene graph (bottom) is updated accordingly by moving the corresponding node (pointed by a black arrow)

(a) An entry event   (b) An exit event   (c) A move event

Fig. 4. We model three event types: (a) entry, (b) exit, and (c) move. The document that moved is pointed by an arrow. The top and bottom images correspond to I_{e-} and I_{e+}, images immediately before and after the event e

These assumptions somewhat restrict the range of possible user interactions, and generalizing the tracking and recognition algorithm to relax these assumptions is an important topic for future work. Nevertheless, these assumptions still allow many useful and natural interactions, which enable the paper tracking and photo sorting scenarios presented in this chapter.

Finally, it is important to note that we do not require the desk to be initially empty: each document is discovered the first time it moves.

3.3 Algorithm

The recognition and tracking algorithm works in 4 steps: event detection, event interpretation, document recognition and updating scene graphs. An overview of the algorithm is provided in Fig. 5.

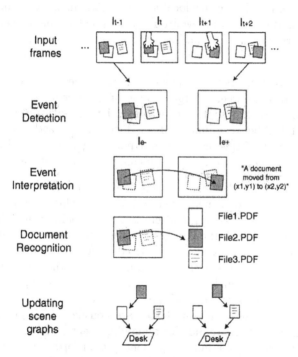

Fig. 5. An overview of the document recognition and tracking algorithm.. For each event, we extract a pair of images I_{e-} and I_{e+}, before and after the event. Then, these images are analyzed to determine the type and motion of the event. Next, the document that moved is recognized by matching it with the electronic file on disk. Finally, the scene graph is updated accordingly

Event Detection

An event starts with the motion of a document and lasts until the motion ends. To detect events, we first compute frame differences between consecutive input frames. If the difference is large, we assume that an event is occurring. Then we extract two frames immediately before and after the duration of the event. Let e denote an event, and I_{e-} and I_{e+} denote the frames before and after the event, respectively.

Event Interpretation

To interpret an event e, we analyze I_{e-}, I_{e+} and frames during the event to determine the type and motion of the event. We use the Scale Invariant Feature Transform (SIFT) [15] to accomplish this goal.

SIFT computes descriptive local features of an image based on histograms of edge orientation in a window around each point in the image. The following characteristics make it suitable for reliable matching and recognition of documents.

- **Distinctiveness**: its high-dimensional (128D) descriptor enables accurate differentiation between a large number of features.
- **Invariance to 2D scale, rotation and translation**: features are reliably matched between images of the document in vastly different poses.
- **Robust matching**: detection and matching is robust with respect to partial occlusion and differences in contrast and illumination.

The event is first classified as a move event or otherwise, by looking for a valid motion of a document from I_{e-} to I_{e+}. This is done by matching features between I_{e-} and I_{e+} and clustering the pairs of matching features that have similar motion. If the largest cluster with a non-zero motion contains sufficiently many matches, it is considered a valid motion and the event is classified as a move. If the event is not a move, it is either an entry or an exit.

The SIFT features in I_{e-} and I_{e+} are split into two groups *foreground* and *background*, for use in the rest of the procedure. For a move event, features in the largest non-zero motion cluster are considered foreground, and the remaining features background. For remaining events, a feature is background if a matching feature is found under identity transform across the event, and foreground otherwise.

Distinguishing between an entry and an exit requires running three tests in sequence, described below. We run each test only if the previous test fails.

- **Test 1**: Foreground features of I_{e-} and I_{e+} are matched against the image database of electronic documents. For an entry event, if the entering document overlaps with multiple underlying documents or there is no underlying document (Fig. 6a), the foreground features of I_{e+} will yield a good match with one document, whereas those of I_{e-} will match either

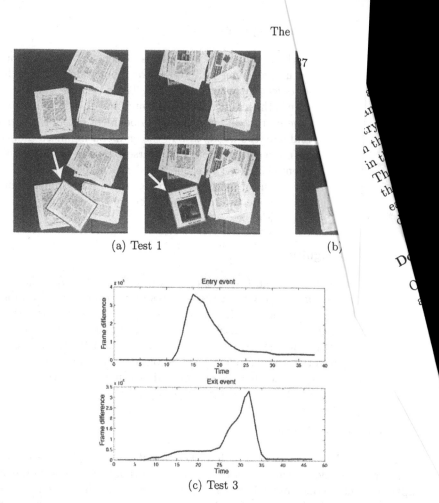

(a) Test 1   (b)

Entry event

Exit event

(c) Test 3

Fig. 6. Three tests are performed in sequence to distinguish between an entry and an exit. The document that moved is pointed by an arrow. (a) Test 1: The entering (or exiting) document overlaps with multiple underlying documents (left) or there is no underlying document (right). (b) Test 2: The exiting (or entering) document aligns fairly well with the underlying document, and the system has seen the document beneath that underlying document. (c) Test 3: The system has not seen the document beneath the underlying document, and looks for the peak in the function that measures the amount of motion during the event

parts of multiple documents or no document (and vice versa for an exit event).

- **Test 2**: If the entering or exiting document aligns fairly well with the underlying document (Fig. 6b), Test 1 will fail to classify the event. However, if the system has previously seen what lies under the foreground region of I_{e-}, it can compare the new foreground region of I_{e+} with that underlying document. If they match, it is an exit event; otherwise, it is an entry.

Finally, if the system does not have sufficient knowledge about ıent stack structure to perform Test 2, the input frames during the ıre analyzed to determine the event type. There is an asymmetry in ıount of change in the image between an entry and an exit. During an event, both the user's hand and the new document enters the scene e beginning and only the hand exits in the end, causing more change ıe beginning than the end, whereas the reverse is true in an exit event. erefore, the system classifies the event based on the peak location in function of the amount of motion over time, measured by differencing ıch frame with I_{e-} outside the region occupied by the entering/exiting ocument, as shown in Fig. 6c.

cument Recognition

ınce the event is interpreted, the foreground SIFT features of I_{e-} (I_{e+} for ın entry event) are matched against the features of each image of electronic documents on the computer and clustered according to the relative transformation. The matching score is defined as the ratio of the sum of matching scores for the features in the largest cluster to that of all matching features. The document with the best matching score is considered the matching document. We assume that all documents have enough features to perform reliable matching between the physical and electronic copy.

Updating Scene Graphs

The interpreted event is used to update the current scene graph representing the structure of document stacks on the desk. Initially, the scene graph is empty, and new nodes are added as new documents are discovered. If the current event is the first event for the document, a new node representing that document is introduced into all scene graphs up to that point, and new edges are added to connect the new node to all scene graphs.

For an exit, all edges are disconnected from the node representing the exiting document. For an entry event, new edges are introduced between the entering document and all documents directly under it. For a move event, these two steps, i.e., exit and entry, are performed in sequence.

3.4 Desktop Browser Interface

We have developed an interface to support the tasks in each scenario that we call the *desktop browser interface*. Some screenshots are shown in Figs. 7 and 8 along with descriptions of each element of the interface. The interface provides four different ways to browse the document stacks: visual query, keyword search, sort and remote desktop. It also allows users to organize electronic documents by assigning a folder to the corresponding physical stack on the desk.

Thumbnail View   **Desktop Visualization**

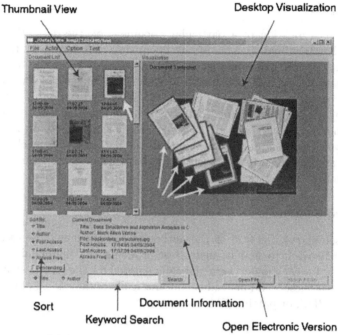

Sort   **Document Information**
        Keyword Search
                Open Electronic Version

(a) Screenshot of the desktop browser interface

(b) The interface in remote desktop mode

Fig. 7. (a) Screenshot of the desktop browser interface. The user selects a document (pointed by arrow, left) by either clicking on its thumbnail on the left or performing a keyword search. The view of the desktop on the right expands the stack (items pointed by white arrows, right) and highlights the selected document (at the bottom of the stack). (b) Screenshot of the interface in remote desktop mode. Figures show the current state of the desk (left) and a new state after the user moves around the document images to search for a document (right). The documents that were moved by the user are highlighted with thick borders

Visual Query

To query the location of a particular document on the desk, the user can browse the thumbnail images of the documents discovered by the system, shown on the left panel of Fig. 7a. When the user finds the document of interest and selects it by clicking on its thumbnail image, the visualization of the desk on the right of Fig. 7a changes to show its location in the stack by expanding the stack containing that document and highlighting the document.

When a document is selected, various information related to the document is displayed, including its title and author, the pathname of the electronic file on disk, and usage statistics, such as the first and last access time, and the total number of accesses.

Keyword Search

If the user knows the title or the author of the document, he can perform a keyword search to find it, instead of browsing the thumbnails. The title and author for each paper were manually entered for the results shown in this chapter, but these could instead be automatically obtained, e.g., by extracting text from PDF, or parsing XML metadata.

Sort

The thumbnails can be sorted based on various criteria, such as author, title and usage statistics to facilitate the search. For example, the user can sort them in order of their last access time to find recently used, or old documents on the desk.

Remote Desktop

The user can directly search through the stacks by clicking and dragging on the image of the desk, as shown in Fig. 7b. We call this mode of interaction the "remote desktop" mode, as it provides a way to search for a document on a desk in a remote location. It is analogous to the Remote Desktop application on a Microsoft Windows system [2] or the VNC application [4] that allow the user to interact with the electronic desktop of a remote machine. This interface mode can be useful when the user wants to quickly find out what is on the desk from a remote location. The user can also open the electronic version of a document by shift-clicking on its image.

Assigning a Stack to a Folder

In the photo sorting scenario, the user can select each stack in the visualization panel by clicking on it and assign a folder, as shown in Fig. 8. The system then copies all digital images in the stack into the folder and pops up the folder in thumbnail view.

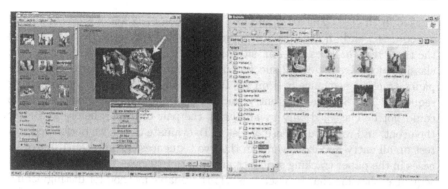

Fig. 8. Screenshot of the interface showing the user select a stack of photographs and assign it to a folder (left, pointed by an arrow). The system copies the corresponding digital photographs into the folder on disk and pops up the folder in thumbnail view (right)

4 Results and Discussion

In this section, we discuss our results and present a performance analysis on document recognition. A video demonstrating the results can be viewed on our web site [3].

4.1 Experimental Setup and Input Sequences

We used the Dragonfly video camera from PointGrey Research, Inc. that records 1024×768 images at 15 frames per second. We streamed the video frames to memory using the firewire port on a PC. The paper tracking sequence was recorded over approximately 40 minutes. It contained 49 events in total (27 moves, 9 entries and 13 exits). There were 20 printed paper documents and 2 books in the sequence. The photo sorting sequence was recorded over approximately 10 minutes, with 30 events in total (11 moves, 19 entries and no exits). There were 30 photographs in the sequence, all of which were printed on paper sheets of almost identical size (approximately 6×4 inches). Most of them contained a mixture of people and landscape. The user distributed photographs from two source stacks, one held in her hand and the other on the desk, into three target stacks. These input sequences were processed offline after the recording session was over. It took about 1 hour to process the paper tracking sequence and about 40 minutes to process the photo sorting sequence using Matlab on a 2.8 GHz Pentium IV PC, averaging 1-2 minutes per event.

4.2 Event Classification

The event classification method described in Sect. 3.3 had a 100% success rate on the two input sequences. The move vs. entry/exit classification test worked in all cases. For entry and exit events, tests 1, 2 and 3 were conducted in sequence, and all of these events were classified correctly. Because each of the three tests handles different situations, all three are required for a perfect classification. Tests 1 and 2 succeeded on 14 out of 22 entry and exits in the paper tracking sequence and on all 19 entry and exits in the photo sorting sequence. The 8 remaining entry and exits in the paper tracking sequence could not be classified only by analyzing the pair of frames before and after the event, and required the use of test 3. To evaluate test 3, we performed this test on all entry and exit events in the two sequences. It failed on 1 out of 22 cases in the paper tracking sequence and 1 out of 19 cases in the photo sorting sequence, showing that by itself it is a fairly reliable method for distinguishing entry and exit events.

4.3 Document Recognition

All 22 documents in the paper tracking sequence were recognized correctly against a database of 50 documents. The database included not only the cover page of a document, which usually has a more distinct text layout than the rest of the document, but also internal pages, some of which contained only text. The images of electronic documents in the database were approximately 400×500 pixels (width$\times$height), and the captured images of the documents were approximately 300×400 pixels.

The photo sorting sequence contained 30 photographs. In the input video, the photographs were approximately 300×400 pixels. There were 50 image files in the database, with resolutions varying between 640×480 and 901×676. Many of them had people posing in front of a background landscape, and some of them contained only scenery. All 30 photographs were recognized correctly against the database.

We conducted a simple test to further analyze the performance of document recognition based on SIFT feature matching. We took pictures of approximately 20 documents and 20 photographs with varying number of detected features, and tried to match them against a database of 162 paper documents and 82 photographs, respectively. We also varied the resolution of the captured image, to examine the effect of the image resolution on the recognition performance.

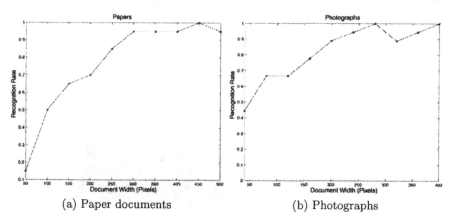

Fig. 9. Plots of document recognition rate for (a) paper documents and (b) photographs under varying image resolution. The y−axis represents the percentage of correctly recognized documents, and the x−axis represents the width of the document (defined as the length of the longer side in pixels) in the captured image

The recognition rate increased in proportion to the image resolution, as shown in Fig. 9. It can be seen that papers must be at least 230×300 (all papers were letter size) and photographs 150×200 pixels (all photographs had 4:3 aspect ratio) in the captured image to achieve a recognition rate of 90%. The recognition rate does not reach 100% even at fairly high resolutions, because a couple of documents had too few features to be reliably recognized (Fig. 10a).

The images in the database also had a varying number of SIFT features, ranging from 248 to 8409 for papers and from 35 to 9526 for photographs. We found that the recognition performance is not significantly affected by the number of features, except for a few cases with an insufficient number of features. This is an expected result because the matching score is normalized with respect to the total number of features on the document, as described in Sect. 3.3. It shows that our document recognition method can be successfully applied to a wide range of document resolution and numbers of features.

5 Future Work

There are a number of directions to extend the current work in the future. In the near term, we would like to build a robust desktop system that responds to user queries in real-time and supports a wider variety of user interactions with documents. In the long term, we hope to extend the system beyond the desktop to the entire office, realizing our vision for The Office of the Past.

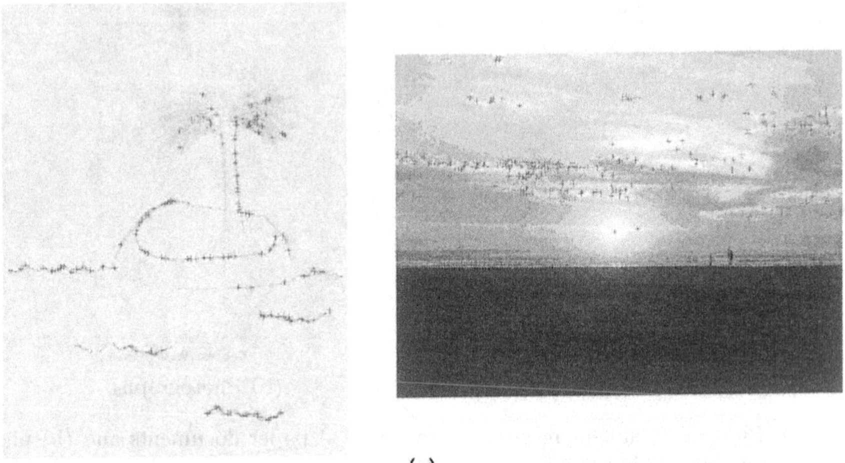

(a)

(b)

Fig. 10. (a) Documents that generate too few SIFT features cannot be handled reliably by our recognition technique: a simple drawing (left, 660×773 pixels, 248 features) and a picture of sunset (right, 800×600 pixels, 508 features). SIFT features are overlaid as cross marks. (b) Documents with average numbers of SIFT features for comparison: a research paper (left, 460×589 pixels, 1404 features) and a picture of a waterfall (right, 614×819 pixels, 2919 features)

5.1 Relaxing Assumptions

Although the current system enables interesting and useful user interactions on the desk, our observation of real users working on their desks indicates that many of the assumptions we made are violated in practice.

Most assumptions were made to enable the system to make unique decisions about the interpretation of each event. Therefore, relaxing such assumptions inevitably introduces uncertainty to the algorithm. For example, if the user moves a stack of documents together, the documents under the top of the stack move without being observed by the camera, making it difficult to know which documents moved. Allowing duplicate copies of the same document or documents that look very similar to each other provides another source of uncertainty. We think that such uncertainty can be handled by maintaining multiple hypotheses and pruning incorrect ones over time. For example, particle filtering technique has been successfully applied to multi-target tracking problems in computer vision and robotics [24, 12], and may be a good method of choice for our system as well.

We assumed that there are three types of events, namely, move, entry and exit. However, users also commonly interact with paper documents in other ways, such as flipping a paper document from front to back, turning the pages of a multi-page document, opening an envelope and extracting material from inside, etc. To handle such events, we may have to examine video frames during the event in addition to before and after the event, to track the user interactions more closely.

While the proportion of documents with electronic versions is increasing, many documents such as mail, the majority of books, and hand-written documents still have no corresponding electronic version available. To handle such documents, the current document tracking algorithm can be modified to use the camera-captured image of each document for tracking and recognition after the initial observation. Also, the first two of the three event classification tests described in Sect. 3.3 are based on the assumption that every document has an electronic version before it is observed the first time. Relaxing this assumption will cause the algorithm to rely more on the third test. While our initial results show that this test is fairly reliable, it will be necessary to further improve its robustness.

5.2 Real-Time Performance

The current implementation of the system processes the input video offline, i.e., after the recording is over. However, the system should be able to respond to user queries in real-time.

The system can utilize idle time for the processing. Since the system performs no computation while nothing is happening on the desk (e.g., at night), it can use such time to process the recorded video.

Furthermore, as we have not optimized the performance of tracking and recognition algorithm, there is much room for speeding up the computation. Currently the most time is spent on matching features between two images for document recognition, where we search for the exact nearest neighbor by comparing all possible pairs of features. As pointed out in [15], the matching can be performed faster by employing approximate nearest neighbor algorithms [6, 10] that have been shown to result in nearly an order of magnitude acceleration over the naive method. Also, PCA-SIFT [11] is an improvement over SIFT that uses a more compact descriptor by modeling image gradient patches with PCA. Its small descriptor size makes it faster to compute than original SIFT. This method may be particularly suitable for our work because the images of documents correspond to a small fraction of all possible images and thus can be readily modeled by a low-dimensional representation.

5.3 Supporting Additional Queries

We can imagine other useful queries that may be supported by our system. For example, the system can allow users to attach reminders to documents, so it can alert the user when a bill is due, or a book must be returned to the library. The system may also assist the user to organize the desk. For instance, the user can ask the system to identify all documents that were not used for the past 30 days, so that they can be cleaned off the desk, or find all credit card bills that look alike, so that bills from the same card company can be filed together. Also, if the system can detect changes on the document surface as users make written annotations on documents, the written annotation may be automatically "lifted" by the system, recognized, and incorporated into the electronic version of the document. A more thorough user study on how people actually interact with documents on the desk can help us determine the types of user tasks that can benefit from our system.

5.4 Extension Beyond the Desktop

Our ultimate goal is to extend the tracking and recognition framework to the entire office. To achieve this goal, we need to handle objects other than standard paper documents, such as mail, books in bookshelves, CDs, and 3D objects like keys, pens, staplers, etc. A more general object recognition technique must be devised that recognizes a large number of objects that may appear in different shapes and viewpoints. We also need to cover the entire office space with cameras. Crabtree and Rodden [7] found that a small number of fixed predictable locations are commonly used to place and interact with physical artifacts in the home environment. It is likely that a similar principle applies to the office environment. To extend our system to the entire office, we can place a few cameras to observe such locations and track objects across the cameras.

6 Conclusion

We proposed a vision for future offices where the physical and electronic worlds are merged by tracking and recognizing physical artifacts with video cameras. As a step towards this goal, we demonstrated a system that tracks the locations of paper documents in the stack, links them to their electronic versions, and provides a user interface that allows the user to browse the document stacks and query documents of interest. We demonstrated our system in the context of two scenarios, paper tracking and photo sorting. Our system provides a seamless unification of the physical and electronic desktops, without the need to convert to a new physical infrastructure. Further work remains to be done to make the system faster and more realistic, and extend it to the entire office.

Acknowledgments

This work was supported in part by National Science Foundation grant IIS-0049095 and Intel Corporation.

References

1. http://desktop.google.com
2. http://www.microsoft.com/windowsxp/remotedesktop
3. http://grail.cs.washington.edu/projects/office
4. http://www.realvnc.com
5. T Arai et al. Interactivedesk: A computer augmented desk which responds to operations on real objects. *Proc Conf on Human Factors in Computing Systems*, 1995.
6. S Arya and D Mount. Approximate nearest neighbor queries in fixed dimensions. *Proc SODA*, 1993.
7. A Crabtree and T Rodden. Domestic routines and design for the home. *Comput Supported Coop Work*, pp 191–220, 2004.
8. K Fujii et al. Tangible search for stacked objects. *Proc Conf on Human Factors in Computing Systems*, 2003.
9. H Hile et al. Microbiology tray and pipette tracking as a proactive tangible user interface. *Proc Int Conf on Pervasive Computing*, 2004.
10. P Indyk and R Motwani. Approximate nearest neighbors: Towards removing the curse of dimensionality. *Proc STOC*, 1998.
11. Y Ke and R Sukthankar. PCA–SIFT: A more distinctive representation for local image descriptors. *Proc CVPR*, 2004.
12. Z Khan et al. An MCMC-based particle filter for tracking multiple interacting targets. *Proc ECCV*, 2004.
13. J Kim et al. Video-based document tracking: Unifying your physical and electronic desktops. *Proc UIST*, 2004.

14. H Koike et al. Integrating paper and digital information on enhanceddesk: A method for realtime finger tracking on an augmented desk system. *ACM Trans Computer-Human Interaction*, pp 307–322, 2001.
15. D G Lowe. Distinctive image features from scale-invariant keypoints. *Int J Computer Vision*, pp 91–110, 2004.
16. W E Mackay and D Pagani. Video mosaic: Laying out time in a physical space. *ACM Multimedia*, pp 165–172, 1994.
17. D Moore et al. Object spaces: Context management for human activity recognition. *Proc Annual Conf on Audio-Visual Biometric Person Authentification*, 1999.
18. R Nelson and I Green. Tracking objects using recognition. *Proc ICPR*, 2002.
19. R E Peters et al. Finding lost objects: Informing the design of ubiquitous computing services for the home. Technical Report GIT-GVU-04-01, Georgia Institute of Technology, 2004.
20. R Raskar et al. The office of the future: A unified approach to image-based modeling and spatially immersive displays. *Proc SIGGRAPH*, 1998.
21. J Rekimoto and Y Ayatsuka. Cybercode: Designing augmented reality environments with visual tags. *Proc Designing Augmented Reality Environments*, 2000.
22. D Rus and P deSantis. The self-organizing desk. *Proc Int Joint Conf on Artificial Intelligence*, 1997.
23. B C S Sanders et al. Discovering objects using temporal information. Technical Report 772, University of Rochester, 2002.
24. D Schulz et al. People tracking with anonymous and id-sensors using Rao-Blackwellised particle filters. *Proc Int Joint Conf on Artificial Intelligence*, 2003.
25. N Takao et al. Tele-graffiti: A camera-projector based remote sketching system with hand-based user interface and automatic session summarization. *Int J Computer Vision*, pp 115–133, 2003.
26. J Y A Wang and E H Adelson. Representing moving images with layers. *IEEE Trans Image Processing*, pp 625–638, 1994.
27. R Want et al. Bridging physical and virtual worlds with electronic tags. *Proc Conf on Human Factors in Computing Systems*, 1999.
28. P Wellner. Interacting with paper on the DigitalDesk. *Comm ACM*, pp 86–97, 1993.

MPEG-4 Face and Body Animation Coding Applied to HCI

Eric Petajan

face2face animation, inc.
eric@f2f-inc.com

The MPEG-4 Face and Body Animation (FBA) standard provides a comprehensive description of humanoid geometry and animation with a very low bit-rate codec for Face and Body Animation Parameters (FAPs and BAPs) enabling transmission of MPEG-4 FBA streams over any digital network. Human behavior captured on video can be converted to an FBA stream for subsequent use in HCI systems that operate locally or over a network in a client-server architecture. Visual communication, animated entertainment, audio-visual speech and speaker recognition, and gesture recognition can be performed directly using the FBA stream anywhere in the network when local resources are limited.

1 Introduction

The flow of human audio/visual information to local and remote machines and people passes through a number of bottlenecks and is processed with coding and recognition algorithms that introduce artifacts and distortion. Digital video from one or more cameras must be either compressed or analyzed in real-time in order to avoid the expense of storing a gigabit per second on a disk array. Real-time video processing is also required by HCI and should be implemented close to the camera to avoid transmission costs and network problems, and to more easily protect the user's visual privacy. The recognition of the human face and body in a video stream results in a set of descriptors that occur at the video frame rate. The human behavior descriptors should contain all information needed for the HCI system to understand the user's presence, commands, and state. This data is highly compressible and can be used in a communication system when standardized. The MPEG-4 Face and Body Animation (FBA) standard [1, 2] provides a complete set of Face and Body Animation Parameters (FAPs and BAPs) and a codec for super low bit-rate communication. This chapter describes the key features of the MPEG-4 FBA specification.

The control of a computer by a human using the visual mode is best implemented by the successive processing of video into features and descriptors that are more compact and more efficient to manipulate as the abstraction is refined. The descriptors that are transmitted or archived should only be as abstract as required by network and storage capacity limitations. The MPEG-4 FBA standard provides a level of description of human face movements and skeleton joint angles that is both highly detailed and compressible to a 2 kilobits per second for the face and 5–10 kilobits per second for the body. The MPEG-4 FBA stream can be transmitted over any network and can be used for visual speech recognition, identity verification, emotion recognition, gesture recognition, and visual communication using an alternate appearance. The conversion of video into an MPEG-4 FBA stream is a computationally intensive process which may require dedicated hardware and HD video to fully accomplish. The performance of recognition tasks on the FBA stream can be performed anywhere on the network without risking the violation of the users visual privacy when video is transmitted. When coupled with voice recognition, FBA recognition should provide the robustness needed for effective HCI. As shown in Fig. 1, the very low bit-rate FBA stream enables the separation of the HCI from higher level recognition systems, applications and databases that tend to consume more processing and storage than is available in a personal device. This client-server architecture supports all application domains including human-human communication, human-machine interaction, and local HCI (non-networked). While the Humanoid Player Client exists today on high-end mobile phones, a mobile Face and Gesture Capture Client is still a few years away.

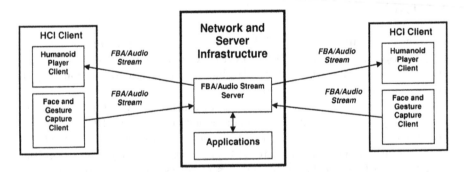

Fig. 1. FBA enabled client-server architecture

Increasing consumer demand for visual content has motivated the development of new delivery systems which provide higher quality over practical (low bit-rate) networks. Traditional video coding systems have reached a performance plateau while network bandwidths have not increased enough to satisfy the demand at reasonable cost. Simultaneously, advances in electronics have enabled cost-effective graphics rendering for the consumer, and encouraged the widespread use of graphics in visual content production.

2 Face Animation

MPEG-4 contains a comprehensive set of tools for representing and compressing content objects and the animation of those objects. Virtual humans (faces and bodies) are treated as a special type of object in MPEG-4 with anatomically specific locations and associated animation parameters. While virtual humans can be treated as generic graphical objects, there are particular advantages to representing them with the Face and Body Animation (FBA) Coding specification.

As shown in Fig. 2, Face Definition Parameter (FDP) feature points have been defined and located on the face. Some of these points only serve to help define the shape of the face. Those remaining are displaced by FAPs, which are listed in Table 1. FAPs 1 and 2 are sets of descriptors for visemes and expressions respectively, as described below. The remaining FAPs (except for the rotation FAPs) are normalized to be proportional to one of neutral face mouth width, mouth-nose distance, eye separation, iris diameter, or eye-nose distance.

FAPs are displacements of the feature points from the neutral face position. Neutral position is defined as mouth closed, eyelids tangent to the iris, gaze and head orientation straight ahead, teeth touching, and tongue touching teeth. The head orientation FAPs are applied after all other FAPs have been applied within the face. In other words, All but the head orientation FAPs refer to the local face coordinate system. If the head is animated with a body, the head orientation FAPs express rotations relative to the top-most vertebrae (the connection point between the face/FAPs and body/BAPs).

FAPs which are not transmitted for a given frame may be interpolated by the decoder. For example, if the inner lip but not the outer lip FAPs are transmitted, the decoder is free to synthesize the motion of the outer lips. Typically, the outer lip motion would closely follow the motion of the inner lips. While the behavior of face models can vary in response to FAPs, lip and eyelid closure are guaranteed. Lip closure is mandated in the neutral face and is defined during animation when the corresponding upper and lower lip FAPs sum to zero. Eyelids are open and tangent to the iris in the neutral face. Since the eyelid FAPs are expressed in units of iris diameter, the eyelids will be closed during animation when the upper and lower eyelid FAPs sum to the iris diameter. Thus, lip and eyelid closure are known regardless of the vertical contact position.

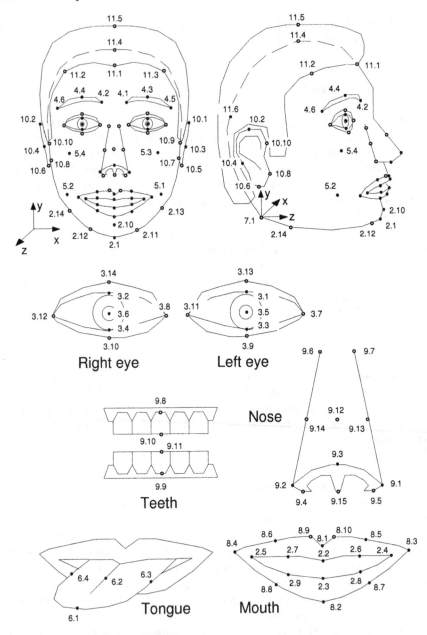

Fig. 2. Feature Points. Note that filled points are subject to displacement and/or rotation by FAPs

Table 1 is presented as a series of sub-tables each containing a related set of FAPs. FAPs 1–2 in Table 1a are the Viseme and Expression FAPs.

Table 1. (a) FAPs 1–2: Visemes and expressions

#	FAP name	FAP description	Units	Uni- or Bidir	Pos motion	Grp	FDP sub grp
1	viseme	Set of values determining the mixture of two visemes for this frame (e.g. pbm, fv, th)	na	na	na	1	na
2	expression	A set of values determining the mixture of two facial expression	na	na	na	1	na

FAPs 3–17 in Table 1b specify the basic oral cavity from the front view. The jaw opening is independent of the lips. Lip protrusion is specified at the horizontal midpoints only.

Table 1. (b) FAPs 3–17: Inner lips and jaw

#	FAP name	FAP description	Units	Uni- or Bidir	Pos motion	Grp	FDP sub grp
3	open_jaw	Vertical jaw displacement (does not affect mouth opening)	MNS	U	down	2	1
4	lower_t_midlip	Vertical top middle inner lip displacement	MNS	B	down	2	2
5	raise_b_midlip	Vertical bottom middle inner lip displacement	MNS	B	up	2	3
6	stretch_l_cornerlip	Horizontal displacement of left inner lip corner	MW	B	left	2	4
7	stretch_r_cornerlip	Horizontal displacement of right inner lip corner	MW	B	right	2	5
8	lower_t_lip_lm	Vertical displacement of midpoint between left corner and middle of top inner lip	MNS	B	down	2	6
9	lower_t_lip_rm	Vertical displacement of midpoint between right corner and middle of top inner lip	MNS	B	down	2	7
10	raise_b_lip_lm	Vertical displacement of midpoint between left corner and middle of bottom inner lip	MNS	B	up	2	8
11	raise_b_lip_rm	Vertical displacement of midpoint between right corner and middle of bottom inner lip	MNS	B	up	2	9
12	raise_l_cornerlip	Vertical displacement of left inner lip corner	MNS	B	up	2	4
13	raise_r_cornerlip	Vertical displacement of right inner lip corner	MNS	B	up	2	5
14	thrust_jaw	Depth displacement of jaw	MNS	U	forward	2	1
15	shift_jaw	Side to side displacement of jaw	MW	B	right	2	1
16	push_b_lip	Depth displacement of bottom middle lip	MNS	B	forward	2	3
17	push_t_lip	Depth displacement of top middle lip	MNS	B	forward	2	2

FAP 18 in Table 1c depresses the chin.

Table 1. (c) FAP 18: Chin boss

#	FAP name	FAP description	Units	Uni- or Bidir	Pos motion	Grp	FDP sub grp
18	depress_chin	Upward and compressing movement of the chin (like in sadness)	MNS	B	up	2	10

FAPs 19–22 in Table 1d specify the vertical positions of the eyelid midpoints. Eyelids are defined to be tangent to the iris when in neutral position. Upper and lower eyelid FAPs sum to the iris diameter when closed.

Table 1. (d) FAPs 19–22: Eyelids

#	FAP name	FAP description	Units	Uni- or Bidir	Pos motion	Grp	FDP sub grp
19	close_t_l_eyelid	Vertical displacement of top left eyelid	IRISD	B	down	3	1
20	close_t_r_eyelid	Vertical displacement of top right eyelid	IRISD	B	down	3	2
21	close_b_l_eyelid	Vertical displacement of bottom left eyelid	IRISD	B	up	3	3
22	close_b_r_eyelid	Vertical displacement of bottom right eyelid	IRISD	B	up	3	4

FAPs 23–26 in Table 1e specify eyeball orientation in units of 10^{-5} radian (FAP/BAP angular unit).

Table 1. (e) FAPs 23–26: Eyeball orientation

#	FAP name	FAP description	Units	Uni- or Bidir	Pos motion	Grp	FDP sub grp
23	yaw_l_eyeball	Horizontal orientation of left eyeball	AU	B	left	3	na
24	yaw_r_eyeball	Horizontal orientation of right eyeball	AU	B	left	3	na
25	pitch_l_eyeball	Vertical orientation of left eyeball	AU	B	down	3	na
26	pitch_r_eyeball	Vertical orientation of right eyeball	AU	B	down	3	na

FAPs 27–28 in Table 1f control eyeball thrust for comical animated characters.

Table 1. (f) FAPs 27–28: Eyeball thrust

#	FAP name	FAP description	Units	Uni- or Bidir	Pos motion	Grp	FDP sub grp
27	thrust_l_eyeball	Depth displacement of left eyeball	ES	B	forward	3	na
28	thrust_r_eyeball	Depth displacement of right eyeball	ES	B	forward	3	na

FAPs 29–30 in Table 1g dilate the pupils. Neutral pupil dilation is one third of the iris diameter.

Table 1. (g) FAPs 29–30: Pupils

#	FAP name	FAP description	Units	Uni- or Bidir	Pos motion	Grp	FDP sub grp
29	dilate_l_pupil	Dilation of left pupil	IRISD	B	growing	3	5
30	dilate_r_pupil	Dilation of right pupil	IRISD	B	growing	3	6

FAPs 31–38 in Table 1h specify the eyebrows. Squeeze is specified for the innermost points only while the middle and outer point squeeze is interpolated.

Table 1. (h) FAPs 31–38: Eyebrows

#	FAP name	FAP description	Units	Uni- or Bidir	Pos motion	Grp	FDP sub grp
31	raise_l_i_eyebrow	Vertical displacement of left inner eyebrow	ENS	B	up	4	1
32	raise_r_i_eyebrow	Vertical displacement of right inner eyebrow	ENS	B	up	4	2
33	raise_l_m_eyebrow	Vertical displacement of left middle eyebrow	ENS	B	up	4	3
34	raise_r_m_eyebrow	Vertical displacement of right middle eyebrow	ENS	B	up	4	4
35	raise_l_o_eyebrow	Vertical displacement of left outer eyebrow	ENS	B	up	4	5
36	raise_r_o_eyebrow	Vertical displacement of right outer eyebrow	ENS	B	up	4	6
37	squeeze_l_eyebrow	Horizontal displacement of left eyebrow	ES	B	right	4	1
38	squeeze_r_eyebrow	Horizontal displacement of right eyebrow	ES	B	left	4	2

FAPs 39–42 in Table 1i specify the horizontal and vertical cheek displacements of two different points respectively on a given cheek.

Table 1. (i) FAPs 39–42: Cheeks

#	FAP name	FAP description	Units	Uni-or Bidir	Pos motion	Grp	FDP sub grp
39	puff_l_cheek	Horizontal displacement of left cheeck	ES	B	left	5	1
40	puff_r_cheek	Horizontal displacement of right cheeck	ES	B	right	5	2
41	lift_l_cheek	Vertical displacement of left cheek	ENS	U	up	5	3
42	lift_r_cheek	Vertical displacement of right cheek	ENS	U	up	5	4

FAPs 43–47 in Table 1j control the tongue.

Table 1. (j) FAPs 43–47: Tongue

#	FAP name	FAP description	Units	Uni-or Bidir	Pos motion	Grp	FDP sub grp
43	shift_tongue_tip	Horizontal displacement of tongue tip	MW	B	right	6	1
44	raise_tongue_tip	Vertical displacement of tongue tip	MNS	B	up	6	1
45	thrust_tongue_tip	Depth displacement of tongue tip	MW	B	forward	6	1
46	raise_tongue	Vertical displacement of tongue	MNS	B	up	6	2
47	tongue_roll	Rolling of the tongue into U shape	AU	U	concave upward	6	3, 4

FAPs 48–50 in Table 1k specify head orientation relative to the highest vertebrae which, in turn, is oriented according to spinal BAP values.

Table 1. (k) FAPs 48–50: Head orientation

#	FAP name	FAP description	Units	Uni-or Bidir	Pos motion	Grp	FDP sub grp
48	head_pitch	Head pitch angle from top of spine	AU	B	down	7	na
49	head_yaw	Head yaw angle from top of spine	AU	B	left	7	na
50	head_roll	Head roll angle from top of spine	AU	B	right	7	na

FAPs 51–60 in Table 1l specify the outer lips. If inner lips are specified without outer lips, then the inner values are copied to the outer lips by default.

Table 1. (l) FAPs 51–60: Outer lips

#	FAP name	FAP description	Units	Uni- or Bidir	Pos motion	Grp	FDP sub grp
51	lower_t_midlip _o	Vertical top middle outer lip displacement	MNS	B	down	8	1
52	raise_b_midlip_o	Vertical bottom middle outer lip displacement	MNS	B	up	8	2
53	stretch_l_cornerlip_o	Horizontal displacement of left outer lip corner	MW	B	left	8	3
54	stretch_r_cornerlip_o	Horizontal displacement of right outer lip corner	MW	B	right	8	4
55	lower_t_lip_lm _o	Vertical displacement of midpoint between left corner and middle of top outer lip	MNS	B	down	8	5
56	lower_t_lip_rm _o	Vertical displacement of midpoint between right corner and middle of top outer lip	MNS	B	down	8	6
57	raise_b_lip_lm_o	Vertical displacement of midpoint between left corner and middle of bottom outer lip	MNS	B	up	8	7
58	raise_b_lip_rm_o	Vertical displacement of midpoint between right corner and middle of bottom outer lip	MNS	B	up	8	8
59	raise_l_cornerlip_o	Vertical displacement of left outer lip corner	MNS	B	up	8	3
60	raise_r_cornerlip _o	Vertical displacement of right outer lip corner	MNS	B	up	8	4

FAPs 61–64 in Table 1m control the nose for sneering and nostril flaring.

Table 1. (m) FAPs 61–64: Nose

#	FAP name	FAP description	Units	Uni- or Bidir	Pos motion	Grp	FDP sub grp
61	stretch_l_nose	Horizontal displacement of left side of nose	ENS	B	left	9	1
62	stretch_r_nose	Horizontal displacement of right side of nose	ENS	B	right	9	2
63	raise_nose	Vertical displacement of nose tip	ENS	B	up	9	3
64	bend_nose	Horizontal displacement of nose tip	ENS	B	right	9	3

FAPs 65–68 in Table 1n control the ears for animals or characters with animated ears.

Table 1. (n) FAPs 65–68: Ears

#	FAP name	FAP description	Units	Uni- or Bidir	Pos motion	Grp	FDP sub grp
65	raise_l_ear	Vertical displacement of left ear	ENS	B	up	10	1
66	raise_r_ear	Vertical displacement of right ear	ENS	B	up	10	2
67	pull_l_ear	Horizontal displacement of left ear	ENS	B	left	10	3
68	pull_r_ear	Horizontal displacement of right ear	ENS	B	right	10	4

MPEG has defined a limited set of visemes (visual phonemes) and facial expressions (defined in Tables 2 and 3) which can be used as either hints or to specify sets of low-level FAPs (2–68) for a given frame. For a given frame, two visemes and two expressions can be specified with a blend factor between the visemes and an intensity value for each expression. The viseme and expressions parameters provide an efficient labeling scheme which accommodates coarticulation and separates speech unit labeling from facial expressions.

Table 2. Values for viseme_select

Visemeselect	Phonemes	Example
0	none	na
1	p, b, m	put, bed, mill
2	f, v	far, voice
3	T,D	think, that
4	t, d	tip, doll
5	k, g	call, gas
6	tS, dZ, S	chair, join, she
7	s, z	sir, zeal
8	n, l	lot, not
9	r	red
10	A:	car
11	e	bed
12	I	tip
13	Q	top
14	U	book

The viseme_def and expression_def flags, when true, signal the decoder to store low-level FAPs in a lookup table while using the combined viseme/expression values as an index into the LookUp Table (LUT). In this mode, for subsequent frames which have only the viseme/expression FAPs specified, the decoder must lookup the low level FAP values from the LUT, thus providing additional compression efficiency. If the viseme_def and expression_def flags are not true then the viseme/expression FAPs are simply hints that the decoder may use to better interpolate unspecified FAP values. In either case the viseme/expression FAPs serve as visual speech and emotional expression labels for use by a variety of content manipulation, content query and human-computer interaction applications.

Table 3. Values for expression_select

Expression_select	Expression name	Textual description
0	na	na
1	joy	The eyebrows are relaxed. The mouth is open and the mouth corners pulled back toward the ears. Corners pulled back toward the ears.
2	sadness	The inner eyebrows are bent upward. The eyes are slightly closed. The mouth is relaxed.
3	anger	The inner eyebrows are pulled downward and together. The eyes are wide open. The lips are pressed against each other or opened to expose the teeth.
4	fear	The eyebrows are raised and pulled together. The inner eyebrows are bent upward. The eyes are tense and alert.
5	disgust	The eyebrows and eyelids are relaxed. The upper lip is raised and curled, often asymmetrically.
6	surprise	The eyebrows are raised. The upper eyelids are wide open, the lower relaxed. The jaw is opened.

FAPs are normalized to be proportional to one of the key facial dimensions listed in Table 4. The third column of Table 1 indicates the Facial Animation Parameter Units (FAPU) used for each FAP. The normalization of the FAPs gives the face model designer freedom to create characters with any facial proportions regardless of the source of the FAPs. The mouth and eyelids will close when they are supposed to, mouth opening will be proportional to the face, etc. FAP normalization also allows face models to be designed without the need to transmit the face model. MPEG-4 compliant face models can be embedded into decoders, stored on portable media (e.g., CDROM), downloaded as an executable from a web site, or built into a web browser. From the user's perspective, MPEG-4 face models can be freely exchanged at any time, and FAP streams which are broadcast can be decoded as soon as the next I-frame is received. More advanced face models will allow the user to deform the model during the animation while maintaining proper facial movements. FAP normalization should also provide better visual speech recognition accuracy for speaker independent applications.

Table 4. Facial Animation Parameter Units

IRISD0	Iris diameter (equal to the distance between upper and lower eyelid)	IRISD = IRISD0 / 1024
ES0	Eye separation	ES = ES0 / 1024
ENS0	Eye - nose separation	ENS = ENS0 / 1024
MNS0	Mouth - nose separation	MNS = MNS0 / 1024
MW0	Mouth width	MW0 / 1024
AU	Angle Unit	1e-5 rad

3 Body Animation

MPEG-4 body animation coding represents the joint angles of a humanoid skeleton. Joint and joint angle names are harmonized with the H-Anim specification [3]. Almost all bones in the human body are included (some foot bones are missing) and the spine can be represented with a lower number of segments for simpler characters. Each Body Animation Parameter (BAP) represents one Euler angle in Angular Units shown in Table 4. Ten of the 186 BAPs are shown in Table 5. FAPs and BAPs are compressed using either predictive coding or temporal DCT coding depending on the application. The coding of FAPs and BAPs is specified in the visual part of MPEG-4 and does not require the use of MPEG-4 systems. A stream of compressed FAPs and BAPs can be transmitted with embedded timing information and synchronized to any audio stream. The timing information is contained in a temporal header that can optionally be included in an intra coded frame (I-frame).

Timing is typically expressed as a frame rate (up to 256 Hz) but can also be expressed as a time code. The downloading of MPEG-4 face and body models requires the use of MPEG-4 systems. The Face Node and Body Node contain FAP and BAP nodes respectively which contain the decoded animation data. The graphical models for the downloaded humainoids are also contained in the Face and Body Nodes. In addition, the Face Animation Table (FAT) and Body Animation Table (BAT) specify the exact mapping between FAPs/BAPs and vertex displacement of the downloaded humanoid model. When the BAT is used, 110 additional BAPs can be specified to animate any vertices in the downloaded body model. These "free" BAPs can be used to animate body fat, clothing, hair, etc.

Table 5. The first 10 (of 186) Body Animation Parameters

BAP ID	BAP NAME	DESCRIPTION
1	sacroiliac_tilt	Forward-backward motion of the pelvis in the sagittal plane
2	sacroiliac_torsion	Rotation of the pelvis along the body vertical axis (defined by skeleton root)
3	sacroiliac_roll	Side to side swinging of the pelvis in the coronal plane
4	l_hip_flexion	Forward-backward rotation in the sagittal plane
5	r_hip_flexion	Forward-backward rotation in the sagittal plane
6	l_hip_abduct	Sideward opening in the coronal plane
7	r_hip_abduct	Sideward opening in the coronal plane
8	l_hip_twisting	Rotation along the thigh axis
9	r_hip_twisting	Rotation along the thigh axis
10	l_knee_flexion	Flexion-extension of the leg in the sagittal plane

4 FBA Client-Server Architecture

A client-server system architecture is needed for the delivery of high quality animated virtual humans or characters to thin clients over any digital network. While wired and wireless network speeds continue to rise, the availability of ubiquitous broadband Internet connectivity is still many years away. Furthermore, the need for low latency communication for interactive applications (e.g., VoIP and dialog systems) places additional demands on networks that further reduce available bandwidth. The addition of visual communication to a dialog system places heavy demands on the network if video streaming is used. A more practical alternative is to present talking animated faces that are driven by low bit-rate animation streams. In many applications animation is more appealing than live video and acceptable levels of animated face model quality are available today. The MPEG-4 Face and Body Animation standard provides a comprehensive representation of humanoids and characters and very low bit-rate compression of Face and Body Animation Parameters (FAPs and BAPs). The MPEG-4 FBA standard also provides independence between a given face model and the source of the FAP data that drives it by normalizing the facial movements. This allows default models to start animating immediately while new models are transmitted over the network.

4.1 Virtual Human Player Client

A practical dialog system must be able to comfortably interface to the user by presenting pleasing talking faces that respond quickly to user input. Figure 3 shows the virtual human player client. The network or file interface accesses MPEG-4 FBA and compressed audio bitstreams that are associated with each other (as indicated by the dashed line). This association could be implemented by file name convention or streaming multimedia format such as QuickTime which uses the MPEG-4 systems streaming file format. As each frame of FAP data is decoded from the FBA stream, timing information contained in the header of the FBA stream is used to synchronize each frame of rendered animated face with the decoded audio. Since the animated face is usually an object in a 3D scene graph, the FBA player client passes a set of vertex geometry for a given frame to the general 3D player for inclusion in the scene graph before final rendering.

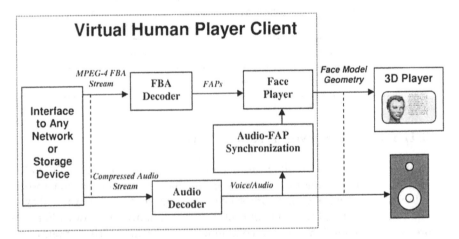

Fig. 3. FBA and audio player client

MPEG-4 FAPs are normalized displacements of standard face feature points from their neutral position (mouth closed, eyes open). Unlike animation based on morph targets, FAP values are specified at a given frame rate that is usually locked to a camera or display frame rate (e.g., 30 Hz). This approach enables FAPs to be generated from either facial motion capture systems or existing animated faces. Thus, the virtual human player client can be used to present any animated face regardless of its origin. The Face Player can be animated from text (TTS), voice (phoneme-to-viseme), or facial motion capture. The use of the MPEG-4 FBA standard allows all face animation output to be mapped to FAPs and delivered to any FBA compliant player.

4.2 Audio/Visual Facial Capture Client

User input to a dialog system could ultimately be a combination of tactile input (keyboard and mouse), voice, face and body gestures, and visual speech. Figure 4 shows an audio/visual input client that captures the voice and facial movements of the user and compresses the resulting audio and FAP data for transmission over low bit-rate networks or for local storage. When a real-time implementation of the facial capture client is available, a full duplex A/V dialog system could be realized across any network by performing compute intensive recognition tasks on server side computers. The MPEG-4 FBA stream is designed for visual speech and emotional state recognition. In a few years, mobile phones will have enough processing power to handle both the player and capture clients simultaneously.

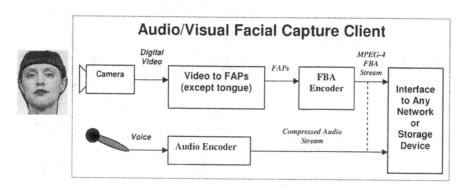

Fig. 4. Audio/visual capture client

4.3 Server-Side Architecture and Applications Interface

The Human-Computer Interface (HCI) is ultimately primarily a personal accessory and will continue to shrink in size over time. The separation between the A/V HCI and the rest of ones electronic information environment is enabled by the MPEG-4 FBA standard and is needed for privacy/security and physical practicality (battery life). The FAP and BAP data is compact and normalized which simplifies analysis and manipulation. Both the synthesis and recognition of human visual behavior are computationally intense and are best located on the server side of the network.

The FBA/compressed audio stream server and applications are shown in Fig. 5 and shows the placement of FBA and audio encoders and decoders to interface with a variety of recognizers and synthesizers. A dialog system would interface to the clients through this server architecture and provide some combination of text, FBA/audio from a database, and any other information to be presented to the user. When a real-time full duplex visual HCI becomes available it will be a source of FBA streams on which to perform recognition tasks for a dialog system. If natural voice is available then ASR, speaker verification, and phoneme recognition for viseme and FAP generation can be performed. Text-to-speech (voice and FAPs) provides tongue FAPs and is an additional source of lip and jaw FAPs. Also, natural language processing (NLP) can provide some facial expression FAPs. All of the different sources of FAP data can then be compared and blended for optimal accuracy or naturalness in a FAP Unification and Interpolation function.

FBA/Compressed Audio Stream Server

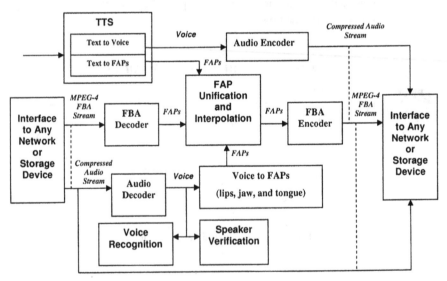

Fig. 5. FBA and audio stream server and applications interface

5 Applications

The compressed FAP stream typically occupies less than 2 kbps of bitrate and can therefore be transmitted over any network that can support coded acoustic speech. As MPEG-4 FBA players proliferate in web browsers and wireless terminals, FAP streams will first be produced for server-based streaming to drive animated characters on web sites. E-commerce and call center applications should benefit from the increased novelty and humanization associated with high quality animated characters. In these streaming content applications, recognition algorithms operating on FBA and audio streams could be used to search content databases for not only speech content, but facial gestures and expressions of emotion as well.

MPEG-4 fills the need for high quality visual communication at low bitrates when coupled with low-cost graphics rendering systems in the terminal. However, MPEG-4 does not specify the analysis techniques needed to create animated objects (e.g., faces) from video. Facial motion capture systems are available today for the generation of MPEG-4 Face Animation Parameter (FAP) data from video [4, 5, 6]. Other systems for representing face and body movements can be easily translated into MPEG-4 FBA as long as these systems provide enough detail to animated face and body models. Specifically, FAPs have often been compared to the Facial Action Coding System (FACS) [7, 8, 9]. FACS was designed to be used by human observers to annotate facial expressions on other humans but was not designed for face animation. FACS does not contain explicit timing information and does not describe visual speech. However, if an animated face were somehow driven by FACS parameters, FAPs could be measured directly off of the face at a given frame rate and a mapping between FAPs and FACS could be developed. Furthermore, the optional viseme and expression FAPs could be used to carry high level descriptors.

The perception of human speech incorporates both acoustic and visual communication modalities. Automatic speech recognition (ASR) systems have traditionally processed only the acoustic signal. While video cameras and video acquisition systems have become economical, the use of automatic lipreading to enhance speech recognition performance is an ongoing and fruitful research topic [10]–[21]. During the last 20 years a variety of research systems have been developed which demonstrate that visual speech information enhances overall recognition accuracy, especially in the presence of acoustic noise. The client-server architecture proposed above should enable earlier deployment of audio-visual speech recognition on mobile devices by performing the recognition processing on the FBA stream on the server side of the network.

MPEG-4 FBA is designed for both traditional videoconferencing applications and character animation. For videoconferencing the face models must be highly realistic to avoid distracting distortions on the face. Humans are extremely sensitive to facial distortions if they expect to see a real face. On the other hand, facial distortion on animated characters is much less noticeable. Figure 6 shows a simple real-time animated face that is pleasing to watch but avoids the pitfalls of realism. The image of the real woman on the right is a frame from a video sequence that was processed into FAP data. The normalization of FAPs allows any FBA compliant face model to be animated by any FAP stream. This enables the face model to be chosen by the viewer if permitted by the application.

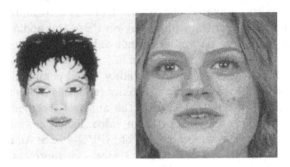

Fig. 6. FBA compliant animated face driven by FAPs extracted from video

FAPs only specify the displacement of standard fixed feature points. In general, the location of these points is independent of the geometric structure of the face model so the designer must take care to collocate the surface with the feature points while deforming the neighboring facial surfaces appropriately. For example, the surface around the lips must be displaced in proportion to the displacement of the lip feature points. Since there isn't a unique solution that satisfies the constraints, the designer must make an esthetic judgment or resort to physical modeling of the skin, muscle and bone. A bones rigged face is shown in Fig. 7. A variety of alternative face model and animation authoring systems have been developed that take advantage of the efficient representation and comprehensive nature of the MPEG-4 FBA standard [22]–[27].

6 Conclusions

As desktop computers and game machines start to accommodate real-time facial motion capture, 3D chat rooms will be populated by virtual humans driven by consumers enjoying visual privacy. At that time, enhanced real-time speech recognition and biometrics will also be enabled. Tactile interfaces (keyboard, mouse, game controller) will also start to be replaced by speech and gesture recognition. Vision-based HCI should then migrate to portable computers (laptops, tablets) and then finally to mobile devices when battery technology and vision processing circuit integration become sufficiently

Fig. 7. FBA compliant bones rigged face model

evolved. The MPEG-4 FBA standard provides the tools to support HCI implementation on a thin client while recognition and manipulation processing is performed on the server side of the network. The ability to capture the entire visual behavior of the human face in a standard 2 kilobit per second bitstream should enable a wide variety of network-based applications in entertainment, communication, security, and personal productivity.

Acknowledgments

The author wishes to thank the members of the MPEG-4 Face and Body Animation group for their contributions to the standard, cooperative attitude, and the hard work in exotic locations leading up to its completion.

References

1. ISO/IEC 14496-1 IS (MPEG-4). Information Technology – Coding of audio-visual objects, Part 1: Systems. www.iso.org
2. ISO/IEC 14496-2 IS (MPEG-4). Information Technology – Coding of audio-visual objects, Part 2: Visual. www.iso.org
3. www.h-anim.org
4. H P Graf et al. Multimodal system for locating heads and faces. *Proc Int Conf on Automatic Face and Gesture Recognition,* 1996.
5. www.f2f-inc.com
6. G Hovden and N Ling. Optimizing facial animation parameters for MPEG-4. *IEEE Trans on Consumer Electronics,* pp 1354–1359, 2003.
7. P Ekman et al. *Emotions Inside Out.* Annals of the New York Academy of Sciences, 2003.
8. P Ekman et al. (Editors). *What the Face Reveals: Basic and Applied Studies of Spontaneous Expression Using the Facial Action Coding System (FACS).* Oxford University Press, 1997.

9. M S Bartlett. *Face Image Analysis by Unsupervised Learning.* Kluwer, 2001.
10. E D Petajan. Automatic lipreading to enhance speech recognition. PhD Thesis, University of Illinois at Urbana-Champaign, 1984.
11. E D Petajan. Automatic lipreading to enhance speech recognition. *Proc Globecom Telecommunications Conference,* 1984.
12. C Bregler et al. A hybrid approach to bimodal speech recognition. *Proc Annual Asilomar Conf on Signals, Systems, and Computers,* 1994.
13. P L Silsbee and A C Bovik. Medium vocabulary audiovisual speech recognition. In: A J Rubio Ayuso and J M Lopez Soler (Editors). *New Advances and Trends in Speech Recognition and Coding.* Springer-Verlag, 1995.
14. A Adjoudani and C Benoit. Audio-visual speech recognition compared across two architectures. *Proc Eurospeech,* 1995.
15. J Luettin et al. Active shape models for visual speech feature extraction. In: D G Stork and M Hennecke (Editors). *Speechreading by Humans and Machines: Models, Systems, and Applications.* Springer-Verlag, 1996.
16. A J Goldschen et al. Continuous optical automatic speech recognition, *Proc Asilomar Conf on Signals, Systems, and Computers,* 1994.
17. J F Baldwin et al. Automatic computer lip-reading using fuzzy set theory. *Proc AVSP,* 1999.
18. J R Movellan and P Mineiro. A diffusion network approach to visual speech recognition. *Proc AVSP,* 1999.
19. P Niyogi et al. Feature based representation for audio-visual speech recognition. *Proc AVSP,* 1999.
20. B Talle and A Wichert. Audio-visual sensor fusion with neural architectures. *Proc AVSP,* 1999.
21. A Senior et al. On the use of visual information for improving audio-based speaker recognition. *Proc AVSP,* 1999.
22. G Fries et al. A tool for designing MPEG-4 compliant expressions and animations on VRML cartoon faces. *Proc AVSP,* 1999.
23. M Escher et al. User interactive MPEG-4 compatible facial animation system. *Proc IWSNHC3DI,* 1999.
24. N Grammalidis et al. Three-dimensional facial adaptation for MPEG-4 talking heads. *J Applied Signal Proc,* pp 1005–1020, 2002.
25. A Raouzaiou et al. Parameterized facial expression synthesis based on MPEG-4. *J Applied Signal Proc,* pp 1021–1038, 2002.
26. C Tolga et al. Efficient modeling of virtual humans in MPEG-4. *Proc ICME,* 2000.
27. I Pandzic and R Forchheimer. *MPEG-4 Facial Animation: The Standard, Implementation and Applications.* John Wiley and Sons, 2002.

Multimodal Human-Computer Interaction

Matthew Turk

University of California, Santa Barbara
mturk@cs.ucsb.edu

Multimodal human-computer interaction seeks to combine multiple sensing modalities in a coordinated manner to provide interfaces that are powerful, flexible, adaptable, and natural. Most research in the area to date has involved various combinations of speech, language, vision, gesture, and haptics technologies, often in concert with graphical interfaces. This chapter gives an overview of multimodal interfaces, discussing their potential advantages and challenges.

1 Introduction

The graphical user interface (GUI), with the associated WIMP (windows, icons, menus, pointing device) implementation of the desktop metaphor, has been a smashing success over the years. Originated at SRI, further developed and commercialized by Xerox PARC, popularized by the Apple Macintosh computer, and spread to the ends of the earth by Microsoft Windows, the graphical user interface was a vast improvement for most users[1] over the command-line interface. Rather than requiring users to remember complex strings of textual input, and limiting the computer's output response to text as well, the GUI with its standard mouse-keyboard-monitor trio (along with some requisite underlying hardware, such as a graphics card) made using a computer easier, and it was instrumental in bringing computing to the masses. The graphical user interface has been dominant for over two decades for good reason, and it has benefited both computer users and the computing industry.

However, the graphical user interface has limitations. As the way we use computers changes and computing becomes more pervasive and ubiquitous, current GUIs will not easily support the range of interactions necessary to

---

[1] Many expert users prefer command-line interfaces, since quickly typing short (often-used) combinations of keystrokes is faster than finding commands in a menu. In addition, most visually impaired users prefer or require the simple layout of the command-line interface.

meet the needs of users. Advances in hardware, bandwidth, and mobility have begun to enable significant changes in how and where computers are used. New computing scenarios, such as in automobiles and other mobile environments, rule out many traditional approaches to human-computer interaction. Computing is becoming something that permeates daily life, rather than something people do only at distinct times and places (as with office productivity applications). In order to accommodate a wider range of scenarios, tasks, users, and preferences, interfaces must become more natural, intuitive, adaptive, and unobtrusive. This is a primary motivation for developing multimodal user interfaces.

We will certainly need new and different interaction techniques in a world of small, powerful, connected, ubiquitous computing. Since small, powerful, connected sensing and display technologies should be available, there has been increased interest in building interfaces that use these technologies to leverage the natural human capabilities to communicate via speech, gesture, expression, touch, etc. While these are unlikely to completely replace traditional desktop and GUI-based interfaces, they will complement existing interaction styles and enable new functionality not otherwise possible or convenient.

The goal of research in multimodal interfaces is to create novel interfaces that combine modalities in a coordinated manner to provide interfaces that are powerful, flexible, adaptable, and natural. While multimodal interfaces may generally refer to both input and output modalities, our focus is on the input side (to the computer). A well known early example of a multimodal interface is the "Put That There" demonstration system developed by Bolt and his colleagues at MIT in the early 1980s [3] (see Fig. 1). In this system, the user communicated in a "media room" via speech and pointing gestures directed at a large screen display, and information from the two modalities was

Fig. 1. Bolt's "Put That There" system. Photo by Christian Lischewski. Copyright 1980, Association for Computing Machinery, Inc. Used with permission

integrated to direct interactions with the system. In the canonical "Put That There" example, two deictic (pointing) gestures, referring to an object and a location, are combined with spoken text to fully understand which object is to be moved to what location. The integration task is to disambiguate the command by matching referents.

Multimodal interfaces may include typical keyboard and mouse input, but may also add visual information (computer vision), spoken conversation (speech and language understanding), touch sensing and force feedback (haptics), and other sensing technologies, as well as "under the hood" components such as user modeling, context/task modeling, reasoning, affect modeling, etc. A key aspect of multimodal interfaces is the possibility for moving beyond the *command/control* oriented interface, where the user initiates all action, to one that is more modeled after *communication*, where the context of the interaction has a significant impact on what, when, and how information is communicated.

This chapter explores the concept of multimodal interfaces and discusses their motivations and background, important and open issues, state of the art, and opportunities for the future.

2 Human-Computer Interaction

The interface between people and computers has progressed over the years from the early days of switches and LEDs to punched cards, interactive command-line interfaces, and the direct manipulation model of graphical user interfaces. The "desktop metaphor" of graphical user interfaces, typically characterized as WIMP interfaces, has been the standard computer user interface for many years. During this time computers have changed enormously, increasing their speed and capacity, and decreasing component size, at an astounding (and exponential) rate. There are now a wide range of computer devices of various size and functionality. In addition, there now are many non-GUI (or "post-WIMP" [37]) technologies, such as virtual reality, conversational interfaces, ubiquitous computing, tangible interfaces, and affective computing, that promise to change the status quo in computer-human interaction. But, in general, hardware has changed much more dramatically than software, especially software for HCI. In fact, one can argue that the disparity in hardware and software improvements has caused the level of dissatisfaction and frustration with computers to increase dramatically, as people's experiences often do not meet their expectations.

Human-computer interaction is more than just a way to get input to, and output from, a computer program. It is more than just a "pretty face," the user interface tacked on to the application before it ships. Rather, HCI is a deep and broad field of study that focuses on the human side of computing, but also includes much about the computer side as well. HCI seeks to understand people, computers, and the ways in which they influence one another, and it involves a wide range of professional disciplines. As such, HCI researchers attempt to think deeply and clearly about:

- People: What are people good (and bad) at? What are their perceptual and cognitive capabilities and limitations? What are their physical capabilities and limitations? What social and environmental aspects of interaction are relevant?
- Computers: What are computers good (and bad) at? What are their technical and mechanical capabilities and limitations (e.g., memory, I/O bandwidth, processing speed, physical design)?
- Context: For what environments and tasks is the system intended? What are the physical and cognitive constraints? Will users be operating when fatigued, rushed, distracted, or otherwise disadvantaged?
- Usability: What does it mean for a user interface to be good, or powerful, or helpful? What must be tested, and what are the independent and dependent variables? Are an adequate range of users being considered and tested?

The general focus of HCI is on the complete user experience – and not just for the "average" user, but for the wide range of users of various ages, sizes, and abilities interacting with computers on a wide range of tasks in a potentially wide range of environments. This requires a user-centered approach (rather than a technology-driven approach) to design, engineering, and testing interfaces. Human-computer interaction comprises four major aspects:

- Design: Intuition, design guidelines, and experience (empirical evidence)
- Human factors: Testing, constructing models of human performance (perceptual, memory, cognitive, etc.)
- Devices: Physical devices (mouse, joystick, keyboard, monitor, HMD, etc.)
- Software: Infrastructure and tools, device drivers

Each of these is an important part of the broad field of HCI. One can view human-computer interaction as a hierarchy of goals, tasks, semantics, and syntax. The goal level describes what a person wants to do, independent of the technology – talk with a friend, for example, or edit a manuscript. Tasks are the particular actions that are required to attain the goal – e.g., locate a telephone, dial a number, talk into the headset. The semantics level maps the tasks onto achievable interactions with the technology, while the syntax level specifies the particular actions (such as double clicking an icon) that accomplish a subtask.

HCI makes use of conceptual models, whether implicitly or explicitly. A conceptual model is a mental model formed through experience, training, or instruction that gives the user a useful mechanism to map the basic elements of interaction to a familiar scenario. A good conceptual model – for example, the desktop metaphor, or a calculator – enables accurate prediction by the user, providing an obvious and natural mapping between system states/events and model states/events.

User interfaces may be viewed as a necessary evil, because they imply a separation between what one wants the computer to do and the act of doing it, i.e., a separation between the goal level and the task, semantics and syntax levels. This separation imposes a cognitive load upon the user that is in direct proportion to the difficulty and awkwardness that the user experiences. Poor design, to be sure, exacerbates the problem, giving rise to the all-too-common experience of frustration when using computers.

This frustrating user experience can clearly be improved upon in many ways, and there are many ideas, initiatives, and techniques intended to help, such as user-centered design, 3D user interfaces, conversational interfaces, intelligent agents, virtual environments, and so on.

One point of view is that direct manipulation interfaces – such as the GUI/WIMP model, where users manipulate visual representations of objects and actions – and "information appliances," devices built to do one particular task well [17], will alleviate many of the problems and limitations of current computer interfaces. Although this is very likely true – and such devices may well be commercial successes – it is not clear that this interface style will scale with the changing landscape of form factors and uses of computers in the future.

To complicate things, it is no longer obvious just what "the computer" is; the largely stand-alone desktop PC is no longer the singly dominant device. Rapid changes in form factor, connectivity, and mobility, as well as the continuing effects of Moore's Law, are significantly altering the computing landscape. More and more, computers are embedded in objects and systems that people already know how to interact with (e.g., a telephone or a child's toy) apart from their experience with stand-alone computers.

There are several alternatives for how interacting with computers (whether embedded or not) can proceed in the future, including the following:

- Simplify: Make the interface obvious and straightforward, giving users direct control and relevant feedback pertaining to the task at hand. Move toward single-task devices and central control to ensure consistency and reliability.

- Disappear: Make the interface disappear into the device, as with embedded computing (e.g., computer control systems in automobiles), so that users may not even know or care that they are interacting with a computer-based device. A more elaborate version of this is the concept of ubiquitous computing, where networks of computers, sensors, and displays become intimately integrated into everyday life.

- Accommodate: Make the interface anticipate, adapt, and react to the user in an intelligent fashion, allowing users to interact in natural ways while the system disambiguates and clarifies users' intentions.

Each of these alternatives has its merits, and each should be (and is being) pursued for future technologies. The first option is the domain of information appliances and direct manipulation interfaces [31]. Clearly, the second option is desirable when it is appropriate to the task at hand, as in an automobile braking system – let the embedding computers do their work while the user steps on the brake as he always has done. This seems most useful in traditional uses of computing devices, such as text editing and information query, and in other situations where the computer appears to the user as a *tool* for a specific set of purposes, such as calculating numbers, controlling a process, or drawing.

The third option – interfaces that accommodate to the user in seemingly intelligent or perceptive ways – has developed a significant following in the user interface community in recent years [15, 34]. It remains controversial [14], however, and the premise is not yet widely accepted and has not been proven in practice by common commercial systems. For example, anthropomorphism (portraying inanimate computers as having a human-like personality or identity) can be awkward and even confusing to the user [32], although it may also have certain advantages [41]. Speech recognition, the individual technology most associated with this style of interface, has not yet turned the corner to become broadly useful, rather than mildly useful in limited domains. Other component technologies, such as computer vision, reasoning, learning, discourse modeling, and intelligent agents, are still primarily in research labs and have not significantly impacted real systems as of the end of the year 2004. The vision of technology portrayed in the movie and book *2001: A Space Odyssey* [5] is clearly not yet at our disposal.

Nevertheless, one should expect these technologies to mature, especially with the common goal of integrating them to improve and advance the interface between humans and machines. There is progress every year and hopeful signs that before long they will begin to profoundly affect HCI. In addition to the desire for these technologies to improve the user experience, there is additional motivation for the computer industry: continuing progress in hardware demands more and more software to drive it and consume all those extra cycles.

These three possible directions for HCI development are by no means mutually exclusive; in fact, the second and third have much in common. As people use computers less and less for text-only processing, and more and more for communication and various media-based applications, the future of human-computer interaction becomes completely intertwined with the future of multimedia systems. The two go hand in hand.

3 Multimodal Interfaces

Since Bolt's early "Put That There" prototype, there has been considerable progress in developing a variety of different multimodal interface systems. Oviatt [18, 22] gives a good overview of the field, defining multimodal interfaces as systems that "process two or more combined user input modes – such as speech, pen, touch, manual gestures, gaze, and head and body movements –

in a coordinated manner with multimedia system output." This implies two main aspects of multimodal interfaces: developing modes of interaction and developing techniques to combine or integrate the modes that enables more flexible, expressive, powerful, and natural interfaces.

Humans interact with the world primarily through the five major senses of sight, hearing, touch, taste, and smell. In perception, a *modality* (or *mode*) refers to a particular sense. A communication *channel* is a pathway through which information is transmitted. In typical HCI usage, a channel describes an interaction technique that utilizes a particular combination of user/computer communication, based on a particular device (such as the keyboard channel or the mouse channel), or on a particular action (such as spoken language, written language, or dynamic gestures). In this view, the following are all channels: text (which may use multiple modalities when typing in text or reading text on a monitor), sound, speech recognition, images/video, and mouse pointing and clicking. In this view, multimodal interaction may refer to systems that use either multiple modalities or multiple channels.

Multimodal systems and architectures vary along several key dimensions or characteristics, including the number and type of input modalities; the number and type of communication channels; the ability to use modes in parallel, serially, or both; the size and type of recognition vocabularies; the methods of sensor and channel integration; and the kinds of applications supported [35].

There are many potential advantages of multimodal interfaces, including the following [20]:

- They permit the flexible use of input modes, including alternation and integrated use.
- They support improved efficiency, especially when manipulating graphical information.
- They can support shorter and simpler speech utterances than a speech-only interface, which results in fewer disfluencies and more robust speech recognition.
- They can support greater precision of spatial information than a speech-only interface, since pen input can be quite precise.
- They give users alternatives in their interaction techniques.
- They lead to enhanced error avoidance and ease of error resolution.
- They accommodate a wider range of users, tasks, and environmental situations.
- They are adaptable during continuously changing environmental conditions.
- They accommodate individual differences, such as permanent or temporary handicaps.
- They can help prevent overuse of any individual mode during extended computer usage.

In addition, recent research [38] indicates that humans may process information faster and better when it is presented in multiple modalities.

Oviatt and Cohen and their colleagues at the Oregon Health and Science University (formerly Oregon Graduate Institute) have been at the forefront of multimodal interface research, building and analyzing multimodal systems over a number of years for a variety of applications. Oviatt's "Ten Myths of Multimodal Interaction" [19] are enlightening for anyone trying to understand the area. We list Oviatt's myths in italics, with our accompanying comments [35]:

- **Myth #1.** *If you build a multimodal system, users will interact multimodally.* In fact, users tend to intermix unimodal and multimodal interactions; multimodal interactions are often predictable based on the type of action being performed.
- **Myth #2.** *Speech and pointing is the dominant multimodal integration pattern.* This is only one of many interaction combinations, comprising perhaps all spontaneous multimodal utterances.
- **Myth #3.** *Multimodal input involves simultaneous signals.* Multimodal signals often do not co-occur temporally.
- **Myth #4.** *Speech is the primary input mode in any multimodal system that includes it.* Speech is not the exclusive carrier of important content in multimodal systems, nor does it necessarily have temporal precedence over other input modes.
- **Myth #5.** *Multimodal language does not differ linguistically from unimodal language.* Multimodal language is different, and often much simplified, compared with unimodal language.
- **Myth #6.** *Multimodal integration involves redundancy of content between modes.* Complementarity of content is probably more significant in multimodal systems than is redundancy.
- **Myth #7.** *Individual error-prone recognition technologies combine multimodally to produce even greater unreliability.* In a flexible multimodal interface, people figure out how to use the available input modes effectively; in addition, there can be mutual disambiguation of signals that also contributes to a higher level of robustness.
- **Myth #8.** *All users' multimodal commands are integrated in a uniform way.* Different users may have different dominant integration patterns.
- **Myth #9.** *Different input modes are capable of transmitting comparable content.* Different modes vary in the type and content of their information, their functionality, the ways they are integrated, and in their suitability for multimodal integration.
- **Myth #10.** *Enhanced efficiency is the main advantage of multimodal systems.* While multimodal systems may increase efficiency, this may not always be the case. The advantages may reside elsewhere, such as decreased errors, increased flexibility, or increased user satisfaction.

A technical key to multimodal interfaces is the specific integration levels and technique(s) used. Integration of multiple sources of information is generally characterized as "early," "late," or somewhere in between. In early integration (or "feature fusion"), the raw data from multiple sources (or data that has been processed somewhat, perhaps into component features) are combined and recognition or classification proceeds in the multidimensional space. In late integration (or "semantic fusion"), individual sensor channels are processed through some level of classification before the results are integrated. In practice, integration schemes may combine elements of early and late integration, or even do both in parallel.

There are advantages to using late, semantic integration of multiple modalities in multimodal systems. For example, the input types can be recognized independently, and therefore do not have to occur simultaneously. The training requirements are smaller, $O(2N)$ for two separately trained modes as opposed to $O(N^2)$ for two modes trained together. The software development process is also simpler in the late integration case, as exemplified by the QuickSet multimodal architecture [7]. QuickSet uses temporal and semantic filtering, unification as the fundamental integration technique, and a statistical ranking to decide among multiple consistent interpretations.

There are several modes/technologies that have been used in multimodal interface systems, though some more than others. The most common are speech recognition, language understanding, pen-based gesture, magnetic (or inertial or optical) sensors for body and hand tracking, non-speech sound processing, haptic (touch- or force-based) input devices, and computer vision. (There have been a few projects that use smell, taste, or balance.) Automatically sensing, detecting, and recognizing various aspects of human behavior – identity, pose, spoken language, visual or pen-based gestures, facial expressions, overall activity – will enable interfaces more closely matching styles of natural human-to-human interaction.

These sensor-based technologies are joined by research in important relevant areas such as user modeling, task/context modeling, and learning. Context obviously plays an important role in human-human communication, and it is a key issue that must be addressed in a significant way in order to achieve truly natural, flexible, and effective multimodal interfaces. The context of an interaction includes all the relevant information: the identity of the user, that user's preferences and experience with the system or task, the subject matter of the task, the location, time of day, urgency of the task, and much more. All but the most limiting and rigid systems will require learning and adapting to the specific context, which is generally far too complex to specify manually.

In addition to publications in the top conferences and journals of each of these individual fields, a number of workshops and conferences have been held in the past decade with the specific intention of bringing together researchers in the various subfields of multimodal interfaces. The workshops on Perceptual/Perceptive User Interfaces were held in 1997, 1998, and 2001, and the International Conference on Multimodal Interfaces has been held several times beginning in 1996. In 2003, the two merged into an annual conference, keeping the ICMI name. Other regular conferences, such as Intelligent User Interfaces (IUI) and ACM SIGCHI (CHI), also feature quality research in, or closely related to, multimodal interfaces. There is also significant interest in multimodal biometric systems in recent years, largely for security applications [11, 28]; while the fields have much in common, the integration schemes and interactivity goals are quite different.

4 The State of the Art

During the past decade, there has been a good deal of research activity in multimodal interfaces, including several different combinations of input modalities. The performances of individual component technologies (e.g., speech recognition and computer vision tracking) have improved, with lower error rates and more robustness to non-ideal conditions. Multimodal architectures that provide software infrastructure and integration techniques have been developed. The number of target applications has grown steadily. The number and, subjectively, the quality of publications in the area have increased significantly. In sum, the state of the art offers an optimistic view that multimodal interface research will soon contribute in meaningful ways to a number of real-world application scenarios, and may possibly fulfill the vision of the "next major paradigm" of human-computer interaction.

Although the "Put That There" system provided a vision in the early 1980s, it was not until several years later that fully operational, real-time recognition capabilities made multimodal research a realistic option. Early examples of such systems combining natural language with direct manipulation (deictic gestures) include XTRA [12] and SHOPTALK [6]. Wahlster [40] created early user and discourse models for multimodal communication. The

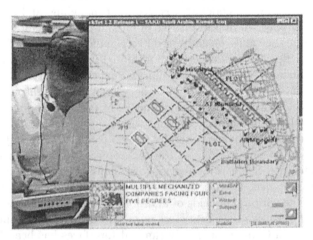

Fig. 2. QuickSet used in the ExInit application, in which a user communicates via multimodal speech and gesture to create initial mission assignments for very large-scale simulated battlefield scenarios. From [8], used with permission

QuickSet system [7], an architecture for multimodal integration used for integrating speech and (pen) gestures, allowed users to create and control military simulations from a tablet or handheld computer. Figure 2 shows the use of a system that incorporates QuickSet in a military application. This system was a milestone in multimodal interface research, both as a practical working prototype system and as an anchor point for a good deal of productive research on various aspects of multimodal interfaces (e.g., [9, 7, 42]). Vo and Wood [38] also presented a framework for multimodal integration of speech and pen input, experimenting with a multimodal calendar application.

Another system for integrating speech and (visual) gesture is described by Poddar et al. [23], applied to the problem of parsing video of a weather report. There have been a number of successful "Put That There" equivalents using computer vision-based gesture recognition along with speech recognition.

Tight integration between modalities has been a critical element in the "speechreading" community [33, 2, 25, 26]. These systems attempt to use both visual and auditory information to understand human speech – adding not just lip reading, but "face reading" to audio speech recognition. Humans appear to do this, as we tend to hear better in noisy environments when we visually focus on the speaker's face.

The area of embodied conversation interfaces, environments where animated characters interact with people (for example, at public kiosks [28], at large wall-mounted displays, or on the desktop), has been moving from characters that are blind and able to understand a limited range of spoken commands to multimodal environments in which the characters interact through speech, vision, gesture, and other modalities [1, 4, 16, 13] (see Fig. 3). Multimodal conversational systems (without visual characters) are being developed for

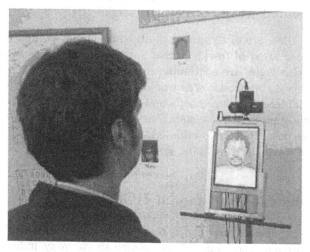

Fig. 3. A multimodal kiosk that uses stereo vision to track head position and recognize head gestures [16]. Used with permission

automobiles, in order to provide intuitive and flexible methods for drivers to control vehicle systems using speech and/or touch [24].

Design guidelines for multimodal user interface design have begun to emerge after the research and prototyping experience of the past decade. Reeves et al. [27] offer a preliminary set of principles for multimodal interface design in six main categories:

- Requirements specification
  - Design for the broadest range of users and contexts of use
  - Address privacy and security issues
- Designing multimodal input and output
  - Maximize human cognitive and physical abilities
  - Integrate modalities in a manner compatible with user preferences, context, and system functionality
- Adaptivity
  - Design interfaces to adapt to the needs and abilities of different users, as well as different contexts of use
  - Provide dynamic adaptivity, with graceful degradation
- Consistency
  - Use common, consistent features as much as possible
- Feedback
  - Keep users aware of their connectivity, available modalities, and interaction options
  - Provide confirmation of after-fusion interpretation
- Error prevention/handling
  - Provide clear exit and undo capabilities
  - Provide task-relevant and easily accessible assistance

Perusing the state of the art in multimodal human-computer interaction reveals a broad array of research areas and goals. Individual recognition and modeling technologies are continuing to improve every year – a summary of the state of each component area would be quite lengthy. Progress continues in multimodal integration methods and architectures, and in tools for creating and testing multimodal systems. Several working prototype multimodal systems have been built and evaluated, and government and industry appear interested in using the developing systems and technologies.

5 Challenges in Multimodal HCI

Despite the significant progress in recent years, still much work remains to be done before multimodal interfaces become an everyday, indispensable part of computing. The research agenda must include both the development of individual components and the integration of these components. Challenges remain in each individual component area; each modal technology (speech and sound recognition, language understanding, dialogue management, haptics, pen-based gesture, vision-based tracking and recognition technologies, user modeling, context modeling, etc.) is an active research area in itself. Fundamental improvements in learning and reasoning are necessary. Multimodal integration methods and architectures are far from mature; in fact, most current systems integrate only two modalities, such as speech and pen or visual gesture. Larger, more ambitious research projects and prototype systems must be developed in order to tackle some of the deep problems that do not surface with simpler systems.

For computer vision researchers interested in applying real-time vision technologies to multimodal HCI, the main areas of interest are well documented, including face detection and recognition, facial expression analysis, hand tracking and modeling, head and body tracking and pose extraction, gesture recognition, and activity analysis. Building systems to perform these tasks in real-world scenarios – with occlusion by objects and other people, changes in illumination and camera pose, changes in the appearance of users, and multiple users – is a huge challenge for the field. A high level of robustness is key for all the recognition technologies, and in the end robustness can only be determined by very thorough and stringent testing under a wide range of conditions. To accomplish given tasks at certain levels of overall system performance, researchers must determine what the accuracy and robustness requirements are for each component. Testing a face recognition system is fairly straightforward, but what are the implications for testing when there are several recognition technologies and underlying user and context models all in one system? The whole is clearly not just the conjoining of the parts.

In addition, there are potentially significant privacy issues with multimodal systems that must be considered early on in order to provide potential users with the assurance that such systems will not violate expectations of security and privacy. Waiting until the technologies are on the way to market is clearly not the way to handle these serious issues.

It is widely believed that truly superior technology does not always win out, and it may be the case that very effective multimodal interfaces could fail to make a significant impact because they are too different from well-entrenched technologies. In order to most effectively bring about a transition to multimodal interfaces, it may be wise to go slowly and to build on, rather than try to replace, current interaction technologies, i.e., the WIMP-based graphical user interface.

There is much work to be done before multimodal interfaces revolutionize the human-computer interface. The grand challenge of creating powerful, efficient, natural, and compelling multimodal interfaces is an exciting pursuit, one that will keep us busy for some time.

References

1. G Ball et al. Lifelike computer characters: The Persona project at Microsoft Research. In: J M Bradshaw (Editor). *Software Agents.* AAAI Press / MIT Press, 1997.
2. C Benoit and R Campbell (Editors). *Proc Workshop on Audio-Visual Speech Processing*, 1997.
3. R A Bolt. Put-That-There: Voice and gesture in the graphics interface. *Proc Annual Conf on Computer Graphics and Interactive Techniques*, 1980.
4. J Cassell et al. Embodiment in conversational interfaces: Rea. *Proc ACM CHI Conf*, 1999.
5. A C Clarke. *2001: A Space Odyssey*, New American Library, 1999 (reissue).
6. P Cohen et al. Synergistic use of direct manipulation and natural language. *Proc Conf on Human Factors in Computing Systems*, 1989.
7. P R Cohen et al. QuickSet: Multimodal interaction for simulation set-up and control. *Proc Applied Natural Language Processing Meeting*, 1997.
8. P R Cohen et al. The efficiency of multimodal interaction for a map-based task. *Proc Applied Natural Language Processing Conf*, 2000.
9. A Corradini et al. A map-based system using speech and 3D gestures for pervasive computing. *Proc IEEE Int Conf on Multimodal Interfaces*, 2002.
10. A Dix et al. *Human-Computer Interaction, Second Edition.* Prentice Hall, 1998.
11. J-L Dugelay et al. (Editors). *Proc Workshop on Multimodal User Authentication*, 2003. http://mmua.cs.ucsb.edu
12. A Kobsa et al. Combining deictic gestures and natural language for referent identification. *Proc Int Conf on Computational Linguistics*, 1986.
13. S Kopp et al. Towards integrated microplanning of language and iconic gesture for multimodal output. *Proc Int Conf on Multimodal Interfaces*, 2004.
14. P Maes et al. Intelligent software agents vs user-controlled direct manipulation: A debate. *CHI-97 Extended Abstracts: Panels*, 1997.
15. M Maybury and W Wahlster. *Readings in Intelligent User Interfaces.* Morgan Kaufmann, 1998.
16. L-P Morency and T Darrell. From conversational tooltips to grounded discourse: Head pose tracking in interactive dialog systems. *Proc Int Conf on Multimodal Interfaces*, 2004.
17. D A Norman. *The Invisible Computer.* MIT Press, 1998.
18. S Oviatt. Multimodal interfaces. In: J Jacko and A Sears (Editors). *Handbook of Human-Computer Interaction.* Lawrence Erlbaum, 2002.
19. S L Oviatt. Ten myths of multimodal interaction. *Comm ACM*, pp 74-81, 1999.
20. S L Oviatt et al. Designing the user interface for multimodal speech and gesture applications: State-of-the-art systems and research directions. *Human-Computer Interaction*, pp 263-322, 2000.
21. S Oviatt et al. Multimodal interfaces that flex, adapt, and persist. *Comm ACM*, pp 30-33, 2004.
22. S Oviatt and W Wahlster (Editors). *Human-Computer Interaction*, Lawrence Erlbaum Associates, 1997.
23. I Poddar et al. Toward natural speech/gesture HCI: A case study of weather narration. *Proc PUI Workshop*, 1998.
24. R Pieraccini et al. A multimodal conversational interface for a concept vehicle. *Proc Eurospeech*, 2003.

25. G Potamianos et al. Joint audio-visual speech processing for recognition and enhancement. *Proc Auditory-Visual Speech Processing Tutorial and Research Workshop*, 2003.
26. G Potamianos et al. Recent advances in the automatic recognition of audio-visual speech. *Proceedings of the IEEE*, pp 1306–1326, 2003.
27. L Reeves et al. Guidelines for multimodal user interface design. *Comm ACM*, 2004.
28. J Regh et al. Vision for a smart kiosk. *Proc CVPR*, 1997.
29. A Ross and A K Jain. Multimodal biometrics: An overview. *Proc European Signal Processing Conference*, 2004.
30. B Shneiderman. *Designing the User Interface: Strategies for Effective Human-Computer Interaction, Third Edition*. Addison-Wesley, 1998.
31. B Shneiderman. The future of interactive systems and the emergence of direct manipulation. *Behaviour and Information Technology*, pp 237–256, 1982.
32. B Shneiderman. A nonanthropomorphic style guide: Overcoming the Humpty Dumpty syndrome. *The Computing Teacher*, 1989.
33. D Stork and M Hennecke (Editors). *Speechreading by Humans and Machines: Models, Systems, and Applications*. Springer-Verlag, 1996.
34. M Turk (Editor). *Proc Workshop on Perceptual User Interfaces*, 1998. http://cs.ucsb.edu/conferences/PUI/PUIWorkshop98/PUI98.htm
35. M Turk and M Kölsch. Perceptual interfaces. In: G Medioni and S B Kang (Editors). *Emerging Topics in Computer Vision*. Prentice Hall, 2004.
36. M Turk and G Robertson. Perceptual User Interfaces. *Comm ACM*, pp 33-34, 2000.
37. A van Dam. Post-wimp user interfaces. *Comm ACM*, pp 63-67, 1997.
38. V van Wassenhove et al. Visual speech speeds up the neural processing of auditory speech. *Proc National Academy of Sciences*, pp 1181-1186, 2005.
39. M T Vo and C Wood. Building an application framework for speech and pen integration in multimodal learning interfaces. *Proc ICASSP*, 1996.
40. W Wahlster. User and discourse models for multimodal communication. In: J Sullivan and S Tyler (Editors). *Intelligent User Interfaces*. ACM Press, 1991.
41. A Wexelblat. Don't make that face: A report on anthropomorphizing an interface. In: M H Coen (Editor). *Intelligent Environments*. AAAI Technical Report SS-98-02, AAAI Press, 1998.
42. L Wu et al. Multimodal integration – A statistical view. *IEEE Trans Multimedia*, pp 334-341, 1999.

Smart Camera Systems Technology Roadmap

Bruce Flinchbaugh

Texas Instruments
b-flinchbaugh@ti.com

This chapter outlines requirements for real-time vision, video and image processing in camera systems for consumer electronics, video surveillance, and automotive vision applications. Related technology trends as they affect the design and development of camera processors and systems are explained. Examples of smart camera prototypes and products are described, including the roles of the embedded digital signal processors (DSPs). Finally, the requirements and trends are extrapolated to speculatively project the future of smart cameras, as well as related implications and challenges for vision research and applications.

1 Camera System Requirements for Real-Time Vision

Let us begin by defining a "smart" camera as a software-programmable camera in which video data digitized from the image sensor is fully exposed to software for processing. We also refer to such cameras as "intelligent" cameras. This concept began to be seriously considered in the 1990s. In the early 2000s it led to the development of programmable processors that satisfy the many demanding requirements for consumer electronics and suggest the future of real-time vision in cameras.

While there are many diverse functions for programmable processors in cameras, in this chapter we focus on enabling vision functions: operations that process incoming video/images to estimate useful information about the environment. Our starting point will be consumer digital camera products available today that use fully-programmable processors and other embedded systems that can be programmed to incorporate vision functions. From there we will consider requirements for other examples of smart camera systems, emphasizing video surveillance, automotive vision, and future toys and games with embedded cameras.

Consumer digital cameras are an important starting point to understand, because any vision system for widespread consumer adoption will need to satisfy the same general requirements.

- **Very low cost.** First and foremost, the solution must be available at a low price. For the consumer to buy at a low price, the bill of materials for the electronics inside must be available at a much lower price. As a rule of thumb, expect the total budget for electronic components in a smart camera to be about 30% of the end-equipment retail price. Thus if a smart camera system concept requires $1,000 worth of devices per unit to produce, it will probably need to sell for about $3,000 to enable a successful business. While digital cameras that cost $3,000+ have been available for many years now, consumers generally do not buy them of course. To reach most consumers, smart camera systems will likely need to be available for less than $300, by analogy with what has happened in the digital camera market.
- **Very low power.** This is a critical requirement for battery-operated smart cameras. For reference, the peak image and video processing power budget of a typical consumer digital still camera is typically below 700 mW. Even for fix-mounted smart cameras with wall power, a processor that runs hotter than a light bulb can easily be unacceptable for many reasons. Thus, while a 150+ W, 4 GHz personal computer processor is useful in the lab for vision experiments, a 0.6 W, 0.6 GHz DSP is much more likely to be required for a smart camera system. Video processing in cellular camera phones faces even lower power requirements for long battery life.
- **Small size.** Clearly cellular phone cameras and other consumer digital cameras must be small enough to be hand carried and ideally to fit in a pocket. The other high-volume electronic camera market, traditional CCTV video surveillance cameras, also demands small size. Practically all future smart cameras will face the same requirements. In contrast to the low-power and small-size requirements for cameras, note that the heat sink alone needed to cool a 4 GHz PC processor is larger and heavier than a cellular camera phone with a high-performance DSP inside.
- **High-speed image and video processing.** The embedded processor(s) must apply the required functions to images and video fast enough to be useful and acceptable. For digital still cameras, the bar is generally regarded as being fixed at a one second shot-to-shot delay – regardless of how many megapixels are in the image. For digital video, 30 frames per second is the typical requirement, again, independent of the image size. While some vision applications may require more or less than this, those that need more will generally need to wait for affordable systems.
- **High-speed general-purpose processing.** Practically all digital cameras run an embedded operating system of some sort to manage system resources, user interaction and data communications. This generates a re-

quirement for a processor, often a reduced-instruction set processor, to re-use existing operating system and applications software.

- **Limited high-speed memory.** The computationally intense image and video processing of digital cameras requires enough high-speed memory to hold several frames of video, and several multi-megapixel uncompressed images for burst-mode capture. This is good for vision algorithms that generally share the same requirements. However, vision algorithms that require the relatively huge high-speed memory capacities of personal computers will need to wait longer for widespread smart camera applications.
- **Modular design.** Smart cameras will likely need to be loosely coupled with other systems, and in most cases will operate autonomously without relying on communications with other/remote systems. High-bandwidth communications for transmitting compressed digital video data will be a standard feature for many smart cameras. But the video communications will be infrequently used in applications where the primary purpose of the vision system is to "watch" the video, in contrast to the traditional purpose of cameras to provide images and video for people to watch.
- **Vision functions.** While an itemization of all algorithms required by various vision approaches could be perhaps as long as the list of all vision research publications, here are a few examples of applications and generic methods to illustrate the diversity of vision function requirements for smart cameras:
  - Video surveillance: motion analysis, object tracking, face detection, face classification, event recognition, ...
  - Automotive vision: range estimation using stereo video, lane detection, face/eye tracking and analysis, obstacle detection, ...
  - Toys and games: object detection and recognition, body tracking, gesture recognition, ...

Of course, for human-computer interaction in general, we regard the many methods described in other chapters of this book as candidate requirements for smart cameras.

2 Technology Trends Behind Smart Cameras

The digital camera and cellular phone industries are well along the way to making programmable DSPs commonplace in camera products. Here is an explanation of that trend and other underlying and contributing trends, providing insight to what has happened behind the scenes to influence current digital camera and cellular phone camera designs. To the extent that these trends are sustained, they also provide a basis for projecting the future of smart camera systems in Sect. 4.

2.1 DSP Crossover Trend from Fixed-Function Circuits to Programmable Devices

Since the first programmable DSPs were designed and produced in the early 1980s, the architectures and silicon technologies have progressed to provide very high processing performance with very low electrical power requirements. For example, the TMS320C64x^{TM} family of DSPs includes processors that operate at various speeds, e.g., 720 MHz at about 1 W [7], with eight parallel functional units for multiple operations in a single instruction cycle, thus enabling over five billion operations per second. Whereas real-time video compression functions were generally beyond the reach of DSPs in the mid-1990s, they have crossed over from circuit-based designs to cost-effective DSP applications now because DSPs are fast enough. Television-quality MPEG-2 video encoding can be implemented entirely in software on a single DSP. And DSP video decoder software for the newest and more-complex video standard, H.264, is poised to receive digital television broadcasts (e.g., DVB-H) to handheld devices such as cellular phones. The accompanying advantages for smart cameras are compelling. These include the flexibility to add new vision applications to existing hardware systems via software without requiring development of new or custom electronics, the capability to upgrade embedded systems in the field via software downloads, and advantages of software re-use in development of next-generation camera systems [5]. Further, what we see is that once a video, image or vision function runs fast enough in DSP software to be useful, it remains in software. That function does not cross back over the line to become a fixed-function circuit implementation, because that would be more expensive all things considered.

2.2 Silicon Technology Trends

The semiconductor industry is undergoing two key changes that are affecting how and when new processors emerge. First, the term of Moore's Law has ended. The technology scaling rate is already slowing. While the industry will continue to develop higher density technology for several more generations, transistor performance is nearing physical limits, and on-chip interconnect is also running into performance limitations. Thus new approaches to architecture and design will be needed to continue to realize performance improvements and cost reductions that have been historically achieved. Clock speeds may not increase much beyond the levels already being produced, but alternate parallel implementations may still provide improvements in performance, power reductions, and cost reductions. At the same time, the industry is facing a form of economic limit: the cost of generating pattern masks to manufacture a new chip design with the most advanced semiconductor production processes already exceeds $1M and is increasing. This nominally means that in order to justify manufacturing a chip to exploit a new circuit or processor architecture, the up-front fixed cost is so high that it significantly increases the risk for a business to invest in the device. Only the very highest-volume markets can justify the expense of developing custom processors using the most advanced semiconductor technology. Unanticipated disruptive technology developments would be needed to avoid these trends.

2.3 From Closed-Circuit Video to Network Communications

Analog CCTV systems for video surveillance have begun to give way to digital network cameras. The transformation appears that it will take many years to complete, but it has begun. Campus-wide networks of video cables connecting dozens or hundreds of analog cameras to a centralized video monitoring room are starting to be displaced by digital systems. In the design and construction of new buildings, the additional expense of video cables is increasingly avoided altogether in favor of using one high-speed digital network for both data communications and video security functions. In Sect. 4, we will discuss some of the interesting opportunities and challenges this trend poses for future video surveillance systems.

2.4 From Wired to Wireless Communications

Perhaps the single trend with the most far-reaching implications yet to be comprehended is the embedding of smart cameras in wireless phones. This trend began almost instantaneously in 2003 when the number of cellular camera phones exceeded the number of digital still cameras sold. With programmable DSPs already in hundreds of millions of cellular phones at that time, many phones had the capacity for substantial digital image and video processing software functions before the image sensor modules were integrated in next-generation designs. The increasing adoption of wireless local area networking technology (e.g., 802.11) to replace wired digital communications networks is also changing the way people think about camera applications.

2.5 Toward Huge Non-Volatile Memory Capacities

The digital camera market drove the high-volume production of low-cost, non-volatile memory cards, which started with about 8 MB capacities around 2000 and exceeded 1 GB in 2004. At the same time, micro hard disk drives were developed in similarly small form factors and now provide tens of gigabytes of storage capacity for music players, digital cameras, and camera phones. While these memory technologies are too slow to meet the high-speed memory requirements for real-time vision, video and image processing, they serve well as storage for digital video recordings and information databases in smart cameras.

2.6 On the Integration of Image Sensors and Processors

The trend at the device level so far is one of status quo. A combination of economics and modular system constraints is keeping these devices from being integrated on a single chip. While CMOS imager technology enables digital processors to be integrated on-chip, and several such devices have been developed, practically all of the world's digital cameras and camera phones continue to keep these functions separate. At the system level, the trend is just the opposite. Whereas digital video processors, as in many machine vision applications for example, have traditionally been remote to the image sensors, the availability of high-performance DSPs has tipped the economic balance to favor co-locating the sensors and processors in the same end equipment in some cases, and sometimes on the same board.

3 Examples of DSP-Based Smart Cameras

This section provides some specific examples of how the technology trends are enabling smart cameras. The systems include research prototypes and consumer products developed by various companies, using DSPs to execute real-time vision, video and/or image processing functions implemented in software.

3.1 Network Camera Prototype

An early example of a DSP-based network camera was prototyped at Texas Instruments in 1998–99. This camera was motivated by vision research for autonomous video surveillance capabilities including object tracking, dynamic position mapping, and event recognition [2, 4]. The system was a network camera with an embedded hard disk drive, using a TMS320C6211[TM] DSP as the processor for all functions.

Image and video processing software demonstrated using this platform included tracking and position mapping of people and vehicles in 320×240-pixel frames at about 15 frames/second. JPEG software compressed video sampled at up to 15 fields/second. While tracking people and objects, event recognition software on the camera distinguished events such as when a person entered a room, placed an object on a table, or loitered in a specified area of the room. With a 6 GB hard disk drive designed into the camera, the camera could autonomously record video or selected snapshots of events as they were recognized. The system had an Ethernet interface to serve web pages and to be remotely configured. Remote web browsers could receive live or previously-recorded motion JPEG video, dynamic maps of where people and vehicles were moving in the field of view, and other information as it was produced by the vision algorithms in real-time, or stored in the database. Portions of the design of this prototype and its digital video recording software were used in the Panasonic WJ-HD100 hard disk video recorder product for video security applications.

DSP software in systems such as this is typically written almost entirely in C, relying on compiler-optimizations to achieve high performance, and an embedded operating system to manage system resources. When higher performance is needed, usually only a few of the most computationally intensive image processing functions need to be optimized using a high-level assembly language. For example in this prototype, key "kernels" of the JPEG encoder (e.g., the DCT) were manually optimized, as well as image differencing and connected components labeling algorithms that provided inputs for tracking and event recognition. Other functions, e.g., face recognition, can also be implemented in C to achieve high-speed performance using the same kind of processor [1].

The DSP embedded in this early network camera prototype was much slower than the fastest available today. It operated at 166 MHz. In 2004, newer compatible DSP processors were available that operate at up to 1 GHz. Thus as smart cameras and software for autonomous video surveillance and monitoring are designed and developed as products, similar functions will run about six times faster than was possible with early prototypes, or process six times the amount of video data.

3.2 Consumer and Professional Digital Cameras

Keeping in mind that our definition of "smart" cameras means "programmable" cameras, here are some early examples of consumer digital cameras in which the image processing pipeline was implemented entirely in software: the 2 megapixel HP Photosmart 315 digital camera in 2000 and the Kodak DX3500 in 2001. In these systems the particular DSP was a multi-processor camera system-on-a-chip, the TMS320DSC21^{TM} .

Since then several other system-on-a-chip camera processors have been developed to enable many cameras with more megapixels, improvements in algorithms, and video-rate processing. Among the latest and most advanced digital cameras based on DSPs are the 14 megapixel Kodak Professional DCS Pro SLR/n and SLR/c cameras announced in 2004. These cameras face a computational per-picture burden that is nominally seven times greater than the early 2 megapixel cameras.

Processing multi-megapixel images, starting with the raw Bayer pattern of sub-sampled colors from the image sensor and proceeding through JPEG compression, requires billions of operations per second to keep the photographer from waiting to take the next picture. The specific algorithms and parameters used are proprietary to camera companies. Generically, the operations include functions such as color filter array interpolation, color space conversion, white balance, faulty pixel correction, Gamma correction, false color suppression, edge enhancement, and lens distortion correction, as well as image compression at the end of the pipeline [8]. See also reference [5] for other insights to software camera systems and software designs.

3.3 Cellular Phone Cameras

Cellular phones with digital still camera, digital video recording, and interactive videoconferencing features are rapidly evolving. The early camera phones introduced VGA-sized picture snapshot capabilities. Now the image sizes are moving up to 3–5 MP in current and next-gen phones. Whereas the early video recording and streaming capabilities of various phones were limited to SQCIF, QCIF, or QVGA-sized video, they are moving up to VGA and are anticipated to reach television quality for digital camcorder-like video recording capabilities.

As in other smart cameras, the high-complexity video encode and decode computations of cellular phones can be implemented in DSP software. Video standards such as H.263 and MPEG-4 are used [3], as well as some proprietary formats. Various camera phone products are using programmable multimedia applications processors such as OMAP1510^{TM} and OMAP-DM270^{TM} for the image and video functions. These multi-processor systems-on-a-chip also enable many other software functions of camera phones.

3.4 Stereo Video Range Camera Prototype

David Hall, of Team Digital Auto Drive (Team DAD) that participated in the DARPA Grand Challenge of March 2004, designed and developed a real-time stereo video range camera prototype [6] to serve as the vision system for their autonomous vehicle entry in the desert race. A vehicle servo-control subsystem takes steering and acceleration commands from the vision system.

The vision system is a rather extraordinary example of a smart camera, comprising six CCD image sensors arranged in two 3-CCD prism modules with a 12" stereo baseline. Two TMS320C64x^{TM} DSPs operate at 1.1 GHz to process the stereo video data. Software on the first DSP reads the digital video data directly from the sensor modules, calculates a range image of the scene, and produces a 3D terrain map in real-time. The second DSP receives the 3D terrain profile, estimates significant objects, and plans a path over the terrain to intersect a way point provided by a GPS and inertial navigation subsystem. Finally the vision system sends commands to the servo-controller to steer the vehicle.

4 Extrapolating the Trends for Future Smart Cameras

In this section, we take a stab at projecting the future design constraints and challenges for smart cameras and related vision algorithm applications. While the speculations here are perhaps stated too boldly and could turn out to be wrong in various ways, this is an attempt to logically extrapolate the trends. To the extent that the trends outlined in Sect. 2 continue and no disruptive processing technology alternative emerges, perhaps much of this will turn out to be true.

4.1 Future Smart Camera Processors, Systems, and Software Products

Considering the trends and examples of DSP-based smart cameras and the already huge economic requirements to justify custom circuit designs for vision algorithms, it appears that smart camera processors will need to be designed and developed once, and then programmed many times in order to afford wide-ranging real-time vision system applications. Re-using system-on-a-chip programmable processors from high-volume consumer cameras will essentially become a requirement for implementing new kinds of low-cost end equipment and vision applications.

Multi-processor systems on a chip are becoming increasingly common-place to achieve higher performance. The importance of power-efficient pro-grammable architecture designs is increasing, and the amount of computation that is available at the lowest cost will eventually become relatively fixed. En-gineers who design new smart cameras will increasingly select commercially available off-the-shelf system-on-a-chip processors that include many features that are overkill for the requirements – except the need for low cost.

A new trend seems likely to emerge: widespread availability of camera products that are designed to be programmed by the purchaser instead of the vendor. Then new smart camera systems will not need to be designed at all, for the most part, because cameras will be available in a variety of form factors and costs, ready to be programmed for custom vision, video and image processing applications. These cameras will enable the independent software vendor business model for vision applications software, to populate smart cameras and create new kinds of products that were previously cost-prohibitive.

Thus, for vision technology to be embedded in high-volume consumer prod-ucts, the solutions will be provided in smart cameras. A strategy to develop such products is to look for where smart cameras are deployed now, or where they could be cost-effectively deployed to provide useful added value in the future, to see which vision applications can emerge next.

4.2 Generic Implications of Smart Cameras for Vision Research

Future smart cameras will provide powerful new tools for vision research. Ana-log cameras, frame grabbers and laboratory workstations will be displaced by smart cameras. Vision researchers will work from their office, from home, or anywhere in the world for that matter, while conducting real-time data collection and algorithm development experiments with remote cameras directly via network. The smart cameras can be in a jungle on the other side of the world, in the depths of a mine or at the bottom of the sea, in controlled laboratory lighting conditions, in a car, or in a child's toy at home. Program the cameras for real-time data collection and in situ vision processing, and have the results emailed or streamed when they are ready. Or the remote camera can call a cellular phone to report results.

Vision research that aims to be useful to society someday, in the form of wearable, handheld or household appliances, must increasingly be computationally constrained. Whereas in the first forty years of vision systems research many computationally complex approaches could be justified by using the argument that processor technology may one day make applications affordable, that argument is going away. The premium will be on vision research that produces algorithms that can run on available smart cameras. We will not be able to afford vision research approaches that require custom algorithm-specific circuits for adequate performance unless the advantage is so compellingly valuable that it will be adopted by a mass market or command a very high price in a low-volume equipment market.

Traditionally, the viable locations of cameras have been extremely limited – and not many cameras in the world. As cellular phone cameras go into the hands of hundreds of millions of consumers, programmable cameras will be everywhere people are. The same technology will also enable cameras to be deployed in fixed positions that were cost-prohibitive to consider before. What new vision functions can these cameras be programmed to take on? While vision research has developed algorithms and prototypes that suggest many potential applications, there is a world of needs out there that vision research has only begun to address. New motivations will focus future vision research.

4.3 Future Human-Computer Interaction

As the field of human-computer interaction evolves to exploit smart cameras, new problems of human-system and human-environment interaction will arise. Some methods may find new applications as software add-ons for digital cameras, cellular phones, and personal data assistants. For example, multimodal human interaction methods could be adapted for smart camera systems. With a microphone and speaker already in camera phones, techniques that recognize speech and emotions using both audible and visual cues can be implemented using the same embedded processors. Thus interactive dialogue systems may emerge where smart cameras are deployed.

New ideas will lead to new kinds of handheld and wearable vision system tools. Among the possibilities: Gesture-based recognition algorithms can be implemented in personal smart cameras for rooms and vehicles to provide interactive remote controls. Mount a camera phone on the back of a bicycle helmet to serve as a proactive "rear view mirror" monitoring system. And small smart cameras will enable new concepts for interactive toys and games.

Challenges for algorithms in this regard are to achieve sufficient robustness in wide-ranging imaging conditions. To be most useful, algorithms will need to operate reliably amid diverse ambient lighting conditions and backgrounds, indoors and out. Perhaps the biggest challenge facing the use of handheld vision systems for human interaction, or to devise new kinds of handheld vision tools, is that the cameras are moving during operation. In the classic human-computer interaction environment, the computer and connected camera(s) are in fixed positions, and the user is in a chair, providing key geometric constraints to help reduce the complexity of image and video analysis. Much more vision research is needed to develop reliable algorithms and applications for human interaction using smart cameras in motion.

4.4 Future Video Surveillance Systems

In the trend from closed-circuit video to network communications so far, most digital video security system products are essentially using the network as a replacement for analog video coax cable. For example, network video server equipment digitally compresses and transmits data from analog CCTV cameras to a remote network video storage system, or streams the data to a remote display for live observation.

While that approach provides several advantages and may be required for many security needs, smart cameras enable more. The traditional video surveillance security functions of centralized monitoring rooms will migrate to smart cameras, greatly reducing the overall cost of ownership and enabling new video security applications in homes, vehicles, schools, hospitals, etc. Using low-cost, high-capacity mass storage and system-on-a-chip processors embedded in smart network cameras to record video data and real-time observations from vision algorithms, centralized digital video storage systems will be avoided. Security personnel can obtain live or recorded video feeds direct from cameras via ordinary network communications when needed, without requiring separate network video server equipment. Traditional out-of-reach mounting positions of security cameras provide sufficient physical camera security for most applications, while real-time encryption algorithms and passwords protect smart camera data if the camera is stolen. In large campus installations, camera data can be backed up periodically on ordinary remote storage systems if needed, like computers are backed up, without requiring continuous streaming of video data to custom storage equipment.

But the big autonomous video surveillance and monitoring opportunities and challenges for vision research go far beyond the first-order cost-saving advantages of smart camera systems, and remain largely unrealized today. Security needs will continue to drive vision research for years to come, to help make the world a safer place. Smart camera systems will enable affordable deployment as research provides the useful, reliable, and computationally constrained algorithms.

4.5 Future Automotive Vision Systems

Automotive vision systems are starting to emerge. A prominent current example is the recent deployment of lane-departure warning camera systems in some car models in the industry. The economies of modular automotive designs, coupled with the expense of cabling, makes it preferable to co-locate the camera and the processor in such systems. As other automotive vision algorithms deploy, smart camera processors are likely to be adopted because automotive systems share the requirements outlined in Sect. 1.

A distinguishing challenge for automotive vision research is to assure a very high degree of reliability. Whereas limitations and mistakes of visual analysis may be acceptable or even exploited in smart camera applications such as interactive toys and games, the consequences of errors are clearly more serious for automotive safety. Vision research faces substantial challenges to collect sufficient image and video databases to measure reliability, in conjunction with human-system interaction research, to determine how reliable is reliable enough.

The large body of ongoing research and development for automotive vision systems is taking on this challenge to develop numerous new roles for smart cameras in cars. The longstanding quest for safe robotic driving continues, while research for other important automotive vision functions appears closer to improving safety for consumers. Stereo/multi-camera video analysis techniques may prove to be sufficient and cost-effective to meet increasing standards for air bag deployment safety. Prototype methods for visual analysis of drivers, to detect and alert if they start to fall asleep at the wheel, fit the smart camera approach as well. Examples of other smart camera applications in the works that seem likely to emerge for automotive safety include automatic monitoring of blind spots, obstacle detection, and adaptive cruise control.

What else will smart cameras do?

Acknowledgments

The observations in this chapter derive largely from lessons learned over the past twenty years in R&D projects for businesses of Texas Instruments, and involving the contributions of numerous others, but the speculative views expressed and any errors of fact that may appear are solely the author's.

References

1. A U Batur et al. A DSP-based approach for the implementation of face recognition algorithms. *Proc ICASSP*, 2003.
2. F Z Brill et al. Event recognition and reliability improvements for the Autonomous Video Surveillance System. *Proc Image Understanding Workshop*, 1998.
3. M Budagavi. Wireless MPEG-4 video communications. In: J G Proakis (Editor). *The Wiley Encyclopedia of Telecommunications*. Wiley, 2002.
4. T J Olson and F Z Brill. Moving object detection and event recognition algorithms for smart cameras. *Proc Image Understanding Workshop*, 1997.
5. B E Flinchbaugh. Advantages of software camera designs. *Electronic Products*, 2002. http://www.electronicproducts.com
6. D S Hall. Team Digital Auto Drive (DAD) White Paper. Personal communication, 2004.
7. T Hiers and M Webster. TMS320C6414T/15T/16T^{TM} Power Consumption Summary. Application Report SPRAA45, Texas Instruments, 2004.
8. K Illgner et al. Programmable DSP platform for digital still camera. *Proc ICASSP*, 1999.

Index